The Problem of Evil in the Western Tradition

From the Book of Job to Modern Genetics

Joseph F. Kelly

A Michael Glazier Book

THE LITURGICAL PRESS
Collegeville, Minnesota

www.litpress.org

A Michael Glazier Book published by The Liturgical Press.

Cover design by Greg Becker. Eyewire Photo.

2	3	4	5	6	7	8

Library of Congress Cataloging-in-Publication Data

Kelly, Joseph F. (Joseph Francis), 1945–
    The problem of evil in the Western tradition : from the Book of Job to modern genetics / Joseph F. Kelly.
    p.   cm.
    Includes bibliographical references and index.
    ISBN 0-8146-5104-6 (alk. paper) (softcover)
    ISBN 0-8146-5149-6 (hardcover)
    1. Good and evil—History.   I. Title.

BJ1401.K44   2001
170—dc21   2001050265

Alicia, filia mea dilecta

Lilium inter spinas (Canticum Canticorum 2:2)

Contents

Preface   vii

Chapter 1: Some Perspectives on Evil   1

Chapter 2: Israel and Evil   8

Chapter 3: The New Adam   29

Chapter 4: Out of Africa   40

Chapter 5: The Broken Cosmos   51

Chapter 6: The Middle Ages   62

Chapter 7: Decline and Reform and Humanism   87

Chapter 8: The Devil's Last Stand   102

Chapter 9: Rationalizing Evil   119

Chapter 10: The Attack on Christianity   133

Chapter 11: Dissident Voices   145

Chapter 12: Human Evil in the Nineteenth Century   154

Chapter 13: Science, Evil, and Original Sin   172

Chapter 14: Modern Literary Approaches to Evil   188

Chapter 15: Some Scientific Theories of Evil   200

Chapter 16: Modern Religious Approaches to Evil   213

Epilogue   230

A Personal Reflection   233

Select Bibliography   235

Index   242

Preface

This book is a survey of how evil has been understood in the West from the biblical era until today. The topic is vast, but the book is concise. Like most professors, I normally approach a topic with abundant footnotes, citations to texts in the original languages, and a full bibliography. To produce such a study of theories of evil would have meant a multi-volume effort. I am primarily an undergraduate teacher, and one who does a great deal of adult education. In fact, this book grew out of classes I teach at my university and from lectures given to popular audiences in the greater Cleveland area. From those classes and lectures I concluded that a general, one-volume study would be useful to students and to the general reader, although I would hope that in the future a fuller effort would be possible.

The book has the basic strength of a survey—putting individual persons and ideas in a larger perspective—and all the weaknesses of a survey, those of both exclusion and inclusion. No doubt many readers will wonder why some authority they consider to be important was excluded, and some of those readers will be colleagues and friends of mine. When colleagues learned that I was working on a book on evil, they invariably said, "Well, naturally you're going to include . . . ." (This was especially true of modern works.) In many cases, their judgment and mine agreed, but in others it did not. In every case I am grateful for their interest and their advice. The issue was primarily one of space. In general, I have chosen authors whose impact was undeniable, but this was difficult to do for the contemporary era. There I tried to choose authors who are representative of different points of view (Fred Katz, Carl Jung, Richard Wright, Flannery O'Connor, Albert Camus).

Friends and colleagues also raised the problem of insufficient inclusion—why has so important an author received what many readers will consider too cursory a treatment? I am sympathetic of this point of view; I know the feeling of seeing a dissertation-length study reduced to a footnote. The answer is again one of space. My intent was to write just one volume, and that necessitated brief treatments even of some important authors.

Since the book is intended for English-speaking, nonprofessional readers, I have limited the bibliography in size to original sources and to relevant secondary sources. There are a few cases where I made my own translation of a foreign text (French, German, Latin), but in general I cite translations. It is my hope that the bibliography will aid readers who like this book to further investigate this fascinating topic.

Since this book covers a period of three thousand years, I turned to colleagues and friends for advice about specific periods. My thanks to Francesco Cesareo, Pamela Mason, Sheila McGinn, John Spencer, and Brenda Wirkus for their advice and for reading specific chapters. Special thanks to my graduate assistants for the last few years, Keith Billman, Jeremy Link, Dianne Alaimo, and Matthew Russ, who read the entire manuscript, caught many errors, and made helpful comments. I received valuable help in the early stages of writing from Richard Valente, director of the John Carroll University office of information services. My thanks also to my department chairpersons, Thomas Sculbeck, s.j., who supported my request for a leave of absence to work on this, and his successor, Paul Laurtizen, a strong advocate of faculty research; to Sally Wertheim, dean of the Graduate School, and the other members of the university committee on research and service who recommended me to the administration for the leave; to Nick Baumgartner, dean of the College of Arts and Sciences, who approved the committee's recommendation; and to Frederick Travis, academic vice-president, who granted me the leave. My thanks also to Dean Wertheim and her committee for financial grants to purchase books for research and to Thomas Zlatoper, acting dean of the Graduate School, for the same courtesy; and to Allen Rome, librarian at Saint Mary Seminary in Wickliffe, Ohio, for helping to find some rare nineteenth-century books. I also want to thank someone I have never met, Professor Jeffrey Burton Russell, whose encyclopedic researches into the devil were crucial to this book. Thanks also to Annette Kmitch of The Liturgical Press, who did the copy editing, and especially to TLP editorial director Mark Twomey for his interest and support not just of this book but of my other efforts for The Liturgical Press.

My most heartfelt gratitude goes to my wife, Ellen, a loving and thoughtful spouse who made myriad small and large sacrifices so that I would have the time to write.

The book is dedicated to my daughter Alicia, a joy to her parents for these twenty-one years.

Joseph F. Kelly
University Heights, Cleveland, Ohio
February 7, 2001

Chapter 1

Some Perspectives on Evil

As the new millennium begins, many peoples of the world endure suffering of all kinds—terrorism, staggering poverty augmented by crushing debt, the seemingly unstoppable spread of disease, totalitarian governments bent on abusing their own citizens. This sadly mirrors the horrors of the past century: the Turkish massacre of the Armenians, the Nazi Holocaust, the Soviet purges, the Japanese rape of Nanking, the American atomic destruction of Hiroshima, the Chinese Great Cultural Revolution, the Cambodian killing fields, and the Rwandan genocide. At times evil seems so universally triumphant that it is difficult to avoid the conclusion that Adolf Hitler, Joseph Stalin, and Pol Pot represent the modern era far more truly than do Mahatma Gandhi, Rev. Dr. Martin Luther King Jr., and Mother Theresa.

These tragedies portray evil at its extreme, but evil is far more extensive than these. The media give daily accounts of murders, assaults, robberies, arson, and muggings. We may take some comfort in thinking that these are the doings of other people, but even good people commit evil in their daily lives—jealousy toward a successful co-worker, hurtful remarks we didn't need to make, failure to help someone, ethnic or religious prejudice. Evil is quite literally everywhere.

Yet ultimately evil does not triumph. If humans were basically evil, why do we recoil from people like Hitler, Stalin, and Pol Pot, and why do we respond warmly to people like Gandhi, King, and Mother Theresa? We want to see an end to war, hunger, and poverty; we want people to

1

be treated with dignity, regardless of race or social and economic status; we want to love and be loved. Basically we are good people.

If we are basically good, then why do we do evil at all? Why do we hurt people instead of help them? Why do we put our own wants and desires ahead of the welfare of others, even ahead of the welfare of the planet? When we know that what we are doing is something that goes against our best instincts and interest, why do we do it anyway? As Paul, the first great Christian writer, lamented, "For I do not do the good I want, but the evil I do not want is what I do" (Rom 7:19). Evil is the most puzzling aspect of human life, especially for people who are theists or believers in God but also for secularists and atheists.

Evil has always presented a unique problem for theists, particularly those of the Western, biblically-centered religions who believe that a good and powerful deity exists and is active in the world. A good god would not want evil to occur and a powerful deity would be able to prevent it, but since evil does happen, obviously the good and powerful God of Judaism, Christianity, and Islam at least permits it for some reason of his own. [Although I prefer inclusivist language, we will follow the biblical image of God as masculine.] Theists recognize this problem, and every major religion has produced a theodicy, the technical term for the attempt to explain the relation of God to evil.

In this book we will trace how thinkers in the West have tried to understand and explain evil. Until the eighteenth century, most Western thinkers were religious, and so they created theodicies. In addition, religious people for centuries had to explain evil not only in terms of God but in terms of the devil, a minor figure in Judaism but a major one in traditional Christianity. Believers understand the devil to be a supernatural being who does evil to humans, but who can only act with the permission of God. Although belief in the devil continues to be high today (*The Economist* magazine reported in 1997 that 63 percent of Americans believe in the devil), many educated theists think that scientific advances have driven him from the world and that no serious discussion of evil should include a mythical figure. But we must include the devil because the devil has always functioned as the personification of evil, and believers in the devil, such as Dante and Milton, have provided startling insights into the nature of evil itself.

Defining Evil

In the 1970s, the Public Broadcasting System showed a series entitled "Civilization," hosted by the British art historian Kenneth Clark. The series opened with Clark standing on the bank of the Seine River in Paris. He told the audience that he could not define civilization, but that he could recognize it when he saw it. He then turned and looked toward the magnificent Medieval Gothic cathedral of Notre Dame.

To "civilization" we can add a host of other terms which defy precise definition but which we use every day, terms such as "education" or "friendship" or "success." Evil falls into this category. Ultimately, perhaps, we cannot define it, but we can still recognize it when we see it. If we see an abusive adult savagely beating a small child, we know immediately that this is an evil act; we do not need to measure it against some scientific or philosophical or religious criterion. Evil is too universal a phenomenon to be defined only by scholars.

On the other hand, a book that traces the history of the idea of evil has to provide at least a working definition of the term.

A great American authority on evil, Jeffrey Burton Russell, has written that "the essence of evil is abuse of a sentient being, a being that can feel pain. It is the pain that matters. Evil is grasped by the mind immediately and immediately felt by the emotions; it is sensed as hurt deliberately inflicted" (*The Devil,* 17). We will abbreviate this thoughtful observation to "the deliberate imposition of suffering by a human being upon another sentient being."

"Deliberate" means that the person committing the evil deed knows what she or he is doing. Many people hurt others unintentionally, sometimes even more than they could have done intentionally, but their acts are not evil.

"Imposition of suffering" means that the action harms a sentient being. The harm need not be physical. A man who would never strike a woman could harm his spouse by infidelity; a woman who would never hit her children could harm them with cutting remarks. And too many of us impose suffering upon ourselves without realizing what we are doing.

The phrase "another sentient being" would have surprised previous generations who would have expected "another human being," but humans can inflict harm upon animals, not just as individuals, but also as entire species as we drive more and more of them into extinction. Many modern people who practice eco-spirituality or environmental ethics would add the living planet to the list as well. The phrase "sentient being" can also include God, whom believers offend or disappoint by violation of divine commands or rejection of divine love.

This definition deals primarily with moral evil, the interaction of human beings with other sentient beings. But in the past, and even to an extent today, people have also believed in natural evil.

Natural evil refers to the harm done to us by natural forces, such as storms or disease. At first this does not seem as serious as moral evil because no natural force could ever wreak the havoc that humans have. But natural forces can sometimes be worse than human evil. The pains caused by the theft of your car would pale in comparison to the complete destruction of your home by a tornado, when you might literally lose everything, including many sentimental items which can never be replaced.

But is a natural evil really "evil"? Today most people consider the harm done by natural forces to be just natural phenomena. For a long time, however, destructive acts such as tornadoes, hurricanes, blizzards, floods, or earthquakes went by the name "acts of God," a phrase even used in the insurance business. This echoes the view that God controls the forces of nature, and so if a flood devastated a town, God, for some reason of his own, either sent it or permitted it. But then the "natural" evil is not purely natural because a supernatural being controls it, and it could not be truly evil because God can only do what is good. Both theists and secularists continue to use the term "natural evil," although most accept the scientific explanation that these destructive forces act in a purely natural way and no supernatural involvement is necessary and no moral lesson should be drawn from them. But the suffering caused by natural evil is real. If God acts in the world, then theists cannot completely dispense with natural evil.

A third type of evil, ontological evil, had a checkered career in the past and has almost no relevance today. Ontology means the study of how things exist, and some Western thinkers believed that certain types of beings were inherently superior to others, such as a rational human in comparison to an animal. Applying this concept to evil causes intellectual havoc, as a simple comparison can prove. Ontologically a human, as a rational being, is superior to a dog, but which being is morally superior: A human who commits crimes or a guide dog that faithfully helps a sightless child walk safely down the street? Another aspect of ontological evil was a dichotomy between matter and spirit, treating the spirit as good and matter as evil, a view still widely held in parts of Asia. This has few Western followers today, largely because the biblical book of Genesis asserts the goodness of creation, a view held by Jews, Christians, and Muslims.

This survey of different types of evil leads to an important and enduring theme in the development of the ideas about evil. Western thinkers distinguished between Evil, the inescapable fact that intelligent beings deliberately impose suffering upon other sentient beings, and evils, the manifold ways in which Evil can be manifest. The understanding of particular evils constantly changes. The English writer Francis Bacon (1561–1626) believed that humans ought to tame the natural world and replace the wild woods with cities and towns, yet many modern people consider the human attempt to dominate nature, rather than to live in harmony with it, to be an evil. Oftentimes the changing understanding of specific evils led to a new or different understanding of Evil.

Paths Not Taken

Some theistic explanations for evil have been marginal in the West but have been popular elsewhere.

Much of the difficulty about evil derives from monotheism, belief in one God, often a good and powerful deity who theoretically can stop evil but practically does not. But if people believed in more than one god, that particular problem disappears. Several traditions have opted for dualism, the belief in two divine principles, one good and one evil, while polytheism spreads things out even more, with belief in several good and evil deities. Dualism eliminates the apparent contradiction of a good and powerful God who refuses to stop evil. The good god wishes to stop evil but cannot because she or he lacks the power to do so. Contrariwise, the evil god wishes to propagate evil universally but likewise lacks the power to do so. Two independent beings each strive to achieve their goals, sometimes succeeding, sometimes failing, always struggling. Popular in Persia (modern Iran), dualism has had a real attraction for some people in Western history, such as the Manichees and Cathars (whom we will meet later). In general, however, it has been only a fringe movement in the West, and not just because of biblical monotheism. Greek philosophers reasoned their way to the existence of one deity who would be unlimited in virtually every way. Even atheists disbelieve in one god.

Dualism's problems lie with the relative powers of the two deities. If they are evenly matched, this would result in a kind of cosmic gridlock, with each one stifling the other's actions. And if one were more powerful than the other, would this still be dualism? In fact, history has seen few absolute dualisms. As disarmament conferences, nature preserves, and charity of every kind prove, we really do believe that good can somehow win out over evil. Even in formal dualistic religions, one can frequently find some ray of hope that the good being will save people from the evil one.

Another theory with a long history is the coincidence of opposites, the belief that God can reconcile in his person all that there is. Judaism and Christianity have affirmed the independent existence of diverse forces or elements, but in other traditions, especially Asian ones, emphasis has fallen upon their unity. Traditional Chinese religion teaches that in every individual one finds both yin and yang, the passive and active principles of the universe, and the unity of these opposites is essential to the being of the whole person. In the great Hindu epic the *Bhaghavad Gita*, Prince Arjuna has a vision in which he sees the unity of all that is, even life and death. For some religious thinkers, this principle of the unity of all can be applied to God, who somehow contains in himself both good and evil, not because he is essentially evil but because he is God, and thus all that is, even opposing forces and elements, resides in him. The coincidence of opposites is not completely foreign to the biblical religions; it even appears as a minor theme in the Hebrew Bible (the Christian Old Testament). Throughout Western history, this view has appealed more to mystics than to intellectuals, although some Medieval thinkers took it very seriously, and in the modern era the psychologist Carl Jung has given it a new form and impetus.

Yet another method of explaining evil is the belief that misery or happiness in this life depends upon what someone did in a previous life. This derives from the belief or hope that there is no such thing as innocent suffering. This view has attracted hundreds of millions of adherents in parts of Asia, but, like dualism, it has not caught on in the West. Belief in reincarnation goes against both the Western scientific attitude and the fundamental teachings of the biblically-based religions. Westerners have generally accepted evil as a force in this life, and they have tried to explain it via monotheism or atheism.

Familiar and Unfamiliar Paths

Attempts to solve the problem of evil have usually dealt with philosophy, theology, and, more recently, the social sciences. This history will deal with them as well, yet often our ideas of things arise less from the theoretical than from the concrete. At several points in Western history, most people's understanding of evil derived not from theories but from their attitudes toward the Other, those groups which stood outside or, more often, were made to stand outside the dominant society. In the modern era people respect and celebrate diversity, yet in the past the Other—the heretic, the Jew—was demonized and personified as evil.

This history will consider literary works as well as the traditional scholarly treatises. Christopher Marlowe's drama *The Tragical History of Doctor Faustus* and Mary Shelley's novel *Frankenstein* have influenced the Western understanding of evil as much or more than the writings of Voltaire and Freud. Most of the authors treated in this book are men for the simple reason that patriarchal societies prevented women from receiving an education and writing about evil or about almost any topic. The situation changed somewhat in the nineteenth century, and we will look at how women writers like Mary Shelley, Flannery O'Connor, Nel Noddings, and Marilyn McCord Adams have understood evil.

Until the eighteenth-century Enlightenment, most Western writers on the topic of evil were Christians. They routinely consulted the Hebrew Bible, so Jewish influence on their views is to be expected. Yet Jewish influence was much stronger than is often thought. The Garden of Eden myth provided the basis for the Christian view of original sin, while the book of Job remains the Bible's most commanding theodicy. Another Jewish notion, the cosmic battle between good and evil, had a tremendous effect upon how much of the ancient and Medieval Western world understood evil. Furthermore, although we commonly think of the Greeks impacting Christian culture as much as the Jews, this was not the case with the idea of evil. Christians accepted the biblical notions first and then fit Greek ideas into them.

Finally, many Christian ideas about evil originated on the African continent, in Egypt, and in North Africa. Because of the Muslim conquest and occupation of these lands, their contribution to Christianity and thus to Western culture has been sometimes overlooked. Yet African Christians made significant and long-lasting contributions to Western views about evil.

* * *

About 1000 B.C.E., the ancient Israelites told the story of humanity's beginning in a place called the Garden of Eden. In the fifth century C.E. an African Christian named Augustine used that Hebrew myth to create a wide-ranging and influential theory on the origin of evil. In the eighteenth century French Enlightenment thinkers attacked this theory as oppressive to humanity, and they exalted the role of science in explaining the human condition. Today psychology, a science in its infancy in the Enlightenment, dominates much thinking about evil, although many people still look to the Garden of Eden and many psychological explanations echo biblical views. The significance of the contributions each historical period made to the understanding of evil cannot be appreciated or evaluated without some knowledge of the other periods.

Yet the value of studying the history of evil lies not just in what it tells us about how people thought of evil in the past; it gives us real insights into the very nature of evil.

Chapter 2

Israel and Evil

Western ideas of evil began in ancient Israel, but the Israelites drew some of their ideas from a common stock of ancient Semitic traditions. They interacted constantly with their pagan neighbors, sometimes as allies, sometimes as enemies, sometimes as trading partners. Inevitably some pagan traditions impacted Israelite ones.

When the pagan gods created the world, they established a cosmos, a world which functioned reliably and a world in which the gods and the values they represented were respected. Farmers and shepherds depended upon the regularity of the seasons; they prayed that the gods would guarantee that the patterns remained unchanged. Any force which threatened that ordered world represented chaos or the lack of reliability. The forces of chaos challenged the gods' right from the beginning, and many societies have creation myths about how the gods battled against monsters. The myths often portray the gods as looking and acting like humans, although with more power and knowledge, while monsters represent the forces of chaos.

The most important creation story, the *Enuma Elish,* comes from Babylon (the remains of this ancient city are in modern Iraq) and dates to about 600 B.C.E., although the earliest version may be a millennium older. It is essentially a combat myth, recounting how the young male sky god Marduk battled against the older female sea monster Tiamat. Marduk pierced Tiamat's body with arrows, then crushed her skull with his mace, and finally divided her body into two parts from which he created the world. The figure of Tiamat plainly shows several elements of chaos. She is a monster, different from the gods and thus threatening to them and to the Babylonians. She represents the fathomless dark depths of the sea. And Tiamat was female. Like all patriarchal societies, Babylon justified its social structure by belief in supposed male superiority so that whatever threatened the patriarchy challenged a divinely established order, the cosmos. A strong female deity (or woman) had to be portrayed as evil. [In the better-known tales of Eve and Pandora, the world was perfect until women were created and introduced evil into it.] The Babylonians and other ancient Near Eastern peoples did not completely discredit the role of the female; they venerated goddesses who had great power, but a male god always reigned.

The combat with the sea monster appeared in several other ancient Near Eastern myths which influenced the people Israel. The Canaanites, Israel's neighbors in the Promised Land, venerated Baal, a fertility and warrior god. One account of his deeds recalls that he "smote Lôtan the ancient dragon," the "twisting serpent" with seven heads. The name Lôtan is related to the Hebrew word "Leviathan," the name of a biblical sea monster, and the seven-headed dragon will reappear in both Jewish and Christian texts.

The most famous Near Eastern myth is the *Epic of Gilgamesh*. Gilgamesh reigns as the king of a city-state. In the ancient world, the city represented civilization with walls and markets, rulers and laws, while the forces of nature represented the untamed, the wild, the chaotic. Gilgamesh learns that a fearsome monster, Huwawa, guards the cedar forests of what would be modern Lebanon. [The Greek word for cedar is *lebanon*.] By preventing people from cutting down the cedar forest, Huwawa denies them access to wood needed for building. He represents a threat to the city and thus to civilization. Gilgamesh must guarantee his people access to the forest. He symbolizes cosmos, and Huwawa symbolizes chaos. Gilgamesh journeys to the forest and kills the monster.

The ancient Near Eastern people saw evil at work primarily as chaos threatening cosmos, and so they emphasized natural evil. But what about moral evil? Surprisingly few texts deal with moral evil. The best known is the *Babylonian Theodicy*, recovered from Babylon and dating possibly to 1400 B.C.E. The text is short and fragmentary. The anonymous author writes in the first person about his pitiable sufferings—a rich man has ruined him and no one will stand up for him. He can neither understand nor accept his fate because he has always faithfully worshiped the gods. A friend stops by to offer platitudes, but the sufferer is not comforted. He can only trust in the gods and hope that they will somehow do what is best for their followers.

When the earliest Semitic pagan literature dealt with evil, it paid less attention to individual suffering than to cosmic struggle. People did consider individual suffering to be unimportant, but they saw such localized evil against a larger backdrop.

Some of these ancient themes made their way into the Hebrew Bible, which starts its story circa 1800 B.C.E. It goes through the people Israel's migration to Egypt, their enslavement there, the Exodus (thirteenth century B.C.E.), their settlement and conquest of much of Canaan (Palestine), a period of tribal confederacy, followed by a united monarchy under Saul, David, and Solomon (1020–931). Next came the divided monarchy with the two kingdoms of Israel in the north and Judah in the south. Assyria destroyed Israel in 721 B.C.E., and Babylonia destroyed Judah in 587 and carried off its leading citizens to Babylon. Cyrus the Persian conquered the Babylonians (539 B.C.E.) and allowed the Jewish leaders to return. From this point onward the Jews lived under foreign domination, first of the Persians, then of the Macedonian Alexander the Great and his successors, until the Maccabees liberated Judah in the second century, only to have the kingdom fall to the Romans in 63 B.C.E. Such a long time period meant that many different authors, representing many different points of view, composed the biblical books.

Abraham, Sarah, and the rest of their clan grew up in a pagan Semitic milieu. When they converted to the worship of a new god, they could not shake off all the culture which they had inherited, nor could several of the generations after them. The various tribes who made up the whole people had their own independent traditions, and they reworked myths and legends to suit their own religious needs.

The people Israel understood evil in several ways. The first they appropriated from their pagan neighbors, the chaos-cosmos myth.

The book of Isaiah tells how God "will kill the dragon that is in the sea" (27:1) and identifies God as the one "who cut Rahab in pieces, / who pierced the dragon" (51:9). Psalm 74 declares that God "broke the heads of the dragons in the waters" and "crushed the heads of Leviathan" (vv. 13-14). The book of Job praises God's mighty hand which "pierced the fleeing serpent" (26:13). Job goes on to praise God's power over the monsters Leviathan (41:1) and Rahab (26:12). Psalm 89:10 repeats the theme: "You [God] crushed Rahab like a carcass."

These have similarities not just to pagan themes but to actual pagan texts. Like Marduk, God slew the dragon in the sea; he pierced the dragon, cut it in pieces, and crushed its carcass. Psalm 74 repeats the dragon in the water theme, but adds that this dragon had multiple heads, recalling the seven-headed sea monster slain by the Canaanite god Baal. At one point in Israel's history, the people had a myth about how God battled against a dragon from the sea and how the forces of cosmos defeated the forces of chaos.

Why did these stories not survive as major texts but rather were relegated to occasional passages in poetry and prophecy? After the Exodus, later generations in Israel would advance to speculative monotheism and conclude that the "gods" of the pagans were "the work of human hands—wood and stone" (Isa 37:19). The older, chaos-cosmos view became outdated. In the tenth century B.C.E., King David centered the worship of the one god in Jerusalem, and King Solomon built him a grand temple. To portray God battling against a sea serpent offended his dignity and reduced him to the level of a pagan god, fighting for his survival rather than ruling the cosmos.

These older traditions could survive in other ways. Maybe God was too exalted to conquer the sea monster in battle, but he could conquer the sea at the greatest event in Israel's history, the Exodus, when he opened the Red Sea and allowed the people to cross through it safely. Psalm 106:9 says: "He rebuked the Red Sea, and it became dry," and the prophet Nahum says: "He rebukes the sea and makes it dry" (1:4). Both verses personify the sea as if it were the old monster.

The notion also survives in Genesis 1:1-3: "In the beginning when God created the heavens and the earth, the earth was a formless void and darkness covered the face of the deep, while a wind from God swept over the face of the waters. Then God said, 'Let there be light.'" In this economic way, the sixth-century B.C.E. Jewish author has reduced the chaos-cosmos struggle to its basics. The earth is formless and void. The Hebrew word for primeval waters is *tehom,* a word related to Tiamat, the Babylonian sea monster. The final chaotic element is the darkness which covers the waters. The "wind" from God which sweeps the water symbolizes God's power, and God brings cosmos in a simple, direct way: "Let there be light," the traditional symbol of intelligence and order.

The growing power of the one God of Israel had domesticated the combat myth, and the primeval darkness has usurped the role of the water as the chief symbol of chaos. In this way the older elements survived.

A second view of evil was the coincidence of opposites, the notion that God could reconcile in himself both good and evil. The book of Isaiah puts these words in the mouth of God (45:7): "I form the light and create darkness, / I make weal and create woe; / I the LORD do all these things." The text does not say that God is actually doing good and that humans do not understand what he is doing. It says simply and clearly that he makes weal and creates woe. He acknowledges that both light and darkness, good and evil come forth from him.

Supporting this passage are ones in which God acts in a contradictory and unfair way, and only the most involved interpretative gymnastics can find any good in what he does. In the book of Exodus (4:24-26) God tries to kill Moses, his chosen one, because Moses had not circumcised his son. Fortunately for Moses, his wife Zipporah recognized the threat and circumcised the boy, but why did God act in this way? Why not just warn Moses? Further on Moses asked Pharaoh to let the Hebrew people go, but he refused. God then sent plagues upon Egypt. After seven plagues, Pharaoh had had enough and agreed to let the people go. But God told Moses, "I have hardened his heart . . . in order that I may show these signs of mine among them, and that you may tell your children and grandchildren how I have made fools of the Egyptians" (Exod 10:1-2). God twice repeated this display of power, guaranteeing more plagues for the innocent Egyptians and yet not helping the Hebrews either since it only prolonged their suffering and slavery. In Exodus God has a negative side and has difficulty controlling it.

Clearly these are legendary accounts, but they witness to ancient Israel's belief in a deity who acted in strange and disturbing ways.

The coincidence of opposites could apply to more than evil. In the Genesis creation myth (1:27) we read, "So God created humankind in his image, / in the image of God he created them, / male and female he created them." Both male and female are required to reflect the image of God—and this view from a patriarchal society. In the book of Proverbs, a collection of practical and ethical advice, the anonymous author attributed all true wisdom to God and then personified wisdom as female and an essential part of the divine person. Wisdom speaks to the people in language reminiscent of the prophets who spoke on God's behalf. She is an associate of God in the task of creation, the great act of birth (chapters 1, 3, 9).

The coincidence of opposites is not the necessary explanation for evil. Yet combining passages which show God acknowledging that he makes weal and woe to those passages where he acts in a genuinely contradictory way to those which affirm a female element in the deity, the coincidence of opposites is one possible biblical explanation for the existence of evil, even if it is a minor one not traditionally favored by Jews and Christians.

A more widespread view of evil was based upon ritual purity, that is, the belief that some persons or objects or requirements were so sacred that any violation of them or their status offended the divine honor and usually demanded retribution. This notion has survived in modified form into the modern world. Some religious codes, such as kosher laws, forbid the eating of certain kinds of food, and some Christian denominations require observance of a general fast or an abstinence from meat on particular days. Ancient peoples took ritual purity for granted. In addition to restrictions about food, many societies prohibited marriages outside the ethnic group or demanded purificatory washings. Regulations had to be followed with the greatest care to detail, and only those holding the appropriate office could perform them. These restrictions had such force because people believed that God stood behind them. The ancients accepted these taboos and lived with them every day. In a way, these could be comforting because people knew that if they observed the precepts laid down by God, they were pleasing him.

But this approach had another side. When someone within the group violated the prescribed ritual, God often took terrible retribution. Those outside the group were often thought to be impure, and they could be treated as if they had violated the ritual purity. The book of Joshua recounts the Israelite conquest of Canaan. As the invaders prepared for the capture of Jericho (chapter 6), Joshua told them that the city and everyone and everything in it fell under the Lord's ban, that is, the Israelites had to purify the city for God by annihilating it and its inhabitants, except for the family of a woman who had sheltered and protected two of Joshua's spies. Amid great slaughter, the army followed the command to the letter. The inhabitants of Jericho were unclean and thus undeserving of the Lord's mercy. After the destruction of this city, Joshua moved on to attack another one and suffered a severe defeat (chapter 7). He learned that Achan, an Israelite soldier, had kept for himself some loot which was supposed to be destroyed because it was unclean. Because of this God inflicted defeat upon the people Israel. For the sin of one soldier, God claimed that "Israel" had sinned; one person's sin had rendered the entire people impure before God.

Later in Israel's history, King David had established a new capital city, Jerusalem, where he wanted to place the ark of the covenant, a sacred shrine symbolizing the Lord's presence among the people, which could be touched only by the ritually pure. The ark was brought to the city in an ox cart driven by two men, one named Uzzah.

> Uzzah reached out his hand to the ark of God and took hold of it, for the oxen shook it. The anger of the LORD was kindled against Uzzah; and God struck him there because he reached out his hand to the ark; and he died there beside the ark of God (2 Sam 6:6-7).

Uzzah feared that the ark would fall off the cart, and so he propped it up. He was not ritually pure enough to touch the ark, so God killed him, in spite of his good intentions. "David was angry because the LORD had burst forth with an outburst upon Uzzah" (2 Sam 6:8). But soon even David himself, God's chosen one, was afraid of the Lord and decided to restrain his anger (6:8-11). Moderns can recognize the legendary elements in these accounts, but they still represent the ancient Israelite view.

But ritual purity ultimately cannot be the prime definition of goodness. This was recognized in ancient Israel by the prophets, who introduced an important new view of good and evil by making social justice the centerpiece of their teaching. Israel had prophets for much of its history, but the greatest names lived during the time of the eighth and seventh centuries B.C.E. They focused on the problems of the poor and oppressed, and they often did so by excoriating the rich and powerful. The prophet Micah blamed the government officials who had no concern for the lowly.

> Listen, you heads of Jacob
>   and rulers of the house of Israel!
> Should you not know justice?—
>   you who hate the good and love the evil,
> who tear the skin off my people,
>   and the flesh off their bones (Mic 3:1-3).

Amos denounced those who

> trample on the needy,
>   and bring to ruin the poor of the land, . . .
> buying the poor for silver
>   and the needy for a pair of sandals (Amos 8:4-6).

Speaking on the Lord's behalf, he demands of the people, "Let justice roll down like waters, / and righteousness like an ever-flowing stream" (Amos 5:24). The great Isaiah indicted the people of Jerusalem, his own city:

> Everyone loves a bribe
>   and runs after gifts.
> They do not defend the orphan,
>   and the widow's cause does not come before them (Isa 1:23).

He had special contempt for dishonest judges,

> who make iniquitous decrees,
>   who write oppressive statutes,
> to turn aside the needy from justice
>   and to rob the poor of my [God's] people of their right (10:1-2).

Like all social reformers, the prophets painted a bleaker picture than conditions warranted, but they speak even today with the greatest moral voices in the ancient world. Naturally, the people whom they indicted resented such treatment. Many people defended their religiosity by citing their faithful observation of cultic and ritual purity. But the prophets would have none of that. Claiming to speak in the Lord's name, Amos said, "I hate, I despise your festivals, / and I take no delight in your solemn assemblies" (5:21). Micah asked,

Will the LORD be pleased with thousands of rams,
    with ten thousands of rivers of oil?
    . . . what does the LORD require of you
but to do justice and to love kindness,
    and to walk humbly with your God? (6:7-8).

Isaiah phrased it most forcefully:

Bringing offerings is futile;
    incense is an abomination to me. . . .
    I cannot endure solemn assemblies with iniquity. . . .
Wash yourselves; make yourselves clean;
    remove the evil of your doings
    from before my eyes;
cease to do evil,
    learn to do good;
seek justice,
    rescue the oppressed,
defend the orphan,
    plead for the widow (1:13-17).

These stunning passages make the prophets' message clear. They do not denounce ritual observance as wrong, but they make it clear that ritual observance without a pure heart is useless and its hypocrisy offends God. What good does it do to offer a ritually exact sacrifice to God if you do not care for his people?

In a few generations the moral authority of the prophets had changed the nature of evil. Evil still meant disobeying the divine will, but now the Israelites understood the divine will differently. God wanted social justice more than anything else. But the Law of Unintended Consequences also came into play. By changing the notion of evil, the prophets had also changed the notion of the divine, and this in turn changed again the notion of evil. The prophets emphasized the total goodness of God, and they hesitated to picture the deity savagely avenging every violation of the ritual and legal code. (The coincidence of opposites also faded in the face of an all-good deity.) Yet even the God of social justice could not just walk away from the ritual and moral codes, and their violators still received punishment. But if not from God, then from whom? Enter Satan.

Although the ancient Israelites practiced monotheism, they did not picture God as being alone. Several biblical passages (1 Kings 19; Psalm 82; Job 1) portray him as surrounded by a divine assembly of the heavenly beings called the *bene ha-elohim,* the "sons of God." It also speaks of other heavenly beings, the divine messengers—*mal'ak* in Hebrew, *angelos* (angel) in Greek. Thanks to generations of artists, everyone knows what angels look like, but the Bible never once describes an angel. It does make it clear that they speak and act on behalf of God himself. No passage makes this more clear than the Exodus account of the burning bush: "The angel of the LORD appeared to him [Moses] in a flame of fire out of a bush; he looked, and the bush was blazing, yet it was not consumed" (3:2). Since this event convinced Moses to return to Egypt and liberate his people, this is a pivotal account for the Hebrew Bible, and yet it was not God but his angel who spoke to Moses.

As monotheists the ancient Israelites, like other ancient peoples, were reluctant to drag God out of heaven for every matter. Pagans had lesser deities for minor concerns; Israel envisioned God using lesser beings to effect his will on earth. Inevitably, some of the angels' tasks were negative ones.

Second Samuel 24 portrays God, whose anger "was kindled against Israel," ordering David to take a census of the people, normally considered to be something unholy since only God should have such knowledge. David did so but suffered remorse. "David said to the LORD, 'I have sinned greatly in what I have done. But now, O LORD, I pray you, take away the guilt of your servant'" (2 Sam 24:10). The prophet Gad, speaking on God's behalf, gave David a choice of punishments for his sinful act. David chose three days pestilence in the land, and God's angel spread a plague that killed seventy thousand people. Only when the angel turned to destroy the holy city of Jerusalem did God stay his hand.

As the angels more and more carried out God's "dirty work," they took on evil overtones, even though their actions were theoretically just. The most dangerous heavenly being was a satan. This is a seemingly strange usage: "a" satan, since we normally think Satan was a proper name. Not originally. The Hebrew word *satan* means an adversary or accuser, and, like a prosecutor, he accuses humans of sins against God. Several times the word has a verb form, "to play the satan" or "to act like a satan." The earliest occurrence of the word—as a verb—is in the book of Numbers. When the pagan wizard Balaam sets out to curse the people Israel, God sends an angel to block his path. The angel "plays the satan" (22:22). Later Jewish writers and all Christian ones would make Satan a proper noun and identify him with a fallen angel. The Hebrew Bible uses the word as a proper noun only three times, all in relatively late books, ones written after the Jews had returned home after the Babylonian captivity of the sixth century B.C.E.

In the book of Zechariah, the prophet has a vision in which he sees "the high priest Joshua standing before the angel of the LORD, and Satan standing at his right hand to accuse him. And the LORD said to Satan, 'The LORD rebuke you, O Satan!'" (3:1-2), because Satan has misjudged Joshua and thought he had sinned. Satan stood in the presence of the Lord who did not banish him but rather restrained him from acting too harshly.

The story of David's census appears in another biblical book. Although 2 Samuel says that God inspired David to take the census and then punished him for doing so, this scenario troubled an anonymous Jewish author of the fifth century B.C.E. He decided to do something about it, retelling the history of Israel in the two books of Chronicles and stressing the importance of the House of David. When the Chronicler got to the census he wrote, "Satan stood up against Israel, and incited David to count the people of Israel" (1 Chr 21:1). He simply changed the text. Just as earlier writers had rejected a deity who battled with monsters and killed people for the slightest violation of ritual purity, so the Chronicler rejected a deity who would incite David, his chosen one, to sin. By the year 400 B.C.E. Satan had apparently gained enough independence that the Chronicler could simply attribute such an act to him without having him act on God's behalf.

In the book of Zechariah, Satan acts rightly although mistakenly in accusing the high priest. In the Chronicler's account, however, he directly does something evil. He has acted independently of God, a theme which appears more prominently in the third and longest account of the Satan in the Hebrew Bible, the book of Job.

No one knows when the book of Job was written. Scholarly dates range from the seventh to the fourth centuries B.C.E., although most place it around the year 500. This remarkable book represents the theology of a growing Jewish internationalism, the view that the one God of Israel rules all nations. The anonymous author of Job expresses this view by making his hero not a Jew but a Gentile, a Bedouin, "a man in the land of Uz" (1:1), who experiences a universal problem for religious people: Why do good people suffer? The anonymous Jewish author created the classic theodicy, which we will examine later. For now let us see what he said about Satan, who makes his most important appearance in the Hebrew Bible in the first two chapters of this book.

"One day the heavenly beings came to present themselves before the LORD, and Satan also came among them" (1:6). Satan is not in hell but is a member of the heavenly court. God asks him if he has seen the piety of God's servant Job. Satan logically replies that Job serves God faithfully because he has given him family and riches, but if Job were to lose all those "he will curse you to your face" (1:11). God then authorizes Satan to take power over all that Job has, although not to touch his body. Armed with divine permission, Satan visits evil upon Job, destroying his ten children and their families, most of his servants, and all of his livestock, but Job does not despair or curse God.

God has proved his terrible point with Satan, who should now back off. Yet Satan returns to the attack, claiming that if Job's body suffered, he would curse God. God permits another assault on Job, whose body

Satan covers with "loathsome sores from the sole of his foot to the crown of his head" (2:7). Yet Job still does not despair or curse God. Satan now disappears from the story.

The author of Job does not present Satan as an evil being but as one of the sons of God who can act only with divine permission. Yet Satan still emerges as more than just the divine servant. God proves him wrong about Job, but he does not accept this. He insists on a second test. As with the first test, he can only act with divine permission, but his insistence on the second test shows that he can act on his own and without divine prompting. This Satanic independence would grow.

Three passages from a collection as large as the Hebrew Bible do not provide much to work with, and we cannot draw extensive conclusions about Jewish views of Satan. The biblical authors removed God from direct participation in actions which humans find reprehensible, and they replaced him with the sons of God or, more frequently, angels. Satan, the Accuser, has begun to act independently of God. Later Jewish tradition would expand his role considerably.

Yet an important passage seems to be missing. Did not Satan tempt Adam and Eve in the Garden of Eden? Actually, no, although some later Jewish authors made this claim (Sol 2:24) and so did the Christian author of the book of Revelation (12:9; 20:2). Later Christian authors made much of this identification, and John Milton enshrined it for the English-speaking world in *Paradise Lost*, but the book of Genesis does not mention Satan. The serpent is a serpent, a traditional Semitic symbol of chaos and an echo of the great sea serpents of pagan mythology.

The Genesis story does deal with evil, but on a rudimentary level. Although artists portray the first humans as adults, they were very much like children. They lived in a garden where, like all young children, they had no conception of work or illness or death. They also had no conception of sexual shame since they were naked together. The father figure in the sky watched out for them. But all children reach adolescence, which manifests itself in two ways, rebellion and sexual awareness. These two children defied the father figure by disobeying his commandment, and this act of rebellion was soon followed by sexual awareness: "the eyes of both were opened, and they knew that they were naked" (Gen 3:7). But they quickly found out that growing up brings problems of its own. Eve will bear children in pain, and her husband shall rule over her; Adam shall toil to bring forth food from the ground. Both of them will die. The story ends with the father figure throwing them out of the house.

The patriarchal element is strong. Not only is Eve blamed for listening to the serpent, she must accept her husband's rule over her as a consequence of her action. As for Adam, God reproaches him: "Because you have listened to the voice of your wife, / and eaten of the tree . . ." (Gen

3:17). The man's initial fault was to listen to the woman, a true sign of chaos to the ancient patriarchal mind.

For the ancient Israelites, the Garden of Eden was not the great drama of good and evil. Adam appears in only one other place in the Hebrew Bible, in the opening verse of 1 Chronicles which lists him as the first ancestor of Abraham; Eve literally appears nowhere else. Their story was a creation myth with the traditional themes of chaos and cosmos, but later speculation, Jewish and especially Christian, would transform it.

In addition to providing the Hebrew Bible's longest account of Satan, the book of Job offered the ancient world's most significant theodicy and still one of the best ever written. It dealt with the mystery of innocent suffering, and it challenged the traditional view. For the traditionalists, if people suffered, it was because of something evil that they had done. In this all-encompassing theory, innocent people simply did not suffer. The anonymous Jewish author of Job found this explanation too facile, and he faced up to the question of innocent suffering. He used his considerable skills to frame the issue in a way the conservative religious mind could accept while still making a daunting rejection of the traditional view.

The prologue set in heaven establishes the folkloric nature of the tale. By the time Job was written, the Jewish understanding of God had moved beyond the stage where he had to accept Satan's challenge. All God really had to do was tell Satan that he was wrong and that would be the end of the matter. But the folklore setting meets an important goal of the author. It enabled the traditionalist to read an account which acknowledges innocent suffering, because it is, after all, just a story and need not be taken too seriously. The ending of the book reinforces this because there God gives to Job more children and more wealth. The short-sighted reader could actually finish the book thinking that nothing had really changed, that Job certainly suffered but God made it up to him and even gave him more. Yet between the prologue (chs. 1–2) and the ending (ch. 42) the author has composed thirty-nine chapters of great Hebrew poetry which demolish the traditional view.

At the end of the prologue Job sits in misery among the ashes, and three friends come to see him. These friends will represent the traditional view of evil and thus become foils for Job, but they deserve credit for maintaining another traditional view, that of community—they are there for Job. They naturally assume he has done something to deserve this suffering. When Job proclaims his innocence, they take the logical course and urge him to acknowledge what he has done wrong. How can he be reconciled to God if he denies any wrongdoing? The irony is effective. To admit a wrongdoing would be to lie and thus to do wrong. Job stands his ground, no easy task since he had been brought up with the same viewpoint as his friends.

As the friends persist in trying to get Job to admit how he had sinned, their arguments become more elaborate and increasingly bitter. They ask Job if God can do wrong. They ask if he dares to judge God. All, however, to no avail. Job insists he did no wrong, and he calls on God to acknowledge this. The friends' attitude progressively turns from concern for Job to anger and confusion. As Job steadfastly refuses to admit wrongdoing, he forces his friends to consider the impossible—maybe they are wrong, maybe there is such a thing as innocent suffering, maybe suffering does not result solely from divine retribution for evil. Job reduces his thoroughly shaken friends to silence. At this point in the story a man named Elihu appears (chs. 32–37), advancing the traditional argument by pointing out the redemptive nature of suffering, but he also fails to move Job. Only God can answer him. To Job's surprise, God does.

God speaks to Job out of a whirlwind, demanding that Job answer questions, mostly about the creation and the natural world. "Where were you when I laid the foundation of the earth? / . . . When the morning stars sang together / and all the heavenly beings shouted for joy?" (38:4, 7). God compares his power to Job's: "Can you draw out Leviathan with a fishhook?" (41:1). God even resorts to sarcasm: "Who determined its [the earth's] measurements—surely you know!" (38:5). The reader finds this uncomfortable. Hasn't God already done enough to Job? Does he have to treat him this way?

But such treatment is essential to the author's answer to the question of why a good and powerful deity permits evil. For him, God is simply beyond human ability to comprehend. His intimidating speech emphasizes the gap between divine and human; even a good man like Job cannot bridge it. For some horribly inexplicable reason, a deity who could prevent innocent suffering allows it. Humans can never understand why he does what he does; they can only trust that he cares for them and that somehow innocent suffering fits into a larger plan of his. Ultimately Job acknowledges this: "Therefore I uttered what I did not understand, / things too wonderful for me, which I did not know" (42:3). In a final touch of irony, the author allows Job to maintain his innocence, but he does show Job doing something wrong by challenging God's conduct.

At the end of the book, God restores Job's wealth and gives him more children. Although this device pacified traditionalists by suggesting that the old system still worked, this anonymous author had produced a brilliant and revolutionary theodicy. God does permit innocent suffering and will not reveal why because we cannot understand his ways.

The author of Job advanced the question of evil by insisting that innocent suffering occurs. He also insisted that he and his fellow Jews had to acknowledge and somehow trust a deity who appears distant and silent at times of great crisis when his people need to feel his presence the most. Such a theodicy is a difficult and even a terrible one, but, for religious people, it may be the only one. The book of Job's theodicy presented too decisive a break with the past to win instant acceptance, and the traditional view persisted, but more and more people had to deal with the question Job had raised. To many, a God who permitted the evil of innocent suffering was not much better than a God who caused it. They looked for another reason for evil. Once again, enter Satan.

Apocalyptic

In the second century B.C.E. a new type of Jewish literature flourished, apocalyptic, from the Greek *apocalypsis* meaning revelation. Its authors claimed to have many revelations, often mediated through angels or great figures of Israel's past, such as Enoch or the twelve sons of Jacob. The revelations followed some definite lines: a recapitulation of Israel's history but with an emphasis upon the most recent times; an account of the people's sufferings at the hands of oppressors, coupled with the divine retribution visited upon sinners and salvation offered to the good; and the attribution of evil to a host of demonic forces.

It is quite a jump from the hesitant independence of Satan in the biblical books to a horde of demons in apocalyptic literature. Foreign influences probably caused the change. In 539 Cyrus the Great, king of the Persians, defeated the Babylonians and permitted the Jews who were in captivity in Babylon to return home. He gave them freedom of religion but not political freedom; Persia ruled the Jews until 331 B.C.E.

The Persians practiced Zoroastrianism, a dualist religion, which taught how the good god Ahura Mazda struggled endlessly against the evil god Ahriman. The Persians did not try to convert the Jews, but the Jews inevitably came to know about Persian beliefs and practices. As monotheists, the Jews could not accept dualism, and throughout the Persian period they maintained their belief in the one God of Israel. Yet it is likely that their notion of Satan, initially a punishing angel taking the first few steps away from God, was augmented by the Persian notion of a strict dichotomy between good and evil beings. In apocalyptic literature, the forces of evil would never match those of the good God, but they clearly act independently of God and not on his behalf.

Persian rule lasted until the conquests of Alexander the Great in 331 B.C.E. After his death in 323, his generals divided up his empire, and the Jews had Greek rulers until the Maccabee brothers liberated them in 165. The Jews had endured foreign domination, even foreign occupation, but the Greeks were the first Western people to interact extensively with them. The new rulers knew that a comparative handful of Greeks could not forcibly rule the peoples of the Near East and Egypt, and so they tried to win them over by convincing them of the superiority of Greek culture. Most Jews resisted, but some Greek influences slipped through.

The Greeks influenced Jewish conceptions of evil with their belief in an afterlife with rewards and retributive punishment, not meant to reform sinners but simply to avenge the offenses they had committed against the gods and humans. Before this period, the Jews had a notion of an afterlife, the continued existence of human spirits in a dreary place called Sheol. Some Jews were moving in the direction of the resurrection of the blessed, and the Greek views furthered that trend. The Jews did not appropriate these new attitudes very quickly, and some always rejected them. But this notion of an afterlife clearly altered Jewish views of evil, especially the notion of retributive punishment. (The place of eternal punishment took the name Gehenna from a valley near Jerusalem where infants had been sacrificed by fire.) Now God could reward the good and punish the wicked posthumously, thus evening the score. In recounting the fate of Jewish martyrs who chose to die rather than to abandon their faith, 2 Maccabees, written about 125 B.C.E., embraces the notion of resurrection for the blessed and damnation for the wicked. Since these martyrs clearly did not deserve to suffer, the notion of resurrection offers an answer to the question of innocent suffering. The biblical book of Daniel likewise speaks of postmortem rewards and punishments (12:1-3).

The Greeks also brought some new words with them. The Hebrew word *satan* meant "the accuser," which in Greek became *diábolos,* which in turn became *diabolus* in Latin, and so *diable* in French, *diavolo* in Italian, *teufel* in German, *diabolo* in Spanish, and devil in English. [The word "devil" has nothing to do with the word "evil." It is simply the English form of a Greek word.]

The Greeks also introduced to the Jews the word *daimon,* or demon in English. The word has a long history in Greek. Originally it could mean a god, but gradually demons left heaven and became lesser gods on earth. The philosopher Plato tells how his teacher Socrates had a demon who sometimes inspired him. But just before the Greeks arrived in the Near East, the word had come to mean a minor evil spirit, and that is how the word usually appears in Jewish writings.

Why did apocalyptic literature become prominent in the second century B.C.E.? It arose in times of persecution, when God permitted foreigners not only to dominate the people but also to threaten their religious life. Pious believers could not accept that God had deserted them, so they interpreted their troubles as a time of testing before God would rescue his chosen ones and punish their oppressors.

The oppressors not only afflicted the people, they insulted the people's God. One Greek king, Antiochus IV (175–164), went so far as to prohibit observance of the Sabbath and even circumcision, the sign of Israel's covenant with God. Such evil went beyond the political and into the spiritual realm. It was natural for the Jews to believe that God would intervene again as he did when Pharaoh had persecuted them. But now some Jewish writers saw a more-than-human conspiracy here. Apocalyptic literature regularly vilified oppressors, but it also looked for the influence of evil spirits behind the persecutors.

The influence of evil spirits went beyond the acts of the persecutors. They became responsible for violations of the religious law, and apocalyptic literature filled hell with sinners of all kinds. ["Hell" is an English word, not a Hebrew or Greek one, used here since it is the familiar term for a postmortem place of punishment.] It is not always clear if the demons are inmates or jailers or both in hell, but apocalyptic literature was primarily visionary and exact boundaries cannot apply.

The First Book of Enoch (I Enoch), a composite work begun in the second century B.C.E., tells how the ancient sage had visions of the sweep of biblical history and of the spirit world. Enoch starts his account with the creation and focuses on an episode recounted in Genesis where "the sons of God saw that they [human women] were fair; and they took wives for themselves of all that they chose" (6:2). An angry God barred them from heaven. *I Enoch* expands upon this episode, identifies the sons of God with wicked angels, and claims that this group, led by an angel named Semyaza, taught humans on earth all sorts of wickedness, such as astrology and enchantments. For good measure, they also taught women how to wear makeup, of which the conservative author disapproved. Because they looked at earthly women, they were called the Watcher Angels.

These fallen angels, their sinful descendants, and humans who follow them will have to face the day of judgment, and *I Enoch* paints a vivid picture of an afterlife of rewards and punishments. Significantly, the book directly addresses the suffering righteous who are still alive: "Do not be afraid, you righteous, when you see the sinners growing strong and prospering in their desires . . . for you shall become companions of the hosts of heaven" (*I Enoch* 102; *The Apocryphal Old Testament,* 308).

I Enoch also witnesses to the diversity of views about evil angels since another part of the book blamed the devil (here named Gadreel) for leading Eve astray (Adam is not mentioned), the earliest identification of the Eden serpent with the devil.

The *Book of Jubilees,* written between 160 and 140 B.C.E., elaborates upon the books of Genesis and Exodus, and it has many of the same themes found in *I Enoch*. The Watcher Angels appear again, but here their leader is named Mastema; again they teach people astrology and other pagan practices frowned upon by the Jews. *Jubilees* portrays Noah warning his children that demons will seduce them and their posterity. Noah was right, and Mastema sent his evil spirits into the world, thus introducing a prominent new element to the concept of the devil, the controlling evil leader who sends others off to do his bidding.

Jubilees introduces another important element by extending the devil's range in the Hebrew Bible. Mastema, not God, tried to kill Moses upon his return to Egypt. Mastema followed Moses to Egypt where he helped Pharaoh's magicians in their contest with Moses. And while it was God who demanded that Abraham sacrifice his son Isaac, Mastema was present at the event and was chagrined by God's decision to spare the boy. Since the Hebrew Bible had few references to an independent evil being, the concept of a devil had little basis in Scripture. But as interpreters found him assisting evildoers or even standing behind questionable actions by God, the devil's presence in the Bible expanded far beyond the limited range of the literal text.

Jubilees also emphasized the estrangement of humans from the natural world. When Adam and Eve leave the Garden of Eden, the animals, who up to that time were able to speak, lost that ability. The first parents' disobedience cut them off from God and nature, and it also cut off the animals from one another. The new emphasis on the Garden of Eden eventually provoked the *Life of Adam and Eve,* probably written initially by a Jew in the first century c.e. and then later edited by a Christian in the third century. This book also blames the devil (here called Satan) for the first couple's loss of Paradise.

This growing Jewish interest in Adam and Eve extended well beyond apocalyptic literature. The second-century b.c.e. sage known as Sirach wrote that "above every other created living being was Adam" (49:16). Eve he would not even mention by name, but he made clear what he thought of her: "From a woman sin had its beginning, / and because of her we all die" (25:24). The first-century b.c.e. book of Wisdom did not repeat Sirach's misogynism, but the author still alluded to the Garden of Eden: "But through the devil's envy death entered the world" (2:24).

No Jewish author ever mentioned original sin, and even the apocalyptic writers did not elaborate upon the Garden of Eden, but the story which interested so few writers of the Hebrew Bible was gaining prominence in second-century b.c.e. Jewish circles and would make a great impact on Christian circles.

Not all apocalyptic books retold Israel's history in visionary form. Some claimed to be "testaments," that is, the last words to their children by great biblical figures. The *Testaments of the Twelve Patriarchs,* written in the second century b.c.e., gives the last words of the founders of the Twelve Tribes of Israel. Familiar themes appear. Zebulun witnesses to the resurrection of the good and the judgment of the wicked; Asher speaks of two inclinations, one to good and one to evil, but an evil spirit named Beliar pushes us toward evil.

In the testament of Reuben, the ancient patriarch warns his children against Beliar and the spirits who serve him, and he adds a strong misogynist element. Starting with the basic premise, "Women are evil, my children," Reuben explains the fall of the Watcher Angels:

> They [women] allured them before the Flood; for as a result of seeing them continually, the Watchers lusted after them and changed themselves into the shape of men and appeared to them while they were making love to their husbands. And the women, lusting after these apparitions, gave birth to giants (*Testament of the Twelve Patriarchs, Reuben* 5; *The Apocryphal Old Testament,* 519).

This is an early appearance of the notion of the incubus, the evil spirit who takes on male form, even that of the husband, to make love to a human woman. More importantly, this passage shows that the increased emphasis on Genesis had now focused on women in general as sources of evil. Original sin has not yet appeared, and the Watcher Angels still have the onus of bringing evil to the world, but now their fall can be explained by—and blamed on—the women whose allure pulled them down from heaven. The Watcher myth would eventually fade away, but its replacement, the Fall in the Garden of Eden, would also blame a woman for the human predicament.

The apocalyptic literature offers a combination of old and new, old themes like patriarchy and excusing God from apparently harsh acts, new themes such as independent armies of evil spirits and the notion of an afterlife as a justification for suffering. The image of one devil is forming, even though many names (Gadreel, Mastema, Beliar, Semyaza) appear. The evil spirits occupy the foreground, but God is always in the background. He allows these spirits and the sinful humans who follow them to practice their wickedness, but eventually he will even the score. The combat myth originally depicted an action that occurred at the creation or shortly after, yet now it goes on for generations. God does not battle one monster but a horde of evil spirits. He does not defeat the monster in order to create the cosmos; rather, he judges the spirits and then establishes a new world of eternal life for the blessed and eternal punishment for the wicked.

One ancient image had managed to survive intact. The prophet Daniel "saw in my vision by night the four winds of heaven stirring up the great sea, and four great beasts came up out of the sea" (7:2-3). He described the beasts, one of which had four heads. Next came a heavenly figure called the Ancient of Days, who calls the four beasts to judgment. God was still battling sea monsters.

In the middle of the second century B.C.E., a group of religiously strict Jews rejected the kingdom of the Maccabees and the Temple of Jerusalem, both of which they believed to be too caught up in politics and not religiously pure. These Jews left Jerusalem and set up a community on the northwest shore of the Dead Sea called Qumran. This community disappeared from history in the Roman-Jewish War of 66–70 C.E., but its documents, the famous Dead Sea Scrolls, were discovered in 1947.

The documents portray a community of very pious people, intimately concerned with ritual purity and simultaneously apocalyptic in outlook. One of their books, the *War of the Sons of Light against the Sons of Darkness,* claimed that God had given them the Prince of Light to support them against the wiles of the Adversary (*satan* in Hebrew) whose name was Mastema. The Sons of Light will battle against the Kittim, probably the Romans, who are allied with Beliar, another evil spirit. Furthermore, the Sons of Light, who are now in exile, will return to Jerusalem for the conflict. The Qumran believers had no use for the unclean Gentiles, but they also had no use for those Jews who, they believed, did not keep the Law of God as they should, that is, as the Qumran believers kept it. They claimed that God would destroy those who did not keep his word. Furthermore, those not initiated into the community belonged not to God but to Belial. The Qumran believers took a step no one had taken before: they demonized some of their own co-religionists over a matter of faith. This shocking development found no support among other Jewish groups. Even apocalypticists who often accused others of sin refrained from demonizing them.

At the opposite pole was the writer Philo, who lived from about 20 B.C.E. to about 50 C.E. in the Egyptian city of Alexandria. A member of a prominent local Jewish family, Philo received a superb Greek education but always remained a believing and practicing Jew. Reconciling his classical learning with Jewish tradition posed a great challenge to him. He believed the Bible came from God, but he could not help but be impressed by the achievements of the Greek philosophers. He tried to reconcile but never to compromise the Bible with Greek philosophy. Like many Jewish scholars, Philo had difficulty with the apparent crudities of some biblical passages. He knew the Bible must be true, and so if it did not make sense on the literal level, then the passage was more likely a symbol or an allegory. The scholar has the duty to search for the higher meaning. So when Genesis talks about Cain fleeing from the "face" of God, Philo pointed out that God did not have a face as we do and Jews did not have to take that phrase literally. Rather they should understand "face" to mean God's presence. This approach has an obvious danger. Once the scholar has decided upon an allegory, what is to keep her or him from reading anything into the text? Philo recognized this, and he kept his allegorizing to what was necessary to make sense of the text.

Philo accepted the existence of demons but made little use of them in his writings. Following the Greek philosopher Plato about ontological evil, Philo believed that God had formed matter into a cosmos, but that "matter is recalcitrant, and to the extent that it resists the work of God, it may be considered evil" (Russell, *The Devil,* 167). Evil matter and human free will which could resist God combined to produce evil in us. Such views had little to do with the apocalyptic thinking so prominent in the first century. Philo would impact both Jewish and Christian interpretation of the Bible and understanding of evil but not for more than a century after his death. Instead of Philo, the apocalyptic writers rode high in the first century, and they actually got a war between the Sons of Light and the Sons of Darkness when the Jews revolted against the Romans in 66 c.e. But the revolt failed; the Sons of Darkness triumphed over the Sons of Light. Yet even defeat did not stop apocalypticism. Although diminished, it remained influential enough to spark a second Jewish revolt, from 132 to 135, which also ended with a Roman victory. Now apocalypticism became a marginal movement in Jewish circles. Since the Romans had also destroyed the Jerusalem Temple in the first revolt, the priesthood, which was associated with the Temple, likewise ceased to be a force in Jewish life. The future of Judaism passed into the hands of the rabbis whose strength lay not with the Temple but in the synagogues.

The rabbis who preserved and reconstructed Judaism took a sober and thoughtful path, emphasizing a learned and careful approach to the biblical text and cultural traditions. They initially kept their belief in demons, but evil spirits played a smaller and smaller role in their worldview. Not only did they smack of the excesses of pagan mythology, demons did not solve the problems of a monotheistic theodicy. If they existed, it was because God created them and permitted them to act, so the believer still had to reconcile the one God with evil. Some rabbis even feared that the existence of demons could compromise Judaism, making it a sort of modified dualism.

The ancient rabbis could not explain evil any better than anyone else could, but they chose to center it in humans rather than in evil spirits. They emphasized the goodness of God and the human freedom of the will. They concluded that we all have within us two inclinations, one to good and one to evil, and, using our free will, we must struggle to do the good. If this sounds like a miniature dualism with two inclinations replacing two gods, we must recall that the rabbis believed the one God would help humans if they believed in him and honored him. If they chose evil, they ran the risk of divine punishment, but the God of Israel had repeatedly shown himself to be a forgiving God. For the pious Jew, evil never had a level playing field.

The rabbis earned their reputation for considering every alternative, and many of them had views which modified or even disagreed with this general view. Some thought that even though something might appear evil to us, it was in fact good in God's sight. Others thought that God sent suffering upon people so that they would appreciate the good. Still others emphasized the afterlife as the place where God would right all wrongs.

All rabbis accepted the view of the author of Job that reconciling a good and powerful God with evil is beyond human comprehension. The rabbis' task was to explain it as best they could with the tools at hand (the Bible, tradition). Since they had to erect a code of daily living for Jews in society without a Temple but with foreign domination, they concentrated upon moral evil more than natural evil.

Yet much of the future of evil in the West was about to pass to another circle of Jews, the disciples of an itinerant Galilean rabbi named Yeshua bar-Joseph, and among those disciples both apocalypticism and evil spirits would take on new life.

Chapter 3

The New Adam

Just as sin came into the world through one man . . .
—Paul, Romans 5:17

The New Testament is the name given to the collection of twenty-seven books composed by Christians in the century after Jesus' death (circa 33 C.E.) and included in Christian Bibles. It includes twenty-one epistles or letters, an apocalypse, an account of the earliest disciples, and four Gospels, narrative works about Jesus, called the Christ (the Anointed One or Messiah) by his followers. "Gospel" is a modern form of an Old English word, *godspel,* a translation of a Greek word meaning "the good news." The Gospels are not eyewitness reports of Jesus' life but rather documents composed later on by people who relied upon oral traditions about him and who shaped that material to meet the needs of their communities. Mark wrote the First Gospel about the year 70, Matthew and Luke wrote some time in the 80s, and John about the year 100. None of the authors put their names on their works; the traditional names appear for the first time in the second century.

Between the death of Jesus and the composition of the Gospels, the apostle Paul dominated the period. From about 35 to his execution by the Romans in the 60s, he founded churches in much of Asia Minor (modern Turkey) and mainland Greece, and he wrote the first Christian literature, his epistles. Paul, like all New Testament writers, emphasized the One who had come to save the soon-to-end world from evil; he did not investigate the theoretical origins of evil or create a theodicy. He generally accepted Jewish ideas about evil, including evil spirits. Paul believed that on one occasion Satan prevented him from visiting the Christians in the Greek city of Thessalonica (1 Thess 2:18), and he warned the Christians in Corinth against the deviousness of Satanic temptation: "Satan disguises himself as an angel of light" (2 Cor 11:14). Turning from angels to humans, he contrasted those "who live according to the flesh" with "those who live according to the Spirit," and he concluded that "the mind that is set on the flesh is hostile to God; . . . those who are in the flesh cannot please God" (Rom 8:7-8). This has dualistic overtones which would reappear later in Christian history. It also echoes the rabbinic concern about the different inclinations a person has to do good or evil, possibly because Paul had studied with rabbis. His own words suggest a belief in the two inclinations: "I do not understand my own actions. For I do not do what I want, but I do the very thing I hate" (Rom 7:15).

But Paul contributed most to the question of evil by contrasting Christ to Adam. The Garden of Eden tale had been gaining prominence among Jews in the centuries before the Common Era, and Paul moved it to center stage. "Just as one man's trespass led to condemnation for all, so one man's act of righteousness leads to justification and life for all" (Rom 5:18). Paul did not mention Eve, much less blame her for sin, but instead used Adam as a symbol of the human race. Christ, the new Adam, would set things right. Paul did not directly equate the devil with the Eden serpent, although he claimed that God would crush Satan under the feet of believers (Rom 16:20), an allusion to a passage in Genesis (3:15) where God tells the serpent that the seed of Eve would crush its head. When he did mention Eve, he used her to demonize co-religionists whose teaching about Jesus differed from his own; Paul expressed his fear that as the serpent deceived Eve by its deviousness, his readers might be led astray by these false apostles (2 Cor 11:3).

Paul did not provide a systematic account of evil or of the devil, but he left much for later writers to fill in. He went beyond traditional Jewish notions, and he introduced a powerful new element which would impact all subsequent Christian thinking on evil, that Jesus had been sent by God to liberate the human race from bondage to sin, the second Adam undoing the harm done by the first.

Within a decade after Paul's death, Mark wrote the First Gospel. He revived a traditional theme, the combat myth, but now the devil replaced the sea monster. He set the pattern, and the other evangelists followed, also portraying Jesus battling Satan. Indeed, all the first Christians shared this view. Jeffrey Burton Russell points out that New Testament writers refer to the devil and demons 568 times, compared to only 340 references to the Holy Spirit (*The Devil,* 222, n. 3). Modern liberal Christians may reject belief in the devil, but the founders of the faith all saw evil in demonic terms.

In general, the Gospels record the triumph of Jewish apocalyptic notions. The world has now passed into the power of the demons. According to Luke (4:5-6), when Jesus was fasting in the Judean desert, the devil tempted him by showing him "in an instant all the kingdoms of the world. And the devil said to him, 'To you I will give their glory and all this authority; for it has been given over to me, and I give it to anyone I please.'" Jesus did not dispute the claim. The Gospel of John repeatedly stresses that the world lay in darkness until Jesus came. No writer explained how the demonic forces so escalated their power that they held the whole of creation in their power, but this belief defined the mission of Jesus.

The Christians believed that a new age had begun with him. God had created a pure world, but evil had perverted it. Now Jesus would abolish the chaos and bring in the cosmos. John's Gospel makes this most clear with its opening verse, "In the beginning was the Word and the Word was with God" (1:1). The Word of God is Jesus, and he was with God at the creation of the cosmos. The Gospels repeatedly show Jesus demonstrating his power over demons. He spurns the devil's temptations. He refuses to allow demons to speak, even when they acknowledge his power, because he will not accept testimony from an unclean source (Mark 1:34; Luke 4:41). Most spectacularly, he exorcises demons from possessed people (Mark 5:1-20; 7:24-30; 9:14-29; parallels in Matthew and Luke). So essential was this to Jesus' ministry that Mark reports it almost laconically: "And he went throughout Galilee, proclaiming the message in their synagogues and casting out demons" (1:39). Jesus redeems the world from the forces of evil.

The New Testament depiction of evil is largely demonic. The Gospels clarify basic teaching about the devil. There is one devil but many demons, although devil is sometimes used in the plural. Translations do not always observe the distinction, and "demon" in Greek becomes "devil" in English; furthermore, later generations of Christians often used the word "devil" in the plural. The Gospels also show that the Christians preferred the name Satan for their adversary. The New Testament includes other names for the devil, such as Beelzebul and Beliar, but these are used infrequently. Beliar appears only once (2 Cor 6:15), and while Beelzebul appears seven times, all instances are in the Gospels of Matthew (four), Mark (one), and Luke (two). By contrast, the name Satan appears in all four Gospels, the Acts of the Apostles, four Pauline epistles (Romans, 1–2 Corinthians, 1 Thessalonians), two pseudo-Pauline epistles (2 Thessalonians, 1 Timothy), and Revelation.

The devil leads a horde of fallen angels for whom an eternal fire was prepared (Matt 25:41). The devil roams about the world, harming human beings, occasionally by possession but mostly by temptation. The temptation of Jesus provides a model of how evil works. In the Gospel of Luke (4:1-13), the devil first offers Jesus bread, appealing to his physical desires, but Jesus declines the offer. Next Satan goes up a level, offering him the kingdoms of the world, symbolizing power and wealth, but again Jesus declines. The last temptation is a brilliant one. Jesus has twice turned down powerful temptations, proof of his personal moral strength. Good people often know that they are good and, if they are not careful, can take pride in that knowledge. The devil hopes to reach Jesus in that way, and so he takes him to the parapet of the Temple and urges him to hurl himself down because God will send angels to catch him. Jesus sees through this, too. He refuses to give in to spiritual pride, and Satan departs. Luke brilliantly shows how evil infects people, starting on a rudimentary level and moving up to self-deception.

Although the devil had replaced the traditional sea monster long before in Jewish tradition, the old combat myth slips through on occasion. The evangelist Mark says that Jesus and his disciples were in a boat when a great storm arose (4:35-41). Jesus speaks directly to the raging waters and says "be still," reminiscent of the old myths of God's victory over the sea monster. The personification of the sea is seconded by his disciples who ask, "Who is this, that even the wind and the sea obey him?" (4:41).

Regrettably, the Gospels also contain the first evidence of the demonization of the Jews by the Christians. Late in the first century, when the Gospels were being composed, many Christians had begun to separate themselves from Judaism, unable to reconcile their growing belief in the uniqueness of Jesus' person and mission with Jewish beliefs. Friction occurred, and by the end of the first century the Christians had begun to use intemperate language about the Jews. Matthew and Mark used dualistic language about those who believe and those who do not, and Luke aligned Jesus' Jewish opponents to the powers of darkness, but John blatantly demonized Jews. His Gospel starts off with allusions to Genesis, contrasting the light and the darkness. This theme continues throughout the Gospel as Jesus brings people to the light of his revelation. John had Jesus identify those Jews who believe in him as "the children of light" (12:36), but there are many who do not see the light. John portrayed them as shortsighted and willfully ignorant; when they defended their refusal to change by claiming they are children of Abraham (and so are faithful to Jewish tradition), John had Jesus put conditions on this paternity, conditions the Jews did not meet and which suggest illegitimacy. The Jews reply, "We are not illegitimate children; we have one father, God himself" (8:41). John then had Jesus give a frightful reply: "You are from your father the devil, and you choose to do your father's desires. He was a murderer from the beginning" (8:44). John himself was a converted Jew, and he apparently took it personally that other Jews would not follow the path he took. Internecine conflicts are always the fiercest. Unfortunately, many later generations of Christians would read this verse and see the Jews as the devil's offspring—people of no worth and deserving of persecution. We must respect the integrity of the biblical text and allow John to express himself as he wanted, but, like many other Christians, I wish those words had never been written.

The Gospels depict a world dominated by the forces of evil and Jesus as the savior liberating us from them, but there is something wrong with this picture. Jesus had lived and died and yet evil remained. If he conquered evil, why was it still around? The answer for Christians lay in another element of Jewish tradition, apocalyptic.

Jewish apocalyptic had responded to oppression, and so did Christian apocalyptic. Exiled by the Romans to the prison island of Patmos off the west coast of Asia Minor about the year 95, a Christian seer named John sent copies of his visions to seven churches on the mainland. Christians call this collection the book of Revelation. John's visions make it clear that Rome had become the enemy of the Church, and he demonized the Romans in terms familiar from Jewish apocalyptic. But John the seer also answered that troublesome question about why had evil survived after Jesus.

John faced the same question the Jewish writers had. If the Jews were God's chosen people, why did their oppressors succeed? The Jews believed that God had not deserted them; he could not desert them. What God did do was guard his wrath until some appointed time known only to him. Then he would wreak his vengeance on persecuting Gentiles and sinful Jews. This sounds like a forced explanation, but it is consistent with biblical teaching that there was simply no way that God would desert his people. When it appeared that he had, the Jews knew that this could not be and concluded that they just did not understand his intentions, and had to look more deeply into the matter. The Christians adapted this notion.

By the end of the first century, belief in an imminent end of the world had begun to wear thin. It had hardly disappeared, but many Christians wondered why it took so long for Jesus to return. Paralleling the Jews, they believed that there was simply no way Christ would desert his people. The book of Revelation takes an idea found in the Gospels, the day of judgment, and pushes it back to an unspecified but imminent future date. And so John the seer solved the problem. Jesus had indeed conquered the forces of evil, in the sense that he had broken their power and deprived them of any hope of final victory, but they still fight a rearguard action against us and will until the end of time when Jesus will come in glory to judge the sinners and the righteous.

John's apocalypse did more than solve the problem of the continuance of evil. It also established several Christian ideas about evil. First, John thought about it in cosmic terms. He wrote about the destruction of the world and its new creation, using Genesis imagery throughout the book. Like all humans, he knew the petty evils we practice every day, but these did not interest him. John's world does not consist of good and evil but of Good and Evil.

Second, he provided the Christians with a biblical foundation for identifying the Eden serpent with the devil: "the ancient serpent, who is called the Devil or Satan, the deceiver of the whole world," "that ancient serpent, who is the Devil and Satan" (Rev 12:9; 20:2). Jewish apocalyptic writers had initially made this identification, and John borrowed it from them. When John's book became a part of the Christian Bible, this identification became the standard explanation of the temptation of Adam and Eve.

Third, John demonized his enemies, the persecuting Romans, as well as some Christians he disagreed with. This, too, follows the pattern of Jewish apocalypses.

Fourth, John made an identification which Jewish and Christian writers had been hinting at. Although much biblical literature denies the existence of pagan gods, another tradition begrudged some power to them. In Aaron's contest with Pharaoh's wizards in Exodus, he turned his staff into snakes and they turned theirs into snakes as well. Aaron's snake devoured the others, but the Egyptian wizards still had power to turn staffs into snakes. How could this be? The Jewish apocalyptic *Book of Jubilees* had an answer: Mastema, the evil spirit, helped the wizards. John borrowed from Jewish authors, accusing "the rest of the human race" (pagans) of "worshiping demons and idols of gold and silver and bronze" (Rev 9:20). In the first Christian centuries, this attitude of gods-as-demons would replace the traditional view of empty idols of wood and stone.

Fifth, John created stirring imagery for evil. Like Daniel, he portrayed his current enemy as Babylon, and, borrowing from the biblical image of Israel as the bride of God, he inverted the image, picturing Rome as the Whore of Babylon, a scarlet woman (chs. 17–18). He supported the Christian notion of redemption by picturing Christ as a lamb, but this lamb does not just suffer. On the contrary, it leads his armies against the devil. To portray the enemy, John turned to an old acquaintance, the Jewish combat myth. "And I saw a beast rising out of the sea, having ten horns and seven heads. . . . It was given authority over every tribe and people and language and nation, and all the inhabitants of the earth will worship it" (Rev 13:1-8). As with the old pagan myths, the fate of the world rests on the outcome of this battle which the good deity will win.

John was not quite the lonely voice he may appear to be. More and more biblical scholars recognize the strong apocalyptic strain in much of the New Testament.

The Second Century

By the early second century the Christians had turned their eyes to the Gentile West. The Jewish element in Christianity remained large for some time, even in western areas, but the path of the young religion lay in a different direction from its parent. Thanks to Alexander the Great, his Greek successors, and the Romans, many Near Eastern peoples had accepted some degree of Western, Greco-Roman culture, but this had always lain over a bedrock of native culture. But now the Christians encountered Western culture in its homelands. Much of what the Christians encountered in the Greco-Roman world they had already encountered in the Near East. The Greeks and Romans had creation myths in which the chief deity Zeus overcame a monster named Typhon, a pattern repeated by the god Apollo who killed the great serpent Python, and by the human Cadmus who slew a dragon so that he could create a cosmos by founding the city of Thebes. The Olympian gods who look like humans defeated giants named Titans. The first woman, Pandora, became the classical patriarchy's focus of blame for all that was wrong with the world. And just as the author of the biblical book 1 Chronicles had substituted "Satan" for "God" in explaining why David took the census, so the Greek writer Plutarch in the second century claimed that myths which portray the gods in undignified fashion are actually talking about demons. The Stoic philosopher Epictetus had wondered how a good God could allow evil, and Plato had spoken about immortality and even reincarnation.

The Greek gods combined positive and negative qualities, helping and hurting human beings, often for no apparent reason. Not surprisingly in a patriarchy the divine vindictiveness was blamed most often on female deities such as Hera, wife of Zeus, who routinely and unfairly punished the human women with whom her lascivious husband had had love affairs or had even raped. The philosopher Socrates was not the only Greek who wondered what would happen to the world if humans acted like the gods. By the second century, however, belief in the classical gods had lost ground to mystery religions which stressed initiation rites and communal participation and which promised their devotees immediate, often physical benefits, such as increased virility or fertility. Most challenging to the Christians was widespread dualism.

An ancient Greek religious movement, Orphism, taught a matter-spirit dualism. An Orphic myth claimed that the evil Titans had eaten the young god Dionysius, the son of Zeus, who in turned killed the Titans and rescued the heart of his son. From the Titans' ashes sprang humanity, while Zeus reproduced Dionysius by implanting his heart in the woman Semele. The Orphics thus claimed that humanity has a dual origin, body/matter from the Titans and soul/spirit from the gods. The Titanic element causes wickedness, while the spiritual element, trapped in the body, struggles to be free. This cannot be accomplished in one lifetime, and the Orphics believed in metempsychosis, the transmigration of souls from one body to another, until the soul could be freed. The philosophy of Plato and his successors also had dualistic qualities. Plato believed that the world we encounter with our senses is a pale reflection of the real world, the world of ideas. We see only the reflection, but, in our ignorance, we think it to be what actually exists. We can have only limited apprehension of the real world in our earthly lives; in a famous image, Plato has Socrates say that the body is the prison of the soul.

Not all Greek thinkers agreed with Plato. The Stoic philosophers had defined goodness as living in harmony with the forces of the cosmos and evil as violating that harmony. But the ancient world looked heavily to Plato, and his successors took his notions about the cosmos to their logical conclusions. If this world is but a reflection of the real one, then it has no value. The Neo-Platonist Plotinus (205–270 C.E.) understood the One as a purely spiritual being at the top of an ontological scale, while pure, unformed matter occupied the bottom place. He transferred this to a moral scale; pure spirit represented the ultimate good and pure matter the ultimate evil.

Like most people who separate the spirit and matter, the Platonists had to explain the relation between the two. If the divine One is a pure spirit, then how did evil matter come about? Most thinkers settled for a series of emanations from the divine. The One emanated the Mind. Since the Mind was not the One, it was therefore a lesser being. This first emanation led to others in a descending scale until matter (evil) had been reached. But why would the One emanate anything in the first place? Some Platonists tried to save the One by separating it completely from matter by claiming that a lesser being, the creator god, made this world. This Platonic ideal appealed to many Christians.

Most Christians, however, rejected Greek dualism. Genesis taught that God had created the material world and saw that it was good. The Christians simply could not accept the Hebrew Bible and simultaneously consider the world or material things such as the body to be evil. But what if there were Christians who could not accept the Bible? [At this point in history the Christian Bible did not include the New Testament which was in the process of formation.]

The earliest Christians were Jewish. Most sincerely tried to reconcile the old faith with the new. But in the second century some Gentile Christians called Gnostics found little of value in the Jewish origins of their faith. They claimed that the Hebrew Bible contained a lot of nonsense, like a talking snake (Genesis 3) or a talking donkey (Numbers 22), but, most seriously for them, it told of a spiritual God who created the physical world. This is impossible, they said, claiming that Christians should reject the god of the Hebrew Bible. The Gnostics formed a widespread, variegated movement, united tenuously by the belief that Christ saved humans not by the redemptive death of his irrelevant physical body but by the knowledge (*gnosis* in Greek) which he brought to them. This knowledge of the cosmos he obtained from his father, the true God, who was to be distinguished from the creator god who formed the material world. No one knows exactly when Gnosticism entered Christianity, but it flourished in the second century when Christianity's Jewish background was fading and newly emergent Gentiles imposed their cultural values.

Most Gnostics felt uncomfortable with the Hebrew Bible, but since Jesus had believed in it, they had to reinterpret it to meet their own needs or to justify ignoring it completely. Ignoring the Bible proved surprisingly easy to do. The second-century Christians had no final list of books that belonged in the Hebrew Bible and no firm idea of whether there even were inspired Christian books, much less what they might be. Gnostic leaders claimed that their own teachings originated in the age of Jesus' disciples and had been passed along secretly in Gnostic circles where they were purged of Jewish elements unacceptable to the true devotees, that is, the initiated few who knew these secret teachings. Instead of turning people off, this anti-Semitic elitism actually gave Gnosticism some cachet for educated Gentiles.

This tendency could reach severe depths. About 140, a Gnostic named Marcion took another radical step, identifying the God of the Jews as the devil. Marcion feared the material world and the flesh, and he concluded that a deity who would create matter must be thoroughly evil. Yet other Gnostics feared to abandon the Bible so completely, and so they reinterpreted it to meet their own views of a spiritual redemption from the evil of ignorance. Some imaginative Gnostics simply turned the Bible on its head. In the teaching of the apostle Paul, sin entered the world when Adam and Eve listened to the serpent and disobeyed God. But for Gnostics called the Ophites (*ophis* is the Greek word for serpent), the evil creator god sinned by imprisoning the spirits of Eve and Adam in fleshly bodies, but the hero of the story, the serpent, offered them redeeming knowledge. This generous act infuriated the evil deity, who then punished the two humans and the serpent. This singular interpretation of the Eden myth won no support outside Gnostic circles and not much within them, but it illustrates how fluid the notion of evil was in early Christianity.

Important as the Gnostics were in the second century, the future of Christian thought lay not with them but with the mainstream thinkers who preserved their faith's Jewish heritage and tried to understand the Bible. Yet even these thinkers now routinely used Greek ideas. About the year 95 a Christian named Clement of Rome praised God for maintaining the harmony of creation which flowed on in an orderly manner every day, the same description the Stoic philosophers would have given. Evil violated the cosmic harmony established by God, a view Clement did not develop although later thinkers did. Most mainline Christian thinkers had to adapt their faith to the challenges of Greco-Roman society and especially to the demands of Greek philosophical thought that spoke of the deity and of humans in terms like nature, essence, and substance. This meant that the Christians had to rethink their understanding of God, of Christ, of Christian living, and much more. They did not devote much time to evil but rather continued traditional Jewish and Christian ideas, including apocalyptic ones when it came to the persecuting Romans. The second-century Christians focused their ideas of evil on the devil.

A Palestinian Christian convert named Justin, martyred by the Romans about 165, showed the power of the demonic image. In spite of his philosophic education, Justin accepted the traditional notions that the devil was a fallen angel and the leader of other fallen angels; he was also the serpent in the Garden of Eden, and the gods of the pagans were actually demons. Justin linked the persecuting Romans with the devil. He also rejected the notion that sacrificing to idols was sheer futility. Instead he considered it to be devil worship. But Justin also added to the tradition about demons. He believed that God created all angels with free will and that the fallen ones had somehow abused that gift. Justin did not know what sin they had committed, but he accused them of seducing women and corrupting boys, so he probably leaned toward the Watcher Angels theory of Jewish apocalyptic. If this is the case, he would have considered their sin to be lust. He also believed that each of us has a good or guardian angel to aid us when temptation to sin arises. This reflects the old Greek view of the personal demon like the one Socrates had.

The Eden myth had grown in importance in Jewish and Gnostic circles, and inevitably the mainstream Christians had to deal with it and not just with the serpent-Satan identification. Justin involved Eve but not in a purely misogynist way. He drew a parallel between Mary, the Mother of Jesus, and Eve. One woman had been intimately involved in the introduction of death and sin into the world; the other had given birth to the one who would redeem humans from those evils. He did not develop this theme, but he opened the way for others. One of those others was Irenaeus of Lyons (ca. 130–ca. 200), an Asiatic Greek who lived in Roman Gaul (modern France). He declared that Eve had been a virgin when she listened to the serpent. Since the Gospels taught that Mary was a virgin when she conceived Jesus, Irenaeus made an effective comparison between the virgin who brought death and the virgin who brought life. Eve still represented evil, but he gave another woman a positive role in the salvation of humanity, a role still prominent in Roman Catholic theology. Irenaeus also introduced another remarkable notion that would lay dormant until the 1970s. Most ancient Jews and Christians believed that when humanity's parents disobeyed God and introduced death and sin into the world, they made a conscious, adult decision for which they and their descendants had to pay the price. Irenaeus argued that Adam and Eve were still children when the serpent tempted them and thus not really ready to deal with Satan's inducements. He even hinted that God should have let them mature a bit more before allowing the devil to tempt them. This theme did not catch on in a Church that would not countenance any notion which would compromise God's absolute goodness, but the theologian John Hick would revive it in the modern era.

Yet Irenaeus could go beyond this theme and see Eden in cosmic terms. Adam and Eve had not just disobeyed God, they had broken the harmony of the creation; they had introduced chaos into cosmos. The world had grown steadily worse from Eden to Jesus, who reversed the process. Through Jesus, God would restore the cosmos to its primeval state, and sin could not harm it again. God would recapitulate all in all. Like Irenaeus' views about Adam and Eve, this view did not last long, not because later generations found it offensive to God but rather because they disagreed with his notion of an earthly paradise, preferring a spiritualized heaven. Irenaeus also stressed several traditional themes. He knew John's Gospel, and he alluded to the passage in John (8:44) in which the evangelist says that the Jews are the children of the devil. He also demonized his opponents—not the Roman persecutors but Christians who disagreed with him. He reported a story about a Christian elder who denounced Marcion as "the first-born of Satan." "Heretics" now joined pagans and Jews as allies of the demons in the eyes of some rigorous Christians.

The second century had presented the Christians with a host of problems. The most serious was outright persecution by the Roman Empire, but they also had to adjust to a new culture, a powerful, invasive one that often had little sympathy for biblical thinking. They successfully fought off the Gnostic assault on the Bible, but they still had a long way to go in assimilating their biblical worldview to Greco-Roman culture. They found the answers to this challenge not in Greece or Rome but on the south shore of the Mediterranean.

Chapter 4

Out of Africa

The harvest of the Nile
—Isaiah 23:3

In its earliest centuries the intellectual heart of Christianity was on the African continent, in Egypt and in North Africa. Tertullian of Carthage (modern Tunisia) lived from about 160 to 220. He was a hard man who lived in a hard world, at a time when a Roman emperor of African descent launched a persecution there. Tertullian did not believe in turning the other cheek. He is the first Christian writer to claim that one of the *joys* of heaven would be watching the damned fry in hell, and he had a list of Roman officials he expected to see there. Tertullian wrote against Gnostic dualism. He defended Genesis; God made a good world, but human sin alienates us from the right appreciation of it. But if Gnostics loathed the world, others liked it too much. Tertullian distinguished between the good world and evil worldliness, which for him meant sensual pleasure, such as the theater, going to taverns, and lavish living. God gave us free will but he also gave the devil leave to tempt us, similar to the testing of Job. For Tertullian, Satan also had the power to cause "natural" evils.

Tertullian's puritanism sent him to extremism on the question of sex. He applauded the advance of old age when, he believed, sexual temptation would diminish. Like all temptations, sexual desire came from the devil. Tertullian kept alive the notion of the Watcher Angels who lusted after human women, although he thought the devil's own sin was envy of humanity, made in God's image and likeness. But, since the episode of the Watchers occurred after Adam and Eve's disobedience, Tertullian knew that the libidinous angels were not completely at fault, and he let the other culprits know it. In an appalling book entitled *On the Adornment of Women,* he told women that they were all Eve incarnate, they shared Eve's guilt, the sentence which God passed upon her still applied to contemporary women, and, most strikingly, each woman is the devil's gateway. Tertullian also threw in a new note, one with a long future ahead of it. After personifying all women as Eve and thus as the devil's gateway, he added, "you are she who persuaded him [Adam] whom the devil was not valiant enough to attack." For him, Adam had too much intelligence and strength of will to fall for the serpent's words, but Eve, weak and stupid, could not restrain herself. But how then did the marvelous Adam sin? Because Eve persuaded him to. The prudish Tertullian did not say how but left the impression that Eve used sex to get him to follow her lead. Unfortunately many later and equally shortsighted people would take up this theme. Eve had moved back into the center of evil.

At the other end of the African coast, the majestic Egyptian city of Alexandria presided over a cultural mélange. Initially founded as a Greek city, its commercial and financial success had attracted the immigration of native Egyptians, Jews, Romans, and people from much of the Near East and the African states along the Nile. Christianity in Egypt reflected the city's cosmopolitan attitudes and produced some of the ancient Church's greatest theologians. On the topic of evil, the Alexandrians had more interest in theodicy than in the devil. Clement of Alexandria lived from about 150 to 210. He had migrated to the city from Greece. He had a brilliant mind but wrote in the style most charitably called discursive. Against the Gnostics, Clement asserted that this world is good, but it is only a pale reflection of God's goodness. This attitude determined his view of evil and enabled him to come up with two important theodicies.

The first was that, by definition, only God can be perfectly good. Therefore all created beings must be imperfect, and the rational ones are consequently susceptible of evil. A created being might lead a completely good life, but the possibility of evil is always present. God could have created beings who would always do the good, but he had to respect the integrity of the rational beings, and so he gave them free will, even though he knew they might use it to sin. This interpretation offered a sensible solution to evil in a monotheist tradition. God retained his uniqueness, and his creations took responsibility for their own evil. Clement did not explain how these beings activated the possibility for evil rather than adhering to the good, but he did advance the discussion with this theory of evil as an inevitable consequence of creation. In one form or another, it has survived down to the modern world.

The theory has flaws. Could not God have created goods that attract humans as much as evil seems to? And what about the extent of evil—

does granting humans free will require the deity to allow so much evil? Clement could see these difficulties, but he was not a philosopher who would work only from reason. He stood in a religious tradition and had to reconcile the good deity of the Bible with the reality of evil. His achievement was to maintain his biblical base while incorporating the insights of Greek thought.

Clement's second theodicy was the privation theory of evil, another product of his Greek training. Since God created all and since God is completely good, he could not have created evil. But if God did not create evil, then it cannot exist. Evil, therefore, does not exist in a positive way but rather in a negative one—evil is a lack of good. Russell uses a good example to illustrate this; evil resembles the holes in a wedge of Swiss cheese. The cheese is good; the lack is not (Russell, *Satan,* 112). But Clement quickly found himself in the bind of explaining how something that did not exist could cause such harm in the world and why God could not create creatures that did not lack the good. Clement tried to align this question to ontological evil, seeing God as absolute reality and every other created being, in varying degrees, as ontologically inferior, working down to evil at the bottom of the ontological scale. But that only complicated things by bringing degrees of evil into confusion with degrees of being as well as by disparaging matter. The actual historical situation was that he was very concerned about dualist movements and especially Gnostic claims about the evil nature of the God of the Hebrew Bible. Clement simply could not attribute anything negative to God, no matter what some biblical passages implied, and he could not concede ground to the Gnostics. Clement could not solve this problem, yet, thanks to him, the privation theory—without his complications—would become a standard Christian explanation for evil.

Since Clement's theodicies dealt with the nature of creation, they did not require a devil. Clement accepted his existence as a biblical fact but downplayed his role.

Clement fled a Roman persecution in Alexandria in 202. His mantle fell upon his student Origen, the greatest Alexandrian thinker, who lived from about 185 to 254. Throughout his life, Origen gladly used Greco-Roman culture to advance his own ideas. Virtually unique in his day, he ecumenically studied with rabbis and relied heavily upon the Jewish scholar Philo of Alexandria, particularly upon his allegorical interpretation of the Bible. Origen made it a staple of his own and of later Christian Bible study. It proved to be an effective weapon for his own sometimes radical views.

Origen thought apocalypticism was utter nonsense. Like many Greek philosophers, he considered this world to be only a reflection of the real one. He considered the world to be good because the Bible said it was, but it had only a reflected goodness. Origen simply could not understand why anyone would really believe that Christ would come again in glory to restore the dying physical world. He destroyed apocalypticism by allegorizing it away. The apocalyptists' New Jerusalem was a symbol of the heavenly one; much of the strife that the Bible speaks of actually occurs in our hearts. Christ would redeem us to life in a spiritual heaven, not in a newly reconstituted earth. He also applied allegorizing and rationalizing to the Garden of Eden. He had difficulty accepting a story about two innocent children being tempted by a talking snake and then being harshly punished by a petty God. Taking a step which many other Christians would not take for seventeen more centuries, Origen insisted the Garden of Eden narrative was not a historical account.

He knew that many Jews and Christians had moved Eden into the center of the discussion of evil, and he, too, believed it belonged there but only if properly understood. When God created intelligent beings, he created them as spiritual beings, and the material world did not yet exist. These intelligences, as Origen called them, had free will, and they chose to sin. God could not ignore such behavior, but he did not punish them in a retributive way, as a literal reading of Genesis would imply. Instead God wisely chose to educate the intelligences. Since the intelligences had committed sins of differing gravity, God treated them differently. Those who sinned less God permitted to stay in the ethereal realms, while the worst sinners fell into a demonic state; this explained the existence of angels and demons. God created the material world as a kind of school for the intelligences who became human. They had to take on physical bodies and live their lives here, in the middle of all the temptations the material world could provide. The biblical story of the fall became the explanation for ontological differences among angels, humans, and demons. One intelligence did not sin, and the Son of God would assume that intelligence (soul) when he became incarnate to redeem humanity. Like Clement, Origen had produced a theodicy which did not require the devil.

But no one who relied on the Bible as much as Origen did could ignore the devil, and he actually increased the devil's presence in the Bible. In addition to Philo's allegory, early Christian scholars used a literary device called typology, which found correspondences between events in the Hebrew Bible and in the New Testament and which was gaining widespread acceptance in Origen's day. For typologists, the Israelites' crossing of the Red Sea typified the Christian's watery escape from the slavery of sin to the freedom of life in Christ by baptism. Most Christians believed that God's truth was contained in the Bible; Origen believed it was hidden in the Bible and had to be dug out. The Hebrew Bible made a few surface references to Satan, but Origen found many more under the surface. He rejected the existence of sea monsters, such as Leviathan and Behemoth, but since the Bible spoke of God's combat with them, what else could they be but types or symbols of the devil? This approach impacted the history of the idea of evil by "discovering" previously unnoticed references to Satan. Like Philo and Clement, Origen would never interpret the Bible in such a way as to demean God. Like the Jewish prophets, he simply could not have the creator of heaven and earth lower himself to fight with mythical monsters. The monsters were not myths but symbols of Satan. Origen's approach had an unintended side effect, a new name for the devil. The book of Isaiah (14:12) spoke of a pagan king as the Day Star which had fallen from heaven. But Origen allegorized it as Satan falling from heaven. When Christians translated the phrase Day Star into Latin, they used the word *lucifer* or "light-bearer," thus providing a new and very familiar name for the devil.

Although Origen accepted many traditional ideas, such as the persecuting Romans being in league with Satan and the devil's responsibility for "natural" evils, he also introduced two new ideas, one of them quite radical.

If Satan was a fallen angel, what sin had he committed to get himself expelled from heaven? Jewish apocalyptic literature and many early Christians identified his fall with that of the Watcher Angels of Genesis 6 and said the sin was lust, the angels' desire for earthly women. This caused a chronological problem. If Satan took the form of the serpent in Eden, then he had already sinned before the Watchers Angels' story. Some commentators tried to reconcile the two accounts, but Origen simply dismissed the Watcher Angels theory. Other Christians had suggested that Satan's sin was envy of the new creatures God had made in his own image. This had obvious merit, but Origen could find no biblical evidence for it. It also meant that the angels' fall would have to come after the creation of Adam and Eve, a difficult point for someone who believed in a pre-mundane fall for all intelligences. To answer the question of what sin Satan had committed, Origen turned to the Bible itself.

He brilliantly used the literary notion of the parallel. Satan had promised Adam and Eve that they would be like gods. Origen heard a Greek echo here—*hubris,* pride, the desire to be more than one had a right to be. *Hubris* was a fixture in Greek mythology. Bellerophon wanted to ride the flying horse Pegasus to the top of Mount Olympus, home of the gods, but the deities struck him down. Origen realized that Israelites had also used this theme; the pagan builders of the Tower of Babel wanted it to reach into the heavens, but God stopped them by confusing their languages. Origen had his answer. The devil's sin was pride. Satan saw himself in God's place; he wanted to be more than he had a right to be. God knew this and expelled him from heaven. When Satan decided to revenge himself on God by attacking the humans made in the divine image, he cleverly realized that what had tempted him would tempt them; they, too, would want to be like God. Origen had neatly and insightfully combined biblical precedent with simple logic. Since his day Christian tradition has identified the devil's sin as pride.

This interpretation of personified evil's sin still carries weight today, even for those who do not believe in the devil. When a believer sins, she or he in effect says, "I don't care what God says, I am going to do what I want." The believer is putting herself or himself in the place of God, but this behavior is not limited to believers. When anyone goes against the laws of society or the inalienable rights of citizens, this, too, is a form of pride, putting one's self above the legitimate rights of others. Origen had recognized something not simply about the devil but about the very nature of evil.

Origen's more radical idea about the devil was a belief in his salvation. Apocalyptic thinking had decreed that the devil would suffer in hell for all eternity along with all of his angels, but Origen objected that this put a limit on God's salvific power. He cogently argued that God had created all beings to be good, and just because they sinned does not mean that he lost interest in them. God would try to win them back, and he was succeeding. Origen believed that the growing geographical spread of Christianity (he testified that it had reached even faraway Britain by 200) meant that the devil's power was contracting. Why could the devil not see the error of his ways and be won over to God? Surely God's saving power could reach every intelligent being. This optimistic view ran headlong into the remnants of apocalypticism. Even if Origen had weaned people away from a literal interpretation of visionary literature, most still expected a last judgment somewhere off in the future when God would separate the sheep from the goats and send the demons and sinners off to eternal damnation. Origen's opponents also argued that if the devil were evil personified and had nothing good about him at all, then he had no way to respond to God's reaching out to him. But Origen believed that even fallen intelligences kept the potential for good. Most Christians rejected this view.

At the end of third century another African, Lactantius, who lived from about 240 to 320, made the original suggestion that evil is necessary to understand the good. Only by seeing the contrast can humans understand the two. On the surface, this sounds logical, but it contains many problems, especially for theists. This theory literally *forces* God to create evil so that humans could recognize the good. This theory also raised problems for the Christian concept of heaven. Since there can be no evil in heaven, how would the blessed recognize God's goodness? As for atheists, the theory means nothing because there is no one who has to create evil to recognize the good. Lactantius raised an interesting question which would reappear at times in the future, but, in the long run, he did not have great influence on the history of the Western idea of evil.

Egypt's other contribution to the development of Western notions about evil came not from Alexandria but from the desert and not from brilliant scholars but from uneducated peasants. The Romans had persecuted the Christians for three centuries, but in the fourth century the Roman imperial family became Christian and the persecutions ceased. Most Christians welcomed the end of the persecutions and the acceptance of the Church by the government, but some very strict Egyptians believed this would diminish the fervor of the early centuries as the Church became enmeshed in worldly affairs. Like the Qumran monks, these Christians also left society and went into the desert.

The end of the persecutions meant the end of martyrdom, and Christians looked for new heroes. The monks fasted endlessly, and they disciplined their bodies severely, even masochistically. This practice made the monks the parallels of the martyrs; the martyrs died once but the monks died little by little every day. The monks could never condemn the body outright, but they had a very low opinion of it. One Egyptian *abba* (elder) said of his body, "It kills me; I kill it." The monks gained tremendous prestige in the Church. Important people such as nobles and bishops went to the desert to meet prominent monks and ask their advice on spiritual matters. Illiterate peasants advised emperors. Inevitably some of the visitors began to write about the monks, to record their lives, their teaching, and their visions. But the attention of the outside world did not impress the monks who often openly expressed their contempt for non-monks. An *abba* named Pambo said he went into the desert to escape "women and bishops." "Women" represented sexual temptation; "bishops" represented the daily life of the official Church which involved dealing with property.

In the monks' writings or in the works about them, the desert played a great role. On the one hand, it represented a sort of parched Garden of Eden, the return to the primitive life. Monastic biographies showed monks living in harmony with nature; some hermits actually went about naked to parallel Adam and Eve before the Fall. The monks believed that by prayer and self-discipline, they could return that pristine state. They did not need to wait for the last judgment. The effects of Eden could be overcome in this life. Yet the desert also represented a place of evil, the dwelling place of demons. In Jewish tradition satyrs and the she-demon Lilith lived there, and Jesus had met the devil in the desert. Ancient civilizations, both Semitic and Greco-Roman, considered cities to be centers of civilization and deserts to be chaotic. The monks believed that they had entered the devil's territory. This expectation caused them to find the demonic virtually every place.

The rigors of the monks' physical environment was matched by their spirituality. Most people take it for granted that they will lead morally mixed lives, doing mostly good but occasionally evil. They take temptation for granted and learn to live with it. The monks strove for lives of perfection, denying themselves the basics of life: they fasted, abstained from sex, wore simple garments, and renounced ambition. They saw even the smallest temptation as a threat. For them, even something which others would consider good or just neutral—appetizing food, a physically attractive person—was a threat. The monks may not have actually encountered such temptations in the desert, but they could think about them, and many did. The monks knew that such threatening thoughts did not just occur by accident; the devil sent them. And if thoughts did not work, the devil would appear to the monks in some visual form. Monastic literature has tales of monks who would see a hearty meal just lying on the ground in the desert or a seductive young woman reclining inside their huts. If the monks gave in to these temptations, the food or the woman would instantly disappear in a cloud of smoke, usually accompanied by derisive laughter. By entering the desert, the monks had gone into harm's way.

But Satan hardly held the upper hand. He recognized that these invaders of his territory were not ordinary Christians but God's shock troops. He viewed this as both a threat and a challenge. If the devil could get a monk to sin, he had won a great victory, one far more important than getting a farmer or sailor to sin. Yet he also realized how little power he had against them if they stuck to their faith. Monastic literature gloried in showing even the simplest, youngest brother driving away the prince of hell by his prayers. More important figures, such as Antony of Egypt (251–356), routed the devil so routinely that the devil actually complained to him that the monks were driving the demons out of their desert home. Antony's response to this whining was to congratulate Satan for finally saying something that was true.

Monastic literature has many engaging qualities for modern readers precisely because of desert egalitarianism. For countless generations, peasants had to live with the depredations of nobles who took their crops, molested their daughters, and impressed their sons into the army. Folk tales often told how a clever peasant had outwitted some aristocratic man or woman. This may have been a poor substitute for equality, but, in most cases, it was all the peasants could do. In the desert, Satan symbolized the classic aristocrat, depriving the monks of their spiritual freedom and trying to get them to follow him. Monastic tales delight in the monks' outwitting him. One day a monk was walking along a desert trail when he came upon a pile of gold. He knew immediately who put the gold there, and he started to laugh heartily. A demon quickly appeared and demanded to know what was so funny. The monk replied, "Where am I supposed to spend this?"

Stories like this added a new element to the growing tradition about the devil, that he is stupid. It may seem odd for a believer to call a dangerous demonic being stupid, but the demons had freely chosen their situation, that is, they had freely chosen to deprive themselves of heaven. What could be more stupid than that? Later thinkers such as the Italian poet Dante would take this idea and apply it not just to the devil but also to evil itself. After all, when goodness would make us happy, lead people to love and trust us, and bring harmony to a community, why do we do evil which cuts us off from all that? These Egyptian peasants were right; evil is just plain stupid.

Yet most of the monastic stories dealt not with that but with threatening temptations or afflictions. The devil beat the monks, confused them, and caused them to feel dissatisfaction with their calling; their only recourse was prayer. Some monks foolishly thought they could defeat the devil on their own, without asking for divine assistance; inevitably they failed, a lesson to other monks. The Egyptian monks created the religious practice of discernment of spirits, a method for telling whether the spirit they were currently encountering was good or evil. If a monk felt calm and at peace, he believed that a blessed spirit was with him; if he felt dissatisfied or restless, it was a demonic one. Sophisticated psychology it was not, but it met the needs of the monks. Subsequent generations of Christians elaborated upon this process.

The monks' contributions to the demonic tradition also included the first physical descriptions of the devil. The Bible provides no description of an angel or a demon, and in general the Jews did not make images of their god or other biblical beings. When the Christians moved into the Greco-Roman world, their new converts brought the tradition of religious art with them. By the beginning of the third century, Christian artists had begun to practice iconography, that is, using a visual image to portray certain qualities about a person. The devil's iconography had to portray his evil qualities. The standard for this was set by an enormously influential book, *The Life of Saint Antony,* the Egyptian monk; it was written by another Egyptian, Athanasius, bishop of Alexandria (328–373). In *The Life* he created the first demonological treatise in Christian history, recounting Antony's struggles, his discernment of spirits, and his description of the devil.

The devil appeared to Antony in visions, so Athanasius was not limited by any physical restraints. The devil could literally be whatever Antony envisioned him to be. This approach flowed from the philosophical principles to which Athanasius adhered. He believed that evil was the absence of the good. Quite literally, personified evil was nothing. The devil had no true substance, no place in God's cosmos. Cosmos requires form; chaos negates form. The devil had no real essence of his own, and so he could take on any shape he wished. His appearance depended upon the artist or upon the person having the vision. Athanasius portrayed the devil as a giant, several filthy animals, and figures with grotesque shapes.

This principle was a gift to artists who could let their imaginations range freely, and they did. But they generally followed some lines. The book of Isaiah had described the demons as satyrs, goat-like creatures; in the Gospels, Jesus separates the good sheep from the evil goats at the last judgment. The First Epistle of Peter said the devil was "like a roaring lion" (5:8). Jewish tradition identified the devil as the Eden serpent, and Origen's exegesis had extended this to other biblical serpents. Athanasius applied Origen's approach to the book of Job and identified the sea monster Leviathan as the devil in his *Life of Saint Antony* (ch. 24). The book of Revelation portrayed Christ as the Lamb of God, so artists did not use that animal for the devil, preferring instead to use creatures like scorpions, wolves, and pigs. Many Jews and Christians considered the pagan gods to be demons, and so artists routinely gave the demons the features of these gods. The artists stuck to gods whose qualities reflected the demonic. Gods of war and sexuality had obvious relevance, but no god fit the demonic image better than Pan.

Originally a pastoral god in satyr-like form, Pan had developed in many ways over the centuries, slowly becoming a deity who never denied his appetite for sensual pleasure. To the Greeks, the mind should hold sway over this appetite, and Pan came to symbolize the irrational, so much so that the word "panic," the loss of reason, derives from his name. To Christian artists, the mind, not the body, truly reflected the divine image, and they chose for their devil the god who represented the negation of the mind, the negation of the divine image. Visually the devil took on Pan's attributes—pointed ears, horns, heavy eyebrows, a bulbous nose, a hairy body, and the lower body of a goat, complete with cloven hooves.

The history of an idea has traditionally focused on the great thinkers who investigated the concept, but modern historians know that other factors and, more importantly, other people contributed as well. The peasant monks of Egypt did not delve into the nature of evil; rather, they focused on its personification and manifestations. Their stature in the Christian church and the appeal of their stories guaranteed that the wider Western world would now see the devil behind every temptation, would considerably expand the range of those temptations to include monastic values (temptations to pleasure or money), would enjoy stories of simple people outwitting the devious Father of Lies, and would envision and portray the devil pictorially. Evil in the West had taken a new turn.

But the African continent had one more contribution to make to the notion of evil, one destined to influence Western notions of evil down to the nineteenth century.

Chapter 5

The Broken Cosmos

Marcus Aurelius Augustinus, known to history as Saint Augustine, was born in 354 in a small African town. Except for a brief time in Italy (383–387), he spent his whole life in Africa. His Christian mother and pagan father knew they had a gifted son and sent him to the African metropolis of Carthage for his education. He studied rhetoric for a career in public service. He went to Italy to seek his fortune, but had a conversion experience and became a Christian. He returned to Africa, became a priest, and in 395 became bishop of the coastal city of Hippo Regius, a post he held to his death in the year 430. A voluminous author whose ecclesiastical career would have made him an important figure in the history of Christianity, he became a major figure in the intellectual history of the West by his writings on evil. He literally changed the way that people looked at the world. His views remained supreme until the Enlightenment, thirteen centuries later, and many conservative Christians still hold them.

Augustine devoted much of his long and busy life to the problem of evil. No one in history has ever delved into the topic with such intensity or come up with so complete an explanation. In his autobiographical *Confessions* (ii.4) he says that the problem first arose for him in his adolescence. Since the account involves a tree and fruit, it may be literary as well as biographical, but that does not make it less significant. With some friends, he stole some pears. They ate a few and threw the rest to some pigs, but Augustine emphasizes that these were secondary considerations. The boys

51

simply wanted to steal the pears. This act upset him decades later as he wondered why he loved an act of moral self-destruction. He loved his fall and not the object of his fall. These sound like the senseless fears of a hyper-scrupulous person, but Augustine has seen through to the true nature of the problem. We can understand if people steal fruit because they are hungry, but the boys just did it to do it. Why, Augustine wants to know, do we just do what is wrong? He echoes every other human being who has ever been in a similar situation, but he found an answer.

In his youth, the answer was dualism, specifically Manichaeism, a religion founded by the Persian visionary Mani (216–276), whose revelations provided him with an extensive creation myth, which echoed Gnosticism—matter is evil, the body is evil, sex is sinful because it produced more material beings, elite members of the sect can enlighten the others. This explanation appealed to the young Augustine. His parents viewed Manichaeism the way modern parents would view a cult. Augustine estranged himself from his family when he became a Manichee, but his mother persisted in trying to win him to Christianity. After nine years he left the Manichees of his own accord, deciding dualism was too simplistic to answer his questions about evil, although many contemporary opponents and later scholars would claim that he did not completely shed dualistic ideas.

Leaving one religion for another did not answer all of Augustine's questions. The Manichees had interpreted Genesis literally and had mocked a deity who created a material world and whose morals were questionable at best. Augustine defended Genesis against them in several books, and his defense got him interested in the Garden of Eden.

Like most converts, Augustine looked back on his previous life with regret and with relief that he had left it. He believed that God had acted to save him from the Manichees, and he could not think of anything he had done to deserve that. He acquired a strong belief in divine grace, God's freely-given assistance to sinful humans. In the early fifth century, his belief would be put to the test. A British monk named Pelagius (d. ca. 420) taught that humans could be saved by their own free will and without God's grace if they disciplined themselves morally and spiritually. Pelagius did not claim that this happened often, although he believed some great figures of the Hebrew Bible and Mary the mother of Jesus had been sinless. Augustine felt that Pelagius did not take enough account of divine grace in salvation, but the British monk reflected the views of many monks that their rigid asceticism and mortification could take them back morally to the Garden of Eden. Augustine and Pelagius did not start out as antagonists, but other factors and other persons intervened, and Augustine spent the last twenty years of his life battling what came to be called Pelagianism.

The Pelagian controversy took the African bishop down a road he may not have wanted to travel. Augustine was pugnacious. He relished a fight and was a sore loser. When pushed to an extreme, he would not back down but found justification for his views. Few people have written as deeply about the mysterious ways of God, yet Augustine constantly wanted to impose his logic on the divine, and at times he became trapped by his own logic. His native brilliance, his unrivaled knowledge of the Bible, and his formidable rhetorical skills guaranteed him a victory, but the Western world paid the price for his remarkable theory of evil. [Augustine initially accepted the privation theory, that evil is basically the absence of good. He never gave that up because God created every thing, and since God could not create evil, it ultimately could not exist. But he treated evil as the ultimate negativity and, somewhat paradoxically, as a powerful force to be dealt with by grace.]

God created the angels, but some sinned. Why? Augustine asked. Because they wanted to. God gave them all intelligence and free will, and some of them misused it. Augustine agreed with Origen that the angels' sin was pride. He could not explain why they gave in to pride; they just did. And they did so immediately. Augustine recognized that the old theories of the Fall had a fatal flaw. If the angels were in heaven and enjoying the presence of God, how could they ever have turned away? Since the Beatific Vision was what awaited the good in heaven, how could anyone say the devil had fallen away from that? Augustine theorized the devil had sinned literally instantaneously after his creation, and he did so by pride. God promptly expelled from heaven Satan and all other angels who supported him. They fell into hell, where they will suffer forever. Powerless to hurt God, Satan got revenge by corrupting his new creations, Adam and Eve, but Augustine emphasized that the devil could not get them to sin. He could tempt them, but they sinned on their own. Just as Satan gave in to pride, so would they—with his help but of their own free choice.

Augustine knew how difficult the idea of condemning the entire race for eating a piece of fruit sounded, but that was what the Bible said. He justified God's act by arguing that he had created Adam and Eve to be perfect, so that any sin of theirs carried weight that no subsequent sin could. The first parents were the only people in history who, relying upon their free will alone, were able not to sin. They could live happily in the Garden, and they would never endure suffering and death. But, like Satan, they chose themselves over God; their pride caused them to commit what Augustine called Original Sin, a term created by him in 396. Like Satan's sin, the first parents' sin was a falling away from the good. By this, they introduced evil into the world. This is one of Augustine's remarkable contributions to the theory of evil. Contrary to what previous thinkers had argued, he said that *sin caused evil and not the other way around*. He reversed centuries of thinking on this point; individual sin did not derive from a cosmic evil, but the decision of two people infected the entire world. Furthermore, he insisted that evil resulted from one historical act and not from multiple, numerous acts of the will.

Augustine could not understand their sin any more than he could his own, but he did recognize that by emphasizing the perfection of Adam and Eve in order to make their seemingly trivial sin look so heinous, he ran the risk of making the Genesis story unbelievable. If they were so perfect, how could they have sinned? First, because they were fallible. Second, Augustine hauled out misogynism to explain it. He believed that, even before she encountered the serpent, Eve, as a woman, already had within her a love of power and a presumptuousness that the serpent could exploit. Eve had to win Adam over with persuasive words, and Augustine hinted that she used more than words.

Original sin determined human history. Augustine believed that the entire human race was contained in seed in the persons of Adam and Eve. This was not a unique idea. The Bible commonly suggested that children suffered for the sins of their parents (Exod 20:5), but Augustine carried the idea to a new level. Not only could the guilt of the first parents' sin be passed along to their descendants, their sin had literally corrupted human nature itself. So corrupted was human nature that humans could do nothing good on their own. Augustine had answered Pelagius; there was no way anyone could be saved by his or her own free will because, as a part of human nature, that will was corrupted and incapable of doing the good.

That answered Pelagius, but now what? If human nature was corrupt and humans could do no good, what happened to them? Very simple. They sinned their way into eternal damnation. Augustine referred to humanity as a *massa damnata,* literally a "damned lump," born condemned and destined to hellfire. Humans are sinful automatons, driven by original sin. But this made no sense. Surely God would do something about it.

He would. God would give humans grace, divine assistance, to overcome sin and be saved. This sounded like a good solution, until Augustine concluded that God would not give grace to everyone but only to those to whom he chose to give it. But isn't this unfair? Why should God give grace to some and not to others? Augustine's answer combined philosophy and the Bible. By definition, the divine nature is good. To say God is not fair in his distribution of grace is to say he does something morally wrong, and that is simply impossible. Augustine also used a theme from the book of Job: who are humans to question God? For reasons of his own, God has chosen to save some people and not to save others, and in doing so the deity, as always, acts justly. Augustine speculated that at the last judgment we would understand God's justice, but we could not do so in this life.

But what does this do to us as humans? Since we are born with the effects of original sin, how can we be held guilty for our sins if God does not give us grace? Augustine replied that we must accept what our first parents passed along to us. We act according to our fallen nature, and we must accept the consequences. Yet is our nature completely fallen? Can we not cooperate with God's grace? Several of Augustine's contemporaries, fearful of where his theories led, suggested this, but his frightful rigidity squelched it. To cooperate with God's grace would be to do something good without that grace, and that was impossible. We cannot earn grace; we simply get it freely from God.

So have we become good automatons, just acting out what divine grace directs us to do? Not so, Augustine replied. Our free will was damaged, and God fixed it. If we had a truly free will, we would always choose the good. Augustine recognized that we always believe that we choose the good because we rationalize our evil acts. ["If I fail this sociology test, it will pull down my average and keep me out of medical school. My parents will be crushed, and why do doctors need to know anything about sociology anyway? There's nothing wrong with cheating in this situation."] We may think that we have a free will, free to choose good or evil, but, Augustine contended, when we do wrong, we do not exercise our free will because original sin has guaranteed that our will cannot choose the good. Only God's grace enables our will to be truly free, so that we always choose the true and not the apparent good. We do so not because of divine pressure but because we see clearly for the first time.

This remarkable theory challenged so much of what had been traditional thinking about evil, but, amazingly, Augustine had not finished. He believed that God saw all of history unfolding in front of him because all was present to him at once. This got Augustine stuck in trying to relate time to eternity, and he never really extricated himself from the problem. But he also did not back down. If God could see all of history, he knew who would sin, including the devil and Adam and Eve, and he also knew whom he would place among the elect, those to whom he would deign to give saving grace. To an already complicated problem, Augustine had introduced foreknowledge and predestination.

In discussing God's foreknowledge, he again found himself imposing logic on the divine. If God foreknows that Adam and Eve will sin and corrupt human nature, why does he not do something before they sin? Because if God foreknows that they will sin and then they do not sin, God's foreknowledge was wrong, and that is impossible. Furthermore, God has no obligation to do anything about Adam and Eve's sin. To objections that it is useless for God to foreknow if he cannot act on his knowledge, Augustine replied that knowledge is only knowledge; God knows what people will do because they will do it, not because he causes them to. Augustine separated knowledge from responsibility.

Predestination was something altogether different. Since God has decided before the creation of the world whom he will save and whom he will not, what good are human lives? We are all acting in some farce manipulated by a divine puppeteer, so what difference does it make what we do? And has God not predestined some people to hell, so what difference can it possibly make what they do? And what of the biblical verse (1 Tim 2:4) which says that God wishes everyone to be saved? These were serious questions, and ones not asked just by Pelagians. Many Church leaders feared that if people believed that God had predestined everyone for salvation or damnation and that they could not freely choose the good, they would see no reason to go to church or, for that matter, to follow any religious precept. Even conservative Protestant seminaries use the old nostrum, "Augustine in the classroom, Pelagius in the pulpit."

As a bishop, Augustine recognized the pastoral problems associated with his views. He recognized that people would not believe in predestination unless they expected to be saved, so he shrewdly focused on that theme. No one can be sure of her or his salvation, he warned, but we can have reasonable assurance that if we act like good people, we are probably among the saved. Those who go to the theater to see obscene pagan plays should not count on seeing the pearly gates, but those who lead a good Christian life should be cautiously optimistic. This questionable means of reassurance was a virtual invitation to self-righteousness; the scarlet letter could not be far behind.

Yet Augustine carefully avoided speaking of double predestination. God did predestine some to be saved, but he never predestined anyone to sin and damnation. He believed that God simply allowed some people to sin their own way to damnation. He could not explain why. His explanation of 1 Timothy 2:4 shows Augustine at his worst. When the Bible said that God wishes *all* to be saved, what it really meant, Augustine claimed, was *all of the elect*. This was a specious interpretation, but he had no choice. He simply did not believe that God wished to save everyone, and so he had to read the passage in a way that preserved his interpretation of evil.

For Augustine the elect were more than just modern replicas of the first parents. Adam and Eve were good by nature, but the elect derived their goodness from God's grace, which made them better than Adam and Eve. Many Christians had written about how the Son of God had to take on human nature to redeem us by his death. For them it was a gloomy story, involving the suffering of a perfectly innocent being. Augustine did not minimize Jesus' redemptive work, but he could envision the *felix culpa,* the "happy fall," the belief that redemption and grace raised the human race to a new state, to a unique sharing in God's life which Adam and Eve would never have had. If they had not sinned, the Son of God would not have elevated human nature by becoming human himself. This is the chief example of another one of his theories about evil, that God could always bring good out of evil.

Augustine could not envision evil triumphing over God in any way, yet every evil act seemed a triumph, no matter how petty. Augustine found no goodness in evil, but he believed that God would find a way to bring good even out of the worst situations. If a city fell to barbarian invaders, it would remind the Romans of the transience of earthly glory and recall them to the true glory found only in the divine. That did not remove the tragedy of the conquest or of the suffering of the city's inhabitants; evil was evil. But in no way would it frustrate the basic goodness of God's activity in the world. Yet Augustine prudently observed that no one was completely good in this life, so deeply had evil penetrated the human condition.

Augustine had created a theodicy which did not require the devil since Adam and Eve had it within their natures to sin without demonic assistance; besides, Satan had sinned without being tempted by anyone else. Since the devil had a prominent place in Scripture, Augustine kept him, but the devil occupied a new place. He now had humanity in his power, and his powers of persuasion were great. Humans *inherit* the sin of Adam and Eve, but, in their daily lives, they *imitate* the sin of the devil.

The devil was but one of many traditional ideas which underwent a change.

To make the first parents responsible for original sin, Augustine demolished Irenaeus' idea that they were children. No one knew how old or mature they actually were, but, after Augustine, everyone considered them to be adults.

Baptism, too, had changed. Before the fifth century, people usually undertook baptism as adults on the grounds that they had to make a mature decision to become a Christian. Infant baptism was practiced occasionally, especially if a child were sick. Thanks to Augustine, all humans were deemed sick with sin. He taught that baptism could wipe away the guilt of original sin, and most Christians chose to baptize their children rather than run the risk that they might die before making an adult decision.

This notion had a frightening corollary. If only Christian baptism could remove the guilt of original sin, what about those who were not baptized? Augustine did not shrink from the horror involved. Although God in his infinite mercy might choose to save some Jews and pagans, in general heaven would be open only to baptized Christians.

In yet another turn on the question, the Pelagians asked, if baptism removed the effects of original sin, why cannot baptized people will themselves to salvation? For that matter, if original sin is the cause of all the trouble, why do baptized people sin at all? Augustine made a significant distinction. Baptism removes the guilt of original sin, so that the baptized can avoid the damnation associated with that sin, but the tendency to sin remains. Baptism put Christians over the obstacle still facing non-Christians, but they still had to struggle.

Augustine found himself sticking fingers in the dike, but, to give him his due, the dike held. If God gave someone grace, did that person have nothing to worry about for the rest of her or his life? Understanding that such a view could lead to complacency, Augustine theorized that God gave us grace in particular situations, but the effect did not last forever. God would have to keep on intervening. But surely there must be a point at which people can relax and feel secure that they have God's grace? No, said Augustine. In an angry debate with an Italian Pelagian, he cited the example of an eighty-four-year-old man who had lived a life of continence for twenty-five years and had recently taken in a mistress. Does this mean that we can lead good lives, only to sin on our deathbeds? Yes, he replied, but, inventing a new grace, he said that God could give us the grace of perseverance so that we would not fail at the end.

In spite of his insistence that he was merely explicating more fully what the Bible had implied, Augustine knew he was changing the traditional understanding of evil. He rightly feared that compromising on even one point would jeopardize his whole synthesis, and so he persevered, even if that meant bequeathing to the world a deity who seemingly capriciously chooses to save some and damn others, who knowingly condemns the majority of human beings to eternal damnation because they had no physical access to baptism, and who knew all this before he created the world but chose to do nothing about it. Augustine would find such objections spurious, and he had arguments to answer them, but there can be no denying the pessimism of his views. The great Catholic patristic scholar Fr. Bernhard Altaner (1885–1964) lamented "Augustine's doctrine of grace which is based upon a frightening conception of God . . ." (*Patrology,* 526).

Astonishingly, there is still more. Not only did Augustine's theory of evil change the Christian view of God and evil, it also changed the Western view of the everyday world. When we look at the world around us, we think that although it is always changing, it is qualitatively the same, that natural forces act in the same way they always have. But that is a relatively recent view, dating from the eighteenth century at best and mostly from the nineteenth. Augustine so emphasized the historical reality of the Garden of Eden that for generations people have accepted his notion that once the world had been perfect and that we had lived in harmony with all creation. We had nothing to fear from animals nor did they have anything to fear from us. The lion did indeed lie down with the lamb. Our first parents spoiled all that with original sin, and the world as we know it is a broken one, one distorted by sin and the evil that accompanied it. People brought up on evolutionary concepts, on the belief that all life forms struggle for survival, usually against other life forms, see Augustine's theory as something fantastic. But he meant it literally. At one time this physical world was free of strife, illness, suffering, and death. God told Adam that when he tilled the ground, "thorns and thistles it shall bring forth for you," and "by the sweat of your face / you shall eat bread" (Gen 3:18-19). Augustine interpreted this to mean that no thorn- or thistle-bearing plants had existed before original sin, nor did people sweat. The world as we know it now is simply not the way it was supposed to be.

This distortion stretched beyond our world. If the angels had not sinned, hell would not exist either. The entire cosmos was broken.

The repercussions of this view could be felt everywhere. The classic ancient work on government, Aristotle's *Politics,* portrays humans as naturally political, people who want to be involved in the life of the state. For Augustine, Adam and Eve enjoyed a perfect society in the Garden of Eden until they sinned. After the Fall, people cannot really trust one another since they are all corrupt, but in their selfishness, they recognize that they can protect their own interests only by joining with others who want to protect their own interests. People are not naturally political; government exists to ward off chaos.

In the ancient world slavery was an intrinsic part of the economy. Some religious voices, such as that of the Greek Christian Gregory Nazianzen (329–390) cried out against it, using, logically enough, the Garden of Eden as an example of a time when slavery did not exist, thus proving that it was not inherent to society. Augustine battered such arguments into dust. Maybe we were equal before original sin, but after it we should expect inequalities to exist. Slavery was a consequence of sin, and since sin would survive until the end of the world, slavery probably would too. Besides, the truly evil enslavement is enslavement to sin. Since none of us knows where she or he fits into the divine plan, slaves should accept their lot and hope for a better existence in the next life. Rarely has the "opiate of the people" argument been used more effectively. Augustine's view dominated Christian thinking on slavery for centuries; not until the nineteenth century did many denominations dedicate themselves to abolishing it.

Early in his life Augustine was, to use a modern phrase, "sexually active"; he had two mistresses and a child by one of them. Yet after his conversion, he looked at sex very differently, and he largely created the negative view of sex held by Christians for centuries. Ironically, he once wrote a book against the Manichees on the goodness of marriage. Those dualists considered the flesh to be evil and they declared that the elect should not generate any more children to be born of the flesh. As a Christian bishop who presided over the sacraments, Augustine could never condemn marriage and procreation, but he had new, pessimistic views about sex, even in marriage.

For generations classical Greco-Roman thinkers had defined a human being as a rational animal, a living creature which could use reason to rise above the beasts. Augustine rightfully considered that to be nonsense, and for the first time in history someone defined a human being as a mélange of desires and fears, of wants and distractions, with reason trying desperately to gain control. Sexual desire fit into this understanding. It did not upset Augustine that married people had sex; try as he might, he could think of no other way to produce children. What bothered him was that people *wanted* to have sex, and they wanted it even to an irrational degree. He called this desire *concupiscence*. Treating sex primarily from a male point of view, he complained that concupiscence denied a man control over his own body. For Augustine concupiscence is consequence of original sin. He believed that if there had been no sin, Adam and Eve and their descendants would have to have had intercourse to produce children, but they would have done so without passion or desire. Sin turned intercourse into an irrational outburst that sinful humans take for granted.

Yet surely not all intercourse must have children as a goal? After all, many married people who are past child-bearing age have sex. But, Augustine asked, why do they have sex instead of doing something else, something more rational? Because concupiscence drives them to it. He concluded that even within marriage, sex without the goal of procreation is a venial or minor sin. Many Christian denominations later rejected this particular view, but Augustine's pessimistic view of sexuality dominated Christian and thus much Western thought about sex for centuries.

It would be inaccurate to portray Augustine only negatively. He wrote on many topics, establishing Western Christian views on the nature of God, the Trinity, the interpretation of the Bible, and the use of pagan culture; he significantly advanced Christian culture when the Roman empire was experiencing its death throes. But, in a history of the idea of evil, Augustine sounds a very negative note.

Augustine's relentless logic led to his conclusions, but sometimes it kept him from asking simple, sensible questions, such as, if the majority of humans go to hell, why does a good and loving deity create people just to damn them to eternal punishment? Augustine's theory demanded that God do no less, and that was enough for him; it was rarely enough for others, although it took thirteen hundred years for them to find the tools to answer him.

Augustine deserves credit for creating a system which reconciled the Greek notion of evil with the biblical teaching about the first human sin, which explained the persistence of evil in spite of divine activity, and which related theories of Eden to both the cosmic and the personal. He kept to the tradition that Adam and Eve had broken the harmony of the world, but also saw the primal couple as the cause of all the misery of everyday life. He gave evil a grubbiness and a pettiness which it had never had before as well as an immediacy and a potency it also had never had before. In so doing, he changed how the West looked at the physical world, at humanity, and at society. It is an astonishing legacy, no matter how unpalatable much of it may be to the modern mind. Few people have impacted history as much as he did.

Augustine died while the Vandals, a barbarian tribe, were invading Roman Africa and besieging his episcopal city of Hippo. New peoples had entered the West, and evil would change again.

Chapter 6

The Middle Ages

> *Abandon hope, all ye who enter here.*
> —Dante, *Inferno*

For centuries the Roman Empire had reigned supreme in the West, but starting in the fourth century and for the next four centuries barbarian tribes invaded or just migrated into what had been imperial territory, initiating what historians call the Middle Ages. The barbarians came from a Germanic, tribal, oral culture. As they settled in the West, Christian missionaries brought them Greco-Roman culture along with the Christian faith. But the barbarians' Christianity often remained on the surface, and in some places Christianity was Germanized as much as the Germans were Christianized. Until the eleventh century, barbarian traditions competed successfully with the Greco-Romanized culture of Christianity, and this was especially true of the question of evil.

When the tribes first settled in heavily populated areas such as Italy, the Romans tried to incorporate them into Roman society or at least to win them over to Roman ways. One person who tried was Boethius (ca. 480–524), a Christian nobleman and senator who worked with the barbarian king of Italy, but who fell from power and was executed on a charge of treason. While in prison awaiting execution, Boethius wrote *The Consolation of Philosophy,* a classic of prison literature. He wonders why he, a good man, languishes in prison while criminals roam free and prosper. A woman appears to him. She is Philosophy, come to recall him, one of her disciples, to his senses. She points out to him that evil is an absence of the good, and no evil person can ever be happy because true human happiness resides in the good. In fact, the only way an evil person can become happy is by owning up to her or his deeds and paying the price for them. Boethius in prison enjoys more happiness than his accusers do because he resides in the good while they wallow in evil. *The Consolation* represents the last attempt by a Roman intellectual to impose reason on an increasingly chaotic world.

Philosophy takes up the question of divine providence and free will. Although God knows what will happen in the future, the future is not bound by his knowledge—contra Augustine—nor is the reverse true, that is, if God knows something, he must make sure that it happens. Boethius will not have God be bound by temporal acts. He insists that it is useless to speak of God's knowing anything in advance since time cannot apply to him. God cares for the world and exercises providence over it, but his activity does not obliterate human free will. What people think is fate Boethius defines as the unalterable workings of this world; fate is actually subordinate to divine providence which guides but does not predetermine all that happens.

Boethius could not answer all that Augustine had to say, and since he dialogued with Philosophy, he had to use reason alone. Boethius knew theology well and had written several theological works, but his execution prevented his returning to this theme, so we will never know what he would have done with something like original sin.

The Consolation of Philosophy was the second most popular book of the Middle Ages behind the Bible, but it could not deflect Augustine's awesome influence because the African dealt with evil in great depth and at great length, while the Italian left behind one book on the topic. Furthermore, Christian education in the Early Middle Ages was dominated by monks, for whom Augustine's biblical exegesis, theology, and spiritual works had great appeal, and the works of Augustine played a role second only to the Bible in the educational life of the barbarian West.

In the Early Middle Ages, Christian scholars devoted themselves primarily to preserving and exploring the heritage of Greco-Roman Antiquity, but they did little which was original. On the question of evil, Augustine's views remained supreme. Church leaders had rejected Semi-Pelagianism, a fifth-century theory that humans could, by their own free will, cooperate with God's grace. In 529 the Second Council of Orange in France carefully explained that Augustine's theories did not involve double predestination, that God did not predestine people to hell but merely withheld from them the grace they needed. The emphasis fell more on grace than on predestination, but the Augustinian synthesis stood virtually untouched.

In the ninth century, after the greatest barbarian, the Frankish king Charlemagne (768–814), had established a Christian state, Western intellectuals began to debate theological topics. A monk named Gottschalk decided to take Augustine's teaching to what he believed was its natural conclusion, double predestination. Gottschalk believed that talk about God's withholding grace was a poor cover for the divine decision to send some souls to damnation. This view provoked a strong reaction among the French bishops, who condemned Gottschalk's views at a council in 848. The bishops argued that predestination was a conscious act of God, and so he would never predestine people to hell because that would be an evil act. God foreknew that some people would sin their way to damnation and that he would not give them the grace necessary to accept the offer, but he did not set out to condemn them. The bishops played down predestination in favor of an emphasis on divine grace, but, again, the Augustinian synthesis triumphed.

If Early Medieval Christian scholars showed little imagination in the area of evil, the converted barbarians did just the reverse. They simply accepted the existence of the devil and saw him as the cause of evil. Missionaries told them that they had to abandon veneration of the pagan gods who were either empty idols or demons. The barbarians gave up the veneration but kept the gods, who were now metamorphosed into a variety of evil beings: trolls, dwarves, leprechauns, brownies, sprites, giants, goblins, werewolves, and vampires. Most of these beings appeared in folklore, which varies so much that it is difficult to find patterns, but these beings all became partners of the devil in his attempt to rule the world. Some Christian leaders simply accepted their existence; others became concerned that Satan's empire had just grown a little too quickly and maybe some skepticism was in order. A seventh-century council of Irish bishops stressed that one cannot be a Christian and continue to believe in vampires, but the peasantry largely went their own way.

The barbarians not only added to the devil's extensive retinue, they also changed the understanding of basic biblical passages, especially the Garden of Eden and those in which the devil appears. They remade the existing tradition to suit the values of a warrior aristocracy. Barbarian poetry, such as the Anglo-Saxon epic *Beowulf,* emerged from a society in which poets declaimed in mead halls. Poets relied on the patronage of local nobility, all of whom were male, trained as warriors, and had a strict code of honor. The poets had to balance their own individual vision with the desires of their patrons.

An eighth-century Anglo-Saxon poem entitled *Christ and Satan* records the lamentations of the fallen angels. They blame Satan for their condition and compare it to their lot in heaven. Standard Christian themes appear. The angels claim that Satan deceived them, just as he had deceived Adam and Eve; he lied in heaven and he lied on earth. But the poet also invoked themes reflective of Anglo-Saxon society. The fallen angels sing of heaven's "high halls" and lament that in hell they have no warm and comfortable wine-hall; hell is windy and cold. The angels used to be God's "thanes" (nobles), but now they are in exile, the worst punishment for a barbarian warrior since it cut him off from his family, his land, and his war-band.

The poem includes several traditional and folkloric themes about the devil. Following *The Life of Saint Antony,* it describes the devil as so gigantic that he could not fit in the wide hall. The evil angels have become misshapen monsters. The poem adds that the devil is chained to the fiery floor of hell, he has a son, and dragons guard the doors of hell. Hell has both flames and bitter cold but reflects the Northern European pagan creation myth about the emergence of cosmos from the primeval chaos of fire and ice. The anonymous poet sent the fallen angels back to chaos, something his readers or listeners would have understood.

The theme of rebellion appears in *Genesis A,* another eighth-century Anglo-Saxon poem. The fallen angels boasted in loud voices about their combined power. Heaven is wide and bright, and as God's thanes they enjoyed its riches. Now they dwell in exile, once again in a land of fire and ice. Satan enjoys a limited nobility since the poet describes him as eager for war, a prime barbarian virtue. He sets up his rebellious kingdom in the northern part of heaven. The north symbolized cold and darkness and thus death; these features made it the appropriate place for Satan's proposed kingdom.

Genesis B, a ninth-century Anglo-Saxon poem, expands upon this theme of the leader and his thanes. Satan describes his warriors as brave, firm, and loyal, all desirable qualities for thanes. The poet cleverly contrasted Satan's lying description of his followers with a true description of their leader—arrogant, rebellious, devious. But the poet also described Satan as a warrior who buckles on his armor and puts a helmet on his head to fight God. Satan describes himself as the liege lord who hands out princely treasures to his thanes. (When the *Beowulf* poet wanted to praise kings, he called them "ring-giving.") The *Genesis B* poet made it clear how despicable Satan is, but he simultaneously had to make Satan a worthy opponent for God. These barbarian Christians had revived the old Jewish combat myth.

The need for a worthy opponent stands behind the strangest part of the poem, a reversal of the Garden of Eden narrative. The devil takes on the form of a serpent and tempts Adam first. Augustine and other ancient Christian writers believed that the devil went to Eve because as a man Adam was too intelligent to fall for the devil's lies. The Anglo-Saxon poet shared those misogynistic views, but in the medieval code of conduct, warriors did not attack women. The devil initially shows himself to be a worthy opponent by first taking on Adam, who naturally sees through Satan's wiles. Then he shamefully attacks Eve. The devil has an easier time with Eve because the poet says that God created her with a weaker mind than Adam. Eve is apparently aware of her mental deficiencies because she likes the devil's promise of a stronger mind if she follows his advice. In fact, she would become so smart that she would lord it over Adam. In the Anglo-Saxon world, a woman lording it over a man meant rebellion against the established order, a parallel to Satan's rebellion in heaven. Deluded and deceived, Eve gives in. At this point the poet included a few lines which convince the modern reader that even Early Medieval barbarians could see through to the real question—why God would permit so many of his servants to be deceived by "lies which came as good counsel." This is Job's question but without Augustine's answer. But Augustine has his moments in this poem. After Eve has eaten the fruit, the serpent encourages her to get Adam to do likewise. This means that the simple-minded woman must overcome the brilliant macho man, a daunting task. Augustine implied the answer; the Anglo-Saxon poet said it outright: sex. Eve, the most beautiful woman who ever lived, did not lead Adam to the tree but gathered up some fruit to tempt him to come to the tree. She modestly calls Adam her liege lord so that he will not recognize her new power. The poet repeatedly emphasized Adam's awareness of Eve's beauty and how that breaks down his resistance. The devil stays hidden nearby, encouraging Adam's desires. Sex seduces him, and he eats the fruit. The poet assures the reader that Eve meant well, but she was just too dim to realize what she was doing. She was, of course, smart enough to tempt Adam with her beauty, but the poet countered that women always play on men's weakness. Thus the poet explained the Fall.

The values of a warrior aristocracy are on display. Adam, the archetypal male, cannot be overcome in a fair fight; his enemies must go around his back, clawing at his weakness. The devil bears the ultimate responsibility, but the poet's misogynism focuses on Eve, the equally archetypal woman. The Germanic barbarians did not introduce misogynism into Western culture, but their warrior-aristocracy values, which had no room for "womanish" values, reinforced it. Rarely does the use of the demonic to express the fears of a society appear so clearly.

The greatest Anglo-Saxon poem, the eighth-century *Beowulf,* does not deal with a biblical theme but with a model hero who slays monsters and exhibits the values of the noble class. *Beowulf* includes several references to evil. The monster Grendel and his mother are descended from Cain, the evil child of Adam and Eve. They live in a den at the bottom of a marsh, thus sharing a watery home with the ancient and the biblical monsters. They attack only in the dark, the special time of the devil, the Prince of Darkness. The poet describes Grendel as the enemy of God, a traditional identification of the devil. Beowulf finishes his heroic life by battling against a dragon (= serpent), and, after he kills it, he cuts it in two. The Beowulf poet may have read the book of Isaiah (51:9) where God cuts the monster Rahab into pieces. The old Jewish combat myth would have had a natural appeal to an Anglo-Saxon warrior.

These barbarian tales depended upon the society that produced them. As the newly converted peoples came more and more into the Western cultural mainstream and as Christian values began to replace the traditional pagan ones, these tales faded into history. Some themes survived, such as the newly created monstrous allies of the devil, and some themes reinforced existing ones like misogynism. But after 1100, Christian writers did not refer to angels as thanes or to God as a liege lord, nor did anyone rewrite the Garden of Eden story to have the devil tempt Adam first.

These poets all wrote in the vernacular, which limited their influence, but the popular, non-scholarly Latin works of this period, which had more influence, do not differ much from these poems. The dominant literary form was hagiography, the life of a saint. Its origins go back to the Bible, to pagan lives of famous heroes, and to the monastic literature of the desert, but Early Medieval saints' lives, like the vernacular poems, reflect barbarian as well as Christian values. Pope Gregory the Great (590–604) wrote a life of Saint Benedict, the great monk, which consists heavily of Benedict's outwitting or overpowering the devil. The Venerable Bede (673–735), an Anglo-Saxon monk, wrote a miracle-filled life of the English monk Cuthbert, in which the saint routinely dispatches the devil. The anonymous Irish work *The Voyage of Saint Brendan,* written around 900, has the sailor-saint take his boat right to the gates of hell.

Yet hagiography did not advance the understanding of the problem of evil. The devil caused evil, and that was all anyone needed to know. Questions of theodicy did not concern the hagiographers. The barbarian Christians viewed the devil as an oppressor. The hagiography often shows the saint, a simple man or woman, standing up to the oppressor. The devil sees the saint as a threat to his domination of the people and attacks with vigor, only to be driven off by the saint's virtue. The hagiographers portrayed the battles vividly, since the devil appears in a variety of monstrous shapes. The saint, like Beowulf, must face this threat alone— or so the devil thinks, but he is wrong because God always stands by his own. Since Medieval Western Christianity stretched from Iceland to the southern tip of Italy, local variations abound, but the basic themes prevailed. The few scholars of this period debated predestination and free will, but the bulk of the people knew that evil came from the devil and they liked stories that show the Christian hero defeating this monster. Few educated people read such literature today, but it embodies the authentic views of Early Medieval people.

What the Early Middle Ages started, the High Middle Ages (twelfth and thirteenth centuries) continued. An Italian bishop, Jacob of Voragine

(1228–98), wrote *The Golden Legend,* an enormously influential hagiographical collection widely used by preachers and artists (much Medieval and Renaissance art is unintelligible without it). The devil appears on almost every page, trying to thwart St. Dominic's work by possessing one of his brethren, reminding St. Pelagia of the wealth he had given her, and provoking numerous Roman governors to persecute virtuous Christians. Even today these stories make delightful reading.

* * *

In the twelfth century, when the barbarians had settled down, the West took on the familiar attributes of the High Middle Ages: Gothic cathedrals, universities, an almost completely Christian population, the Crusades, and a strong self-confidence. In the High Middle Ages the Christian Church held great power in Western Europe. The popes rose to prominence in the late eleventh century, and in the twelfth century they extended their authority, bringing order and organization throughout the Church, which reached into every area of life. Scholars worked on the question of evil, but, for most Europeans, evil manifested itself in the Other, the person who differed from the dominant views of society. These Others represented the fears of High Medieval society, and, unfortunately, some teaching and preaching often exacerbated those fears.

Pagans

By the High Middle Ages most of Europe was Christian. The few surviving pagans lived in the north, mostly in Scandinavia and the Baltic regions. Veneration of gods like Thor and Freya and Odin survived in parts of Sweden until the fourteenth century, but pagans lived in remote areas and did not impact the larger society. Yet they could not escape demonization. In the early thirteenth century, some German Christians attacked and ultimately converted the Livonians, a pagan tribe living in what is now Estonia. But the notion of the Other was now focusing in different directions.

Muslims

Starting in the seventh century, Muslim armies had conquered the Near East, North Africa, Asia Minor, and most of Spain. With the First Crusade (1095–99), the Western Christians launched a centuries-long struggle against the Muslims. Few Westerners knew much about the Muslims, which made them easy to demonize and their religion easy to distort. Nowhere is this better seen than in the great French epic *The Song of Roland,* composed anonymously around 1100.

The epic deals with Charlemagne's attack against the Spanish Muslims in 778. On his return to France, his rear guard, led by a count named

Roland, was attacked and destroyed by a local tribe of Basques, but as the story of Roland was told and retold, Muslims replaced the Basques. Charlemagne's successes in Spain grew to monumental proportions, and Roland's defeat was attributed to treachery rather than to the superior abilities of the Muslims. Even with treachery, the Muslims still needed an army many times that of Roland. The great knight fought bravely and killed many of the enemy with his noble sword Durendal. When the Muslims finally fled and the wounded Roland knew he was dying, he propped himself up against a tree and faced south toward Spain so that even in death he did not turn his back to his enemies. This is heady stuff, and it made Roland a model for the chivalrous knight. The work's popularity both reflected and spread Medieval ideas about the Muslims.

Although the Muslims are rigid monotheists, *The Song of Roland* portrays them as no different from polytheistic pagans. Mohammed is not their prophet but their god, or rather one of their gods because they have several. In the Spanish city of Saragossa the Muslims venerate an idol of Mohammed. They invoke their gods in battle. They even have a sort of trinity, combining Mohammed, Termagant, and Apollyon (who appears in the book of Revelation as the angel of the abyss). The unbaptized Muslims cannot go to heaven, so even if a Muslim warrior fights bravely and dies a noble death, Satan still carries him off to hell. Even though many fruitful Christian-Muslim exchanges occurred in the Middle Ages, the image of the Other prevailed for Christians.

Jews

Despite the insistence of modern Christian leaders that anti-Semitism is un-Christian and a perversion of the Church's belief, it was unfortunately a central element of Christian life in the Middle Ages. The Jews represented the Other who worked hand-in-hand with Satan.

The portrayal of the Jews paralleled that of Satan. Since none of what they were accused of actually happened, those who demonized them could literally say whatever they wanted. Some of it is so stupid that it would be ludicrous if we did not know what it led to. The Medieval Christians believed—as do many modern Christians—that in the sacrament of the Eucharist, the bread of the host became the actual body of Christ. Medieval anti-Semites regaled audiences with tales of how Jews would steal the host and then stick pins in it. The host promptly bled. This is a clever rhetorical device, comparing the blood flowing from Christ's body on the cross with the blood flowing from Christ's body in the host, and they could blame them both on the Jews. But this meant that the Jews had to believe that the host was the body of Christ; otherwise there was no reason to stick pins in it. Since the Jews did not, the accusation is not only manifestly false but also inane. To trash like this was added the traditional accusations that the Jews murdered Christ, that they stubbornly refused to convert to what they knew to be the true religion, and that they distorted their own Scriptures to eliminate prophetic references to Jesus. But new charges reflected the new situation of the Middle Ages when Christians were warned about temptations to greed, a sin in which the Jews were believed to indulge.

Church authorities considered usury or paying interest on loans to be a sin, and so they forbade Christians to engage in it. Naturally people were reluctant to loan large sums of money with no interest, and so it was necessary to find people who could engage in usury without harm to their souls. In 1215 the Fourth Lateran Council authorized Jews to practice usury. That way funds would be available for loan but no Christian's salvation would be jeopardized. Thus was born the image of the Jewish moneylender. When capitalism came to the Western economy and the Church had to relax the ban on usury, Italian, German, and Dutch bankers rose to enormous power, but they never encountered the resentment the Jews did. There were historical exceptions to this sad list, as when popes protected Jews from angry mobs, but in too many sermons and too much popular literature, "the good Jew" was the one who "saw the light" and converted to Christianity.

Women

Muslims and Jews were distinctly Other from the Christians, but, on the surface at least, women were not since half the Christian population was female. Yet the misogynist legacy of the ancient and Early Medieval worlds also blossomed in the High Middle Ages. In the tradition of Tertullian, some Medieval preachers presented women temptations to all men. Since Augustine had argued that sex without intent of procreation was a sin even for married people, it was clearly better for married couples to abstain from sex on such occasions. But many Medieval Christians knew that lascivious women wanted sex and so they tempted men into wanting it, too. The poor, innocent men simply never stood a chance.

It was, of course, the women who never stood a chance.

Like the devil and the Jews, women were weak in the face of a good Christian man, and so they, too, had to be devious. They hid their viciousness under attractive exteriors. They not only entranced men sexually, but they lied, gossiped, and worked behind their husbands' backs. As Joan Gregg has demonstrated in her book *Devils, Women, and Jews* (1997), Medieval attitudes constantly imposed male fears upon women, especially the fear of being a cuckold. Preachers harped on any attempt by women to make themselves physically attractive: a vain woman looks in the mirror and the devil's face stares back; tiny demons leap and prance about a woman's elaborate dress; a woman condemned to hell is pierced by as many burning needles as hairs she had plucked from her eyebrows.

Such dangerous beings had to be kept in line. On the positive side, preachers stressed prayer and the sacraments, but since they believed that women were easy targets for the devil, they thought it best to use force. Civil law and ecclesiastical law both restricted the rights of women, and wife-beating was common. The daughters of Eve would not be allowed to destroy the Medieval paradise. But couldn't the critics find any good women? The common sense answer is yes, but Medieval men saw Eve behind every woman. They could recognize the goodness of a particular woman, but she was still Woman and the devil's gateway. Medieval society often idealized virgins, martyrs, or nuns who had renounced marriage. No woman held a higher position in Christian life than the Virgin Mary, but she bore little resemblance to the average Medieval woman who was married off by her parents in her adolescence, was constantly pregnant (if she did not die in childbirth early in her marriage), could be abused by her husband, aged rapidly, and bore throughout her short life the guilt of Eve.

Horrific as it sounds, the worst was yet to come. Misogynism did not reach its apogee until the Witchcraze of the sixteenth and seventeenth centuries.

Heretics

Heresy can be defined as a conscious deviation from the official teaching of the institution. In Early Christianity heresy usually took the form of intellectual dissent from official teaching. In the High Middle Ages, intellectual heresy continued but it was more and more replaced by social heresies, that is, heresies which excoriated the official Church for not living up to its proclaimed ideals. They questioned the very legitimacy of the Church and of Christian society.

The twelfth and thirteenth centuries saw the growth of towns for virtually the first time since the Roman Empire, and with this came a new phenomenon, urban poverty. Accompanying this was the sense of dislocation people felt when they left family farms and land for the comparatively anonymous life of the town. Life on the bottom was hard, but there were people who tried to help the poor. These were rarely monks or bishops. Monks withdrew from society into monasteries, while the bishops usually came from the aristocracy, virtually guaranteeing a hierarchy unaware of the problems of the poor. The parish priests usually came from the ranks of the people, but they were often too poorly trained and educated to make a difference. The two great Christian heroes of the era were the Spaniard Dominic de Guzman (ca. 1172–1221) and the Italian Francis of Assisi (1180–1226), who founded religious orders to work with the poor. The two founders insisted that their friars be mendicants, that is, that they beg for alms and food, so that they would understand in a direct and personal way the plight of society's underclass. The work of the Dominicans and Franciscans with society's outcasts reconciled some dissidents to the Church, even at the risk of their being considered heretics themselves, but some who helped the poor concluded that the Church was not the solution but the problem. Social heretics resented the wealth and power of the higher clergy, who were supposed to practice poverty. Technically they did, via a legal distinction. Individual clergy could not own property, but the institution could. That meant that a monastery could have great wealth which individual monks could share, but the monks themselves were theoretically poor, a distinction lost on the truly poor. (To his everlasting credit, Francis of Assisi insisted upon both institutional and personal poverty for his order, a practice which won it acceptance among the poor and marginalized.)

Social heretics insisted on a comprehensive reform of the Church's way of life. When that was not forthcoming, they felt they had to break from the Church. So radical a move threatened the Church but also the state in an era which envisioned no separation of Church and state. From Augustine's Garden of Eden onwards, the devil had threatened the stability of every society, and the state joined the Church in demonizing the heretics.

The most threatening High Medieval social heresy was Catharism, a descendant and variation of both Gnosticism and Manichaeism. It had all the strengths and deficiencies of most dualist movements, including a simplistic explanation for good and evil and an elitist spiritual hierarchy. The word "Cathar" means "pure." The Cathars rejected the material world and the flesh as evil. They believed that the devil had created the world and imprisoned people's spirits in fleshly bodies. They pointed to natural evils such as earthquakes and storms, and harmful animals such as fleas as proof that a good deity could not have created this world. Sexual desire represented a harmful distraction, and intercourse was forbidden as the ultimate concession to such desires. Good Cathars would not eat meat because animals were born from intercourse by other animals; instead they practiced vegetarianism. The Cathar elite took the name "the perfects" because they rigorously followed the group's most stringent demands. They practiced poverty, dressing simply and owning nothing. A rite called the *consolamentum* marked off one as a perfect. The majority of Cathars were called simply "believers," but all believers hoped some day to receive the *consolamentum* before they died. Failure to become perfect meant that the believer's soul would migrate into another body after death, possibly even to the body of an animal, and the long struggle for spiritual freedom would begin again.

The modern reader may wonder how something like this could ever become a popular movement, but Catharism paralleled the ideals of the Church. Medieval Christianity idealized asceticism, sexual renunciation, and poverty, all of which the Cathar perfects and many believers practiced. But Catharism also presented itself as a prophetic witness against the wealth and power of the Medieval Church and against the pretensions of a noble society. Anyone could become a perfect, regardless of his or *her* social status. In a democratic and revolutionary move, the Cathar hierarchy recognized that women could become perfects, thus achieving a status they could never have in the institutional church. Not surprisingly, Catharism was especially popular among women.

In the late twelfth and early thirteenth centuries Catharism dominated much of southeastern France. The French kings did not rule there, and the local nobility, seeing the strong link between the northern French and the papacy, tolerated Catharism. Several noblewomen belonged openly to the sect and became perfects. Pope Innocent III realized the danger to the Church and opened negotiations with the Cathars, using monks as his ambassadors in the hope that their simple life would impress the heretics. But the negotiations came to nothing, and Innocent allowed the northern French to mount a crusade against the heretics.

In 1209 northern French armies launched the Albigensian Crusade, so called because the Cathars' chief stronghold was the town of Albi. Crusade propaganda portrayed the heretics as being in league with the devil. In twenty years of intermittent warfare, the crusaders eventually defeated the local armies and destroyed the Cathars when they found them. Using massacres to spread terror, the crusaders frequently murdered noncombatants, including children. When the fighting subsided, persecution decimated the surviving heretics. The Cathars perished or fled to mountain regions. Most Cathar children abandoned their parents' faith.

But force did not deal with the underlying problems of poverty and social inequity. The popes did not recognize this, and instead of following the lead of the mendicant orders, they opted for even more force. Unlike Muslims, Jews, and women, heretics could not be easily recognized. Heresy gained ground and became menacing precisely because its adherents could hide behind vague, orthodox-sounding formulas. Pope Gregory IX (1227–41) established the Roman Inquisition in order to train investigators who could spot heresy, burrow through all the heretics' evasions, and win them back to the Church.

The Inquisition soon degenerated into an instrument of terror. Informers proliferated, and those who were arrested received no legal counsel and no right to confront their accusers. Guilt was presumed, and torture reliably produced confessions. Those stubborn enough not to confess only proved how guilty they were. The Inquisition rarely executed heretics. Instead they were handed over to the secular authorities who usually burned the heretics at the stake and then expropriated their property. Execution by burning provided an apt lesson for all heretics and their sympathizers; these partisans of the devil went from earthly fire to hell fire. Such an approach never touched the real problems, and all the efforts of the Dominicans and Franciscans could not make up for the problems of the larger society. Forms of social heresy continued for the rest of the Middle Ages.

Scholasticism

Ironically, at the very time when prejudice and irrationality defined evil for many Medieval Christians, some others were introducing reason into the discussion in one of the most powerful intellectual revolutions of Western history. In the twelfth century the Christian West rediscovered the writings of the great Greek philosopher Aristotle (384–322 B.C.E.) at the same time that a new educational institution, the university, was coming into being. The two interacted fruitfully. Aristotle posed a strong theoretical challenge to the Christians who for generations had depended upon Scripture and tradition to answer questions. The Greek philosopher had literally written an encyclopedia. As one who knew nothing of the Bible or Christian tradition, Aristotle symbolized for the Middle Ages unaided human reason. Augustine had naturally included reason among the human faculties weakened by original sin, and his domination of Early Medieval thought kept later thinkers, with few exceptions, to the same view. But now Christian scholars saw, in awesome form, what reason, independent of faith, could do, and they were mightily impressed. They could never abandon Scripture and tradition for reason alone, nor could they ever place it above them. For example, Aristotle argued that the physical world was eternal, but Genesis said that God had created it and so they followed Genesis. In many other areas Aristotle did not conflict with Scripture, but he did with tradition, forcing the Christians to moderate their views.

The earliest universities, Paris and Bologna, appeared in the 1130s. The university teachers were known as scholastics, the men of the schools. Scholastic teachers of theology and philosophy incorporated Aristotelian ideas into their deliberations and raised the status of unaided human reason in the eyes of the Church. They firmly believed that all good things came from God and that reason could work in harmony with revelation. This optimism enabled them to produce prodigious works of scholarship known as *summas* or summaries of philosophical and theological thinking, marked by astonishing attention to detail, seemingly endless qualifications and distinctions, and rigorous rationality. The size of the *summas* caused some to wonder if things had not gotten out of hand; a thirteenth-century English Franciscan named Roger Bacon derided another Englishman's *summa* as "about as much as one horse could carry."

Although he lived before the full impact of Aristotle and the rise of the university, Anselm (1033–1109), archbishop of Canterbury, tried via reason alone to prove some basic Christian doctrines. He stuck to the old theme of evil's being an absence of good and thus nothing on its own. He likewise denied double predestination, suggesting, as his predecessors had, that God predestined salvation for the elect but simply withheld grace from those who would be damned. Anselm even passed along an old tradition that God created humans in order to fill up the places in heaven left by the fallen angels. (No one ever bothered to explain why God simply did not create more angels.) Anselm could not escape from Augustine, and he did not try, but he did clarify some of his teachings. He brought front and center a point that should have seemed obvious to earlier generations and to which Augustine had alluded. Anselm said that we simply cannot speak of God's foreknowledge because the term always implies that God looked into the future and that is simply impossible because God lives outside time and all history is instantly present to him. After Anselm no scholar presented God standing in front of his blueprints, plotting how history would flow.

Anselm located the origin of evil in Satan's turning away from God in heaven, a pattern repeated on earth. God did not create evil nor did he create an evil will. The good Satan had a good will; he could have remained in heaven because he had the ability not to sin. Then why did he? Anselm had to acknowledge the difficulty of humans discoursing about heavenly beings, but he made a simple, potent suggestion. Satan sinned because he willed to. Satan wanted to be like God, an inappropriate desire for a created being. Satan chose the lesser good, the desire of his own will, over the greater good, following the divine will. God could have given him the grace to avoid the sin but chose not to. God let Satan make the decision on his own, and, with his uncorrupted free will, he freely chose to turn away from God, just as he would tempt Adam and Eve to do. This careful reasoning had lifted some of the impossible Augustinian burden, especially as it was misunderstood by Early Medieval Christians. Satan's sin was not the inevitable consequence of a divine plan; he sinned simply because he willed to. [Augustine had also said this, but he had subsumed Satan's sin within his predestinationist framework.] Once Satan had sinned, evil entered the cosmos. Other angels followed his example, and evil came to the earth as well. Anselm generally followed Augustine's teaching that human evil results from original sin and that we need grace for salvation.

Coincidentally, just as the Christians were discovering Aristotle, the most important Jewish philosopher of the period, Moses Maimonides (1135–1204) brought the philosopher's ideas into Judaism. Born in Spain, Maimonides spent his life in Egypt as a court physician and leader of the Egyptian Jewish community. He interpreted the Torah in light of philosophy, which upset some conservatives, but, like the Christians, he rejected Aristotle when his teaching contradicted the Bible. At a time when Christian scholars were trying to fit the devil into their theodicies, Maimonides simply rejected belief in demons and other traditions he considered superstitious. He accepted the notion of evil as privation, and he accepted evil as an inevitable consequence of creation. He defended the freedom of the will which God's foreknowledge did not affect; we are responsible for what we do. God helps to offset evils with his commandments which guide humans in doing good; Maimonides emphasized the positive rather than the prohibitive role of those commandments. His concerns to reinterpret Torah in the light of modern knowledge meant that he was busy on many fronts besides evil. Writing at a time when Christian scholars dominated Western life, Maimonides made a real contribution to developing Western notions of evil. Christian scholars used his work.

Many scholastics wrote about evil, and the most important was the Italian Thomas Aquinas (1225–74). Thomas admired Aristotle so much that he referred to him simply as "the Philosopher." He knew that many conservative churchmen did not trust the philosopher's influence on Christian intellectuals, and he tried to reconcile Aristotle with Christian teaching without doing violence to either. When Aristotle contradicted revelation, Thomas stood by it, but he was willing to reconsider some traditional teachings, even those of Augustine. Thomas recognized the power of Augustinian tradition, and, in his writings, when he disagreed with Augustine, he did not mention him by name but resorted to the discreet formula, "some have said." But, discreetly or not, Thomas altered the traditional Western Christian view of evil.

He stood in a long tradition, and he knew it. He agreed with much of what his predecessors had taught, but he did not just reaffirm such teaching. He examined it in detail, quoting pagan, Jewish, Muslim, and Christian authors, pro and con, then giving his own view, and finishing with a point-by-point refutation of those with whom he disagreed. Aristotle's influence appears in his view of natural evil. Since Aristotle did not assume that the world is not the way it is supposed to be, he took storms, earthquakes, and the animals' struggle for life for granted. Thomas agreed. He considered some natural phenomena to be evil in the sense that it is better that people see and hear instead of being blind or deaf. God wills the goodness in a person; he does not will the blindness or deafness. Like moral evils, natural evils are deficiencies in the good. Yet could not God have created a cosmos without natural evils? Thomas used an old argument here but with his own bent. God cannot create infallible creatures; only the divine being can have no possibility of imperfection. The fallibility of created beings would then manifest itself in a variety of ways, including natural evils. Contrary to Augustine, Thomas said that these harmful forces exist in the world as a consequence of creation, not as a consequence of original sin. Perhaps humorously, Thomas pointed out that death, the ultimate consequence of original sin, would probably still have been necessary because if no one died, the world would become impossibly crowded.

Like Anselm, Thomas wondered how evil had begun. He used the argument about fallibility, but he raised it to a new level, using the Aristotelian concept of nature which stressed that certain traits are appropriate to each existing being. God creates all that is, and all creation is fallible because it is not divine. God cannot make an infallible creature because that would be contrary to its nature; infallibility can only reside in the divine nature. God must act according to his own nature, and he must respect the nature of his creation. This is not a weakness on God's part. Divine omnipotence does not mean that God can do anything; for example, he cannot sin, he cannot destroy himself, he cannot create a being equal to himself. If he did any of those, he would cease to be God.

By insisting God be true to his own nature and respect the nature of his creation, Thomas altered the Medieval notion of evil. Many Christians believed that goodness resides in the divine will; if God wills something, then it is good. But Thomas placed goodness in the divine nature. God cannot act contrary to his nature. If he wills something contrary to his nature, that thing cannot be good. For Thomas, of course, God could never will contrary to his nature, so in that sense, goodness could be said to reside in the divine will but not in an arbitrary way.

Thomas taught that the deity created a cosmos filled with all kinds of beings. Each being had its place and function in the order of creation, and often one being functioned at the expense of another, as when one animal preyed upon another. If we look at only one action, we may see evil as the fox devours the rabbit. But Thomas said that God sees past the particular. God does what is good for the whole of creation, not for the individual parts of creation, except as they relate to the whole. Thomas would not say that it was good for the rabbit to be eaten by the fox, but each animal acts according to its nature and thus the essential goodness of the whole is preserved precisely because they acted according to their natures. To transfer this to humans, we cannot understand why individuals suffer, but we can understand that God's providence still cares for the whole because God, too, follows his nature and is always beneficent toward us.

With this general understanding of creation in mind, Thomas followed tradition in saying that moral evil exists because in heaven Satan turned away from the divine toward a lesser good. Humans sin because of original sin which corrupted our nature; God provides saving grace to some of them. He suggested that God wished the good for everyone, but he wished less good for some than for others, a notion reminiscent of Augustine's belief that God gave grace to some and not to others.

Thomas believed that free will had survived the Fall, but in a weakened condition. Augustine's language had implied that original sin had vitiated free will. Thomas knew this was impossible since God had created it, so he made a scholastic distinction, that free will had survived in humans but that its full powers had not. Having saved the will from sin, Thomas next saved it from grace. He denied that the grace given to the saved by predestination imposed necessity upon them, even though predestination was certain. Original sin had made us slaves to sin, and God's grace restored to us our freedom from sin. Thomas emphasized that predestination was the giving of grace rather than a vast divine plan to save and damn people. He gave it a genuinely Christian dimension.

But what about those to whom God does not give grace? Thomas could only fall back on God's justice and mercy. Humans sin their own way to damnation, and, when God withholds grace from them, he acts justly. When he gives them grace, he acts mercifully. Unlike Augustine, Thomas had enormous respect for Jewish and Muslim scholars as well as Aristotle, and he was not eager to send masses of non-Christians to damnation. Thomas did not try to demystify predestination, and he was right not to. Anyone accepting Augustine's premise that God chooses to save some and not to save others simultaneously accepts an impossible conundrum; the believer has to join Job in accepting the mystery of the divine actions.

Like Augustine, Thomas had created a theodicy which did not require the devil. Because of the devil's presence in the Bible, Thomas found a place for him in the overall schema of his work, but he did not need him. In fact, he even diminished Satan's presence in Scripture. Thomas recognized the difficulty of interpreting some biblical passages literally, but he feared that allegory and typology, the belief that the Bible must be interpreted on other than a literal level, could be wildly misused. He insisted, as a methodological point, that these could not be used in intellectual arguments, although people could retain them for preaching or spiritual reading. Since the devil barely appears in the Hebrew Bible, for a millennium Christians had followed Origen and typified the biblical monsters such as Behemoth, Leviathan, and Rahab as the devil. By abolishing symbolic interpretation from theological method, Thomas reduced the devil's presence in the Bible and thus his presence in serious scholarly work. This was no small step. After Thomas, the devil played a constantly diminishing role in theories of evil.

In a stark way, Thomas's theodicy highlights the gap between the scholars and their co-religionists. No matter how inadvertently, the scholars were banishing the devil, while the rest of contemporary society found him at work everywhere, especially among the Others. Even if the gap between the two had been occasionally bridged, the situation of the Others would not have improved greatly. It is the fate of scholars in almost every generation to fail to influence large numbers of people.

* * *

Yet it was not a scholar but a poet who produced the Medieval world's deepest insights into evil. No one has ever had better insight into the nature of evil. In his epic poem *The Divine Comedy,* the great Italian poet Dante Alghieri (1265–1321) recounted a startlingly imaginative journey through hell, purgatory, and heaven. In hell *(Inferno),* Dante encountered the damned; in purgatory *(Purgatorio),* those who must do penance for their sins but who would eventually make it into heaven; in heaven *(Paradiso),* the blessed. In the Middle Ages "comedy" meant not something humorous but a tale with a positive outcome. Moreover, unlike tragedy which intended to lift the reader to lofty heights, comedy brought one down to daily life, as Dante did by writing in Italian, the language of his people, rather than in Latin, the language of the scholars.

His basic conservatism manifested itself in an acceptance of a prime Augustinian principle; only good Christians get to heaven. Surprisingly, Dante mentions Augustine only once, in his *Paradiso,* but he did not challenge what had become a fundamental tenet for most Medieval Christians. Yet, as all artists must, Dante often went his own way. He put many prominent Florentines, northern Italian nobles, and foreign dignitaries in hell; several popes, monks, and bishops ended up there as well. He could not put even good pagans in heaven, but he goes out of his way to praise their virtues.

Dante's device to portray evil, a journey through hell, had a long ancestry. In classical literature, the underworld contained both good and evil people as both Ulysses and Aeneas discovered, but by the Middle Ages the good were up in the sky with God and only the evil were below the earth. Several Medieval visionary stories recounted visits to hell; their intent was usually moral, to urge believers to reform their lives. All of this sounds dated, yet it continues today in modern books and films about the earth after a nuclear war or an environmental disaster. The protagonists journey through a wasteland of desolation and violence, the consequence of human evil.

Yet can someone who lived in an era when people routinely believed in the devil have anything to say about evil to skeptical moderns? Yes, and for two reasons. First, Dante followed the scholastic theologians in downplaying the role of the devil. *The Inferno* has thirty-four parts or cantos, and only in the last canto does the devil make an appearance. The poet used him primarily as a symbol. Second, unlike the scholars, Dante wrote not about ideas but about people. The intellectual equal of any scholastic theologian, he chose poetry as his vehicle. He wrote about evil with an immediacy that academics could never have. We may not remember Thomas Aquinas' distinctions on will's functions, but we cannot forget Francesca and Paolo or the last voyage of Ulysses.

Dante starts off in hell and finishes in heaven because he believes that this is the journey the soul takes; furthermore, by experiencing evil, we understand the good more profoundly. This is a variant on the old idea that only by knowing evil do we know the good, but what Dante means is that because of original sin we start off in evil anyway, and so such a journey is inevitable. More importantly, by going through hell, Dante encounters evil in its purest state. In their daily experiences people encounter evil but in a diluted form. They combine good and evil in their lives, and this prevents them from seeing evil in its essence. But there is no good in hell. Evil displays itself as it really is.

This sounds almost apocalyptic, and we prepare ourselves to encounter Evil. But Dante's genius quickly dispenses with that illusion. He shows us evil as in its true manifestations—vanity, stupidity, pettiness, self-delusion, revenge, and hatred. Some important villains and the devil himself appear in the poem, but evil is never heroic or even cosmic. Dante had little use for the Early Medieval device of making the devil a worthy opponent. Evil and its personification literally represent nothing. Dante did not originate the notion of evil as essentially vain and stupid, but he made it a central theme of the epic. His genius guaranteed that his views would be read by later writers, and he set the pattern, common from the sixteenth century onward, that literary artists would play as great a role as philosophers, theologians, and scientists in the discussion of evil.

For Dante, God is good and the world is good. Evil turns all of that upside down, and so Dante did, too. In the Aristotelian universe, the earth was at the center and the planets moved about it in concentric circles. As one went farther out from the earth, the circles became wider. The sphere of the fixed stars lay beyond them, and beyond that the dwelling place of the deity. Contrariwise, in *The Inferno,* Dante journeys from larger concentric circles to increasingly smaller, tighter ones; the cosmos becomes progressively more narrow and the damned become more vicious as the poet descends farther down. In *Paradiso* Dante would journey through the planetary spheres to the realm of God; in *Inferno* he journeyed through the hellish circles to the prison of Satan. The deity lives beyond the spheres and the devil lives at the center of the earth; they are literally as far from one another as they can possibly be physically. This gap is also an ontological one. God is pure spirit, and he lives beyond the physical cosmos. Satan is pure matter, and this great bulk of matter has sunk to the very lowest point in the cosmos. God shines with the warmth of love; Satan lives forever in darkness and in cold. (Contrary to the common image of a fiery hell, Dante portrays the devil encased in ice up to his waist.) The deity represents perfect motion, while Satan is immobile, trapped in the ice and weighed down by evil. The realm of evil is an upside-down world, physically, ontologically, and morally. Dante makes his point well—no matter what we think we are getting away with, when we turn to evil, we turn our lives upside-down.

The epic begins with Dante the pilgrim becoming lost in a deep wood (canto 1). The great Roman poet Vergil appears and offers to lead him to safety, but they must first take a long journey. Dante has reservations, but Vergil assures him that God will watch out for them. Dante admires Vergil's poetry and so trusts him. Moreover, the pagan poet had written an account of the underworld in his own epic poem, the *Aeneid*. The two poets set off. It is impossible to recount the whole poem, but certain cantos shine with insights into evil.

When the poets enter hell (canto 3), Dante sees a nine-line inscription over the gate, ending with the famous words, "Abandon hope all ye who enter here." Pure evil must lead to despair. Dante must discuss evil within hell itself because only there can he get to its real nature.

The first souls the poets meet are those who could not choose between good and evil. They deserve neither heaven nor hell. Since they could not make up their minds in life, in death they spend all eternity blindly following a banner, which, like them, goes in no firm direction. Dante uses a familiar device from the Greek vision of hell: the punishment fits the crime. Vergil observes that these people were so feckless that the world did not even notice their having been there, and, in a brilliant poetic device, neither does Dante: this is the only level of the underworld in which no one is named.

When Dante meets souls who do deserve hell, they are waiting to board a boat to cross the river Acheron. The poet reverses the image of crossing the Jordan to the Promised Land, and he introduces Charon the boatman, a figure from Greek mythology. Here he cleverly makes use of an old tradition. If the gods of the pagans were demons, then why not use them in hell? Dante listens to the moans of those awaiting passage. They curse God, their parents, their country, their era, and the human condition generally. The damned blame everyone and everything except themselves. This self-delusion borders on the ludicrous. These people are in hell; everyone around them is damned, too. Whom do they expect to convince with these denunciations? Like all evil people, they cannot face up to who they really are. Better delusion than the pain of honesty.

On the next level (canto 4), Dante finds himself in limbo. The pastoral impact of Augustine's views proved too much for the Medieval Church. Did God really send unbaptized babies and good Jews and pagans to eternal damnation? Since Adam and Eve had closed the door to heaven and only Christ could open it, the early Christians believed in an unspecified postmortem location for the saints of ancient Israel who waited for the coming of Christ. After Augustine was safely dead, some Medieval Christians began to speculate on another type of place, this one for infants who had died before being baptized and who, in Augustinian theology, went directly to hell. In this place, called limbo, the residents could enjoy natural happiness but were denied the blessedness of the divine presence. The Church never formally taught the existence of limbo, but acceptance of it was widespread and believers in it included Thomas Aquinas. As the Christians became increasingly acquainted with the virtuous Jews and pagans of the ancient world and even of their own world, limbo began to fill up with adults. Dante clearly enjoys his visit to limbo. That was where Vergil lives, and he introduces him to all the great poets of antiquity, such as Homer. This visit also produces one of the poem's most famous lines, when the poet identifies Aristotle as "the master of those who know." In the Middle Ages, master meant *magister* or teacher; Dante here praises Aristotle as the teacher of all those who learn anything. More than the great are there; Dante also hears the voices of infants. Although endless darkness suffuses hell, Dante acknowledges the light of learning in limbo as he heads into eternal night.

Now he encounters the damned enduring their punishments. Each level of hell holds people guilty of a specific type of sin. The farther down ones goes, the worse the sinners and the worse the punishments. On the upper level of hell (canto 5), the poets meet the Lustful. They sinned by the flesh, and they survive as shades. Their punishment for corporal sins is to be eternally insubstantial, blown about like dead leaves in a raging wind. Dante sees several famous illicit lovers, like Paris and Helen of Troy, but the only one who speaks to him is Francesca da Rimini, a young Italian noblewoman who was married off by her family to a politically important nobleman but who fell in love with her husband's younger brother Paolo. Her husband discovered their infidelity and murdered them both. (Dante puts him farther down in hell.)

Francesca and Paolo are linked together in hell. Like all the damned, Francesca passes the buck, blaming their adultery—or at least her own—on a book she and Paolo had read together about Lancelot and Guinevere, two famous Medieval literary adulterers. Francesca says that this passionate story moved Paolo to kiss her, even though in the book Guinevere, the woman, takes the initiative. If the parallel holds, then Francesca is lying, which we would expect in hell. She clearly enjoys Dante's attention, and she may win some sympathy. Everyone in the Middle Ages knew that marriage without love led to love without marriage. Yet Dante stands by custom and tradition. Paolo and Francesca are not martyrs for love; they belong in hell. But his realization of their suffering takes a toll on the poet, who faints. New to hell, he reacts emotionally, but he will harden as he descends.

The next sinners by the flesh are the Gluttons (canto 6). Since excess food becomes excrement, the gluttons wallow about in slime and dung. Dante meets a Florentine nicknamed Ciacco, "the Hog," who, like a hog, roots around in the filth; to this gluttony has reduced him. Evil has robbed him of his humanity. Maintaining the materialist theme, Dante goes from sex and food to money, encountering the Misers and the Spendthrifts, those who hoard money and those who waste it (canto 7). They form two groups which forever crash into one another with huge weights. After each collision, they withdraw and repeat the process. Futility, revenge, mindlessness—and they can never rise above them. The poet cleverly ends this canto by contrasting these furious warriors with the Slothful, who, of course, do absolutely nothing for all eternity. They are encased in muck, and air bubbles offer the only proof that they even exist.

When the poets reach the circle of the Violent (canto 12), they meet the Minotaur, the monster of the Greek Labyrinth and a symbol of the terrifying underworld. The Minotaur threatens them, but he is so caught up in his own boiling rage that he cannot bring himself to attack the poets. Escaping from him, the poets encounter violent humans, immersed forever in a river of boiling blood. Surprisingly, they occupy a place in hell just above the Suicides (canto 13). Today we might wonder why those who harmed others are higher than those who harmed only themselves. This, and the answer to several other apparently puzzling placements, lies in Dante's belief in the importance of the natural functioning of the world.

Evil goes against the natural order, and the more it perverts that order, the worse it is. No matter how deplorable, violence against others is more natural than violence against one's self. Suicide is also less Christian because the violent can repent, but suicides have already despaired. They have abandoned hope.

Below the violent are Counterfeiters, Alchemists, and Fortune Tellers. To modern people counterfeiting is a serious crime but surely less so than violence; alchemy is nonsense; fortune telling belongs in a carnival. But Dante saw all of these people as perverting nature. Medieval people used metal coins, and counterfeiters literally had to change the composition of the coin, which Dante thought unnatural. Alchemists tried to turn base minerals into gold, again contrary to nature. Fortune tellers assumed the role of God, presuming to know the future, and Dante gave them an inspired punishment (canto 20). They walk for all eternity with their heads turned completely around. Those who presumed to see the future will forever see only the past.

As the poets go deeper into hell, the nature of evil begins to change. More and more Dante emphasizes its stupidity, which reveals itself mostly in vanity. He meets noble Florentines in the circle of the Violent who ask him to mention their names if he returns to Florence (canto 16). Even in hell, they worry about their public image. Evil giants, who have been in hell much longer than the Florentines, feel the same way. Vergil bribes them to help the poets by promising them that Dante can spread word of them in the world above (canto 31). Farther down, vanity gives way to the out-and-out lie. For Dante, sin began when the serpent lied to Adam and Eve. That primitive myth showed that people lie to themselves when they find a way to justify evil; it also showed a lie turning the world upside down, another parallel to *The Inferno*. Dante comes down very hard on those who lie: Flatterers who pretend to give rulers advice but merely say what they think the rulers want to hear; Seducers who betray someone else's precious gift of love; Hypocrites who turn on their own values. Dante plunges the Flatterers into excrement, and he has demons whip the Seducers mercilessly, but he finds an imaginative punishment for Hypocrites. They trudge along, forever encased in heavy leaden cloaks with a thin gold exterior, the gold representing the positive front they put up but the lead representing the baseness of their real selves (canto 23).

The poet successfully contrasts the love of earthly glory with real values in his account of Ulysses' last voyage (canto 26). After his epic adventure, the great hero has become bored with domestic life and yearns to return to the sea. He rounds up a band of sailors and urges them on with noble words about virility and fame. They sail past Gibraltar into the Atlantic, only to die in a ferocious storm. At first we admire Ulysses for his courage and sense of adventure, but he is in hell for a reason. He has deserted his wife, his son, and his aged father, who had all faithfully waited for twenty years for him to come home from the Trojan War. Unlike the pious Aeneas, the hero of Vergil's epic, Ulysses shows no familial piety but just a fatal desire for personal glory.

At the base of hell (canto 34) Dante finds the gigantic, bored, ice-encased Satan along with the worst of sinners, the traitors who feigned love of their homeland but turned against it, personified by Brutus and Cassius who assassinated Julius Caesar, and traitors who turned against their benefactors, personified by Judas who turned against the benefactor of the human race. The devil uses his three mouths to chew mindlessly on the three of them for all eternity.

Dante portrays the nature of evil in less obvious ways. When he enters hell, its guardian, Minos, warns him not to trust anyone (canto 5); a demon looks for an occasion to fight with another one (canto 22); souls in hell constantly curse one another. Even in common misery, the sinners' perversity prevents them from having sympathy or respect toward someone else. We see evil as it really is with nothing to modify or blur our view.

The poet also uses an old idea, the slippery slope, but his genius gives it new immediacy: he applies it to himself. Dante the poet shows Dante the pilgrim being changed by the insidious effects of evil. The longer Dante is surrounded by it, the less he can fight it off. He enters hell with his virtues intact, which is why he can initially feel sorry for the suffering sinners, but eventually severity replaces mercy. He faints at the sufferings of Francesca and Paolo, but as he encounters more and more of the damned with their prevarication and self-justification, he slowly becomes indifferent. Eventually he becomes hardened and even harsh; even his language becomes increasingly coarse and vulgar. At the base of hell, Dante accidentally kicks the head of a sinner who is encased in ice up to his neck. The poet recognizes him as a traitor to Florence, so he grabs the helpless man by the hair and threatens to pull it out if he does not tell Dante what he wants to know. The sinner refuses, so Dante does pull out his hair. Any sympathy for the damned is long past. Cleverly, the poet also shows how the stupidity of evil has caught up with the pilgrim. In the hair-pulling episode, he actually threatens someone who is already in hell, as if anything Dante could do would make a difference. He has to get out of hell, and soon. His guide, Vergil, knows this, and the poem ends when the two poets climb *up* from hell by climbing *down* (everything is reversed in hell) the gigantic hairy body of Satan, reminiscent of the Greek god Pan, and emerge into the light of day.

Much of the epic's immediate interest lay in its portrayal of Florentine and Italian politics. The first readers saw in its pages people they knew. That immediacy presents a barrier to the easy enjoyment of the poem, since modern readers must constantly consult footnotes to find out who these now obscure people were. But even for those unacquainted with Medieval history or Italian literature, the poem has tremendous power as an evocation of evil, what it is, how it functions, what it does to us.

The poem incorporates much Christian theology and Dante apparently believed in the devil, but *The Inferno* transcends even basic elements like these. Like all great writers, Dante tells us something about ourselves, and we applaud him for that, even if he tells what we do not want to hear. He pulled evil out of the cosmos and put it into our daily lives—in our vanity, our pettiness, our self-delusion—in a way that only a poet could.

Chapter 7

Decline and Reform and Humanism

> *Why this is hell, nor am I out of it.*
> —Christopher Marlowe, *Doctor Faustus*

As the Middle Ages drew to a close, the Church struggled unsuccessfully against the newly emerging nation-states of Europe and went into a serious decline. Social heresy became prevalent and ultimately unstoppable. Simultaneously, demands for reform mounted within the Church. As in the High Middle Ages, the secular rulers feared heresy and joined the Inquisition in rooting it out. Demonizing enemies went from a belief to a weapon.

The Jews remained primary targets. The Late Middle Ages maintained all the usual accusations, but added a new one. Christians suspected Jews of using poison against them. Like the devil and women and heretics, the Jews were believed to resort to devious means, especially Jewish doctors who, under the guise of curing Christians, were supposedly poisoning them. But since using physicians to poison would be too slow and affect only a few Christians, the Jews were next suspected of plotting to poison town wells and thus to murder many Christians at once. Accusations of well poisoning continued, but the real insanity broke out in 1349 when the bubonic plague or Black Death reached Europe. The plague was carried by fleas which were carried by rats which in turn were carried by ships returning from the Near East, but no one knew that in 1349. The Black Death struck hardest at seaport cities, and it moved along trade routes to many other cities. The death rate seems almost impossible to believe, running as high as 60 percent in some places. There was nothing to stop it, and people looked for other reasons than natural causes to explain it.

In some parts of Germany, France, and Spain, Jews were suspected of causing the plague. No one knew how they did it, and no one bothered to explain why Jews died from it too. Some Christians believed the plague to be a punishment from God, and groups called Flagellants went from town to town, whipping themselves for their own sins and the sins of society, but the Flagellants simultaneously stirred up anti-Jewish frenzy. The situation became so bad that Pope Clement VI (1342–52) condemned the Flagellant movement and offered French Jews sanctuary in Avignon, the papal residence. When the plague had finally burned itself out and the Jews could no longer be blamed for it, accusations of well poisoning returned. For too many Christians, the Jewish Other still represented evil.

Most people of that day were uneducated and simply accepted the devil or the devil-inspired Other as the cause of all evil and did not venture into questions of theodicy or free will or original sin. This attitude appears in sermons, but in the Late Middle Ages another form of popular media, the theater, often reinforced them. Late Medieval plays fall into several categories, such as mystery, miracle, and morality plays. The Church used them to teach the Bible and Christian doctrine to the people. Many English plays survive in collections called cycles, like that from the town of York. These cycles literally took people through the whole of the Bible from the creation to the last judgment. Satan appeared in many plays, but most importantly in the Fall, the Last Judgment, and the Harrowing of Hell. The Harrowing of Hell dates back to the sixth century, and it relies upon an obscure passage in the biblical First Epistle of Peter (3:19) which says that after his death but before his resurrection, Christ had preached to the spirits in "prison." The Christians theorized that the biblical figures before Christ remained in the underworld (the prison), bored but hopeful and certainly not in pain, until Christ came. In the sixth century a book entitled the Gospel of Nicodemus provided the first account of this descent, which became known in English as the Harrowing (despoiling) of Hell because Christ took away from Satan all the souls he thought were his.

Recalling that since the earliest feudal times the devil had represented one more powerful aristocrat who oppressed the people (he is called Sir Satan in some plays), we can see why such a play would be popular. The playwrights spruced up the basic drama with clever dialogue. Biblical figures like Adam, Eve, Isaiah, and David discuss whether enough time has finally passed for their redemption. In another part of hell, Satan (or Lucifer or Beelzebub) and his minions discuss this fellow Jesus. They are concerned because he was able to sneak past them at birth, having been conceived virginally. This concern mounted when he performed the miracles of raising people from the dead, thus demonstrating his power over the underworld. But everything looks all right now since this trouble-maker has just been executed. Usually one demon advises against being too sure that the crisis has passed, but, like the peasants, he finds that the ruler does not care what he thinks. The audience has the satisfaction of knowing that the rejected demon is correct. Soon the demons hear a furious pounding on the door of hell. Christ demands that they open the gates. They refuse, so he breaks open the gates, temporarily blinding the demons with the light, both physical and spiritual, that comes rushing in. Christ releases all the biblical worthies from their captivity and then informs the devil that he can keep hell open because there will be a lot more sinners to come.

The thirteenth century had produced the scholastic synthesis, combining the Bible, tradition, and reason to produce a comprehensive account of Christian doctrine. But the pendulum of history always swings, and a reaction set in against the scholastics by the Late Medieval mystics. What pleases the rationalist often offends the mystics. The scholastics had painstakingly investigated every aspect of Christian teaching, and some mystics charged that they had removed the mystery from the faith. A deity who fit into all the academic categories was reduced in stature to one more proposition. The mystics insisted that God was beyond our knowledge, and if we want to know him, we must stand in reverent awe and accept his overwhelming presence. Even Dante agreed. When he gets to Paradise, the famous mystic Saint Bernard of Clairvaux (1090–1153) carries him to the highest realms while the academics remain below.

The mystics characterized their "knowledge" of God in personal, imaginative terms, such as a blinding light or an overwhelming darkness or a great hunger or a quiet presence. Their experience of evil was also personal, often focusing on the devil, who mocked their meditations and tried to delude them. Many mystics such as Meister Eckhart (d. 1328) and Julian of Norwich (d. 1418) wrote of their struggles, and their writings have attracted far more readers than the scholastics ever have, but while the mystics impacted the understanding of evil, they did not advance it. Their experiences were personal, unvalidated, and incapable of being explained or replicated. The mystics saw no need to offer proof, which they considered irrelevant. The reader must accept the mystic's word that all these experiences actually happened. (Medieval people, unlike moderns, did not look for psychological factors to explain these visions.) But the mystics did make a contribution to the understanding of evil. They had questioned the validity of the scholastic world view into which everything fit neatly. In the fourteenth and fifteenth centuries scholars questioned that too.

The earlier scholastics believed in universals, that there was such a thing as humanity, which existed as an idea in God's mind. Late Medieval scholastics claimed that there were no divine ideas, no archetypes for God to follow. They were led by the English Franciscan, William of Ockham (d. 1349), who established the principle known as Ockham's razor, that anything superfluous to an argument must be discarded. Ockham claimed that we do not know universals, which are thus superfluous; we actually know only individual persons or things. We abstract from these individuals a concept to which we give universal names, such as humanity. This movement was called nominalism (name-ism), and it had both a long-range and an immediate impact on the idea of evil.

The long-range impact was the rise of science. If individual things are real and good in themselves and not just reflections of an ideal, then they deserve to be studied on their own. Nominalism gave the study of the physical world a dignity it did not previously have. Science as we know it began in the Late Middle Ages, and in later centuries it became the formidable enemy of the devil and forced Westerners to rethink the notion of evil. The more immediate impact was to free God from having to follow his universalist ideas, thus making it possible for God to act differently in the world. Evil is not the violation of some absolute standards but rather of the will of God, and he can make evil whatever he wants it to be. This seemingly radical approach actually hearkened back to the Hebrew Bible. For example, there may be no natural reason to keep the Sabbath holy, but God wills that it be so, and thus it is good for believers to observe the Sabbath and evil to ignore it. The nominalists distinguished between God's absolute and ordained powers. The first meant that God could do as he wished, even sending good people to hell. God's ordained power meant that God chooses to govern his creation according to a certain order (= ordained), and this is the world in which we live. We can trust God not to change the rules, but by just positing the existence of God's absolute power, the nominalists had altered the notion of evil.

Ockham defended divine predestination in a traditional way, claiming that God rationally pursues his own ends and cannot be held to standards which are independent of his will, the standards which humans would set. Humans may do good deeds independent of divine influence, but those deeds do not earn humans eternal life unless God chooses to credit those deeds. The nominalists then turned on another explanation for evil, the Augustinian synthesis. Augustine had explained evil in heaven by the sin of the devil and evil on earth as a consequence of original sin. The nominalists did not challenge original sin, but they did question whether all humanity had indeed been hopelessly corrupted by Adam and Eve. They worked within the Christian tradition, but they feared that Augustine's theory had turned humans into helpless robots, ordered around by sin or by grace. Some nominalists suggested that although humans cannot be saved without divine grace, the free will on its own can cooperate with that grace. Augustine had insisted that we can do nothing good without divine grace. For the will to cooperate with that grace meant that the will could do something good on its own.

This challenged the prevailing orthodoxy, and so the nominalists looked to the Bible for support. The apostle Paul had said that the pagans by their own powers could know that God existed. The nominalists asked, if humans can know of the deity via natural knowledge, why could their wills not respond to that knowledge? Why could they not wish to cooperate with this deity in combating the evil they could see all around them?

By the time the nominalists aired these views, Augustine had become the tradition on the question of free will, grace, and evil, and most Christian thinkers kept to his point of view, but cracks were appearing in the monolith.

Renaissance humanism widened the cracks. As the Middle Ages drew to a close, Western Christian intellectuals came into increased contact with ancient classical and Christian writers. Their horizon expanded well beyond Augustine and Aristotle.

The humanists preferred intellectual pursuits which dealt with the recognizably human rather than those that speculated about the divine; they preferred literature and eloquence to theology and philosophy. Their architecture focused more on secular buildings and less on churches. Michelangelo's statue of David is not a biblical saint but a human being of splendid physicality and a representation of the power of the city-state of Florence. The word "Renaissance" or "rebirth" may sound pretentious, but a new world was indeed dawning in the West. The humanists did not completely abandon theology and philosophy, but they found Aristotelianism dry and unimaginative, full of obscure terms and meaningless distinctions, and they found Augustinianism pessimistic, even morbid. The scholastics relied almost exclusively on Latin texts, including Aristotle in translation, while the humanists wanted to return to the ancient sources, both classical and Christian. The sources were more than just newly learned Greek ones. The humanists believed the scholastics did not understand the Bible because they could not read it in the original, and so in addition to Greek, they studied Hebrew. They found scholastic Latin to be barbarous, and so they studied the Roman writers whose polished Latin appealed more to the literary mind. In this new world, evil would take on new dimensions.

Nicholas of Cusa (ca. 1400–64), a German cardinal, believed that Aristotelians put too much faith in reason and relied too heavily upon distinctions. Everything seemed so clear cut that there was no room for gray areas. Like the mystics, Nicholas objected to God's being put into categories, but unlike the mystics, he had an intellectual answer to the scholastics. He returned to an old idea, the coincidence of opposites.

The Aristotelians relied upon the principle of non-contradiction, that A cannot be B. But, Nicholas asked, can we speak that way about God? Can we be sure that if God is A, then he therefore cannot be B? Nicholas wrote that God is beyond our abilities to understand him; all we can achieve is a "learned ignorance," an intellectual recognition of our rational limits. When we recognize this, we can speculate on what God might reasonably be. More importantly, in theology we can leave behind us the constraints of Aristotelian logic. God cannot be both good and evil because these are contradictories—or so we think. But are there contradictories in the deity? Nicholas did not say that God was evil but rather that God is the principle of unity, of identity, bringing together in himself all opposites and then transcending them. He is the opposite of the opposites. He negates the contradictions of the world. God's absolute transcendence is beyond reason, so when the Aristotelians start to place the divine in rational categories, they rely upon reason which simply cannot do the job. Nicholas did not attack reason; on the contrary, he rationally worked to prove how comparatively little reason could do when it came to God.

The traditional coincidence of opposites theory placed evil somewhere in the being of God, with the acknowledgment that humans could not understand how God can reconcile the two. Nicholas admitted that he could not fathom the coincidence of opposites. He could have used that admission to suggest that evil could reside in the divine, but he did not. Instead he fell back on the privation-of-good theory, thus shielding God from evil. Whether this resulted from his own unwillingness to take the last step his theory demanded or from respect for tradition or from concern about being labeled a heretic or some combination of these, we do not know. Nicholas may not have challenged the traditional teaching of the Church on evil, but he did make it clear that the origin of evil required a better explanation than the *hubris* of a fallen angel.

In contrast to Nicholas, the Italian humanist Giovanni Pico della Mirandola (1463–94) took a direct approach. Pico could read both Hebrew and Arabic as well as Latin and Greek, and his thought reflected the diversity of his reading. Although he was sympathetic to scholastic theology, he felt Christians could learn from other traditions, and he had an especial fondness for the Jewish *Kabbalah,* a theosophical treatise. He gave voice to the humanist frustration about Augustinian pessimism. Pico's most famous book is entitled *On the Dignity of Man,* published posthumously. Other Italian humanists had written about that, but Pico carried the struggle for human dignity directly into Augustinian territory by insisting upon human liberty and by emphasizing that unlike the animals we can make our own free choices. Pico thought a good way to exercise that freedom would be to seek out wisdom wherever it could be found. He freely and approvingly quoted pagan and Muslim authors along with the Bible, and he did not elevate the Bible above other sources. Most shocking to traditional thinkers was Pico's discussion of human nature without reference to original sin, the traditional starting point for all Medieval discussions of human nature. Scholars and Church leaders opposed his views.

Dead by age thirty-one, Pico did not live long enough to establish a thorough-going anthropology to rival that of Augustine, but, however unwittingly, he set out on a path others would follow in rejecting or at least passing over original sin as the starting point for understanding human nature. His method of relying upon non-Christian authors who did not bear the burden of the doctrine of original sin also appealed to humanists. Yet, unlike Pico, many humanists shied away from confrontation with the traditions behind much Church teaching. They hoped instead to win ecclesiastical authorities over to their point of view, a realistic hope since many of the Renaissance popes came from the noble and cultivated Italian families who supported the humanist cause.

The major figure in this Christian humanist movement was the Dutchman Desiderius Erasmus (1466–1536), who believed that humanistic values could reform individuals who would in turn reform the Church. He also believed that true learning would push back what he considered the obfuscation of scholasticism. He mocked the scholastics' inability to read the Bible in the original languages; he even edited the Greek New Testament with a Latin translation which deliberately differed in parts from the one used by the theologians. He threw down the gauntlet to the prevailing mores, and part of this offensive included an attack on the notion of evil. A cautious man, he moved indirectly and, if possible, humorously. In 1518 he published his *Colloquies* (conversations). The fourth colloquy deals with demonic apparitions.

Two men discuss how a friend of theirs named Polus played a joke on a local priest. Polus brought some people out to a lonely crossroad and claimed to see a dragon in the sky. No one wanted to admit being unable to see it, and so the story soon spread of a demonic apparition. A local priest went to see the place, and Polus hid there, making weird noises, which the priest assumed to be made by a demon. The next evening the priest went to exorcise the demon, bringing images and holy water and saying the formulas of exorcism. Polus and a friend hid nearby and then suddenly, mounted on dark horses and carrying torches, they rode furiously past the frightened priest who ran away. The priest went back to try again, and now Polus, feigning to be a devil, spoke to him and pretended to be overcome by his powers. As a final prank, Polus sent the priest a letter that claimed to be from a soul which had been liberated from the devil by the priest's exorcism. The priest swallowed the prank whole and showed the letter to his equally credulous friends. The two storytellers observe that they do not put much faith in apparitions because most of them have human or natural explanations.

This clever little piece enabled Erasmus to score his major points. He never denied the existence of the devil but wrote about a false apparition. Even the firmest believer in the devil knew that there were false apparitions and so could not be offended. Since Erasmus was writing for those who could read, he knew that many would agree with him about the superstitious elements associated with exorcism, but he carefully avoided saying that exorcism itself was superstitious or even ineffective. More subtly, he portrayed those who believe in such apparitions as credulous fools, while his sophisticated speakers conclude that "most"—and thus not all—of such things have a simple, non-demonic explanation. The reader naturally wants to be on the side of the sophisticated rather than the foolish. Finally, by writing a humorous piece, he put off his critics who would look ridiculous in taking a comic piece seriously.

Erasmus enjoyed wide influence in ecclesiastical circles, and the humanist cause appeared to have a real future in the Church. But a greater figure than Erasmus entered the scene. A German monk of the Augustinian order, Martin Luther (1483–1546) had a strong personal sense of sin and pathological fear of his own damnation. By the early sixteenth century, the Catholic Church had created numerous methods for dealing with sin. While giving allegiance to classic Augustinian teaching, the Church had emphasized that the sacrament of penance removed the guilt of current sins and that other sacraments, made available by the Church, gave people the grace necessary to fight off the temptation to more sin. Luther found none of this personally satisfying, and so he turned to the Bible for an explanation, particularly to Paul's Epistle to the Romans. Eventually Luther concluded that the Catholic Church had wandered far from any fidelity to the Bible, and he began to question much of the Church's teaching. When ecclesiastical officials tried to get him to recant his views, Luther concluded that he had to leave the old Church (1521). Many Germans followed him, and the Reformation had begun. Protestantism soon became one of the two major traditions of Western Christianity.

Luther concluded that humans can never be righteous before God, but that God can impute righteousness to them if they have faith in Jesus' saving death. The deity can consider them righteous even though they are totally unworthy. God provides them with all they need for salvation. He thus justifies them, and they must trust in him. They can be justified by faith but not by the actions or ceremonies of the Catholic

Church. Like Augustine, Luther insisted that humans must do good works, but they should never believe that these save them. People are saved because God chooses to save them.

The reformer did disagree with his master on some points. Augustine believed that God imparted grace to us and changed us, while Luther and his followers insisted that God declared us to be righteous and helped us on the road to sanctification. But, as far as the nature of evil was concerned, Luther differed little from Augustine. He believed firmly in original sin and predestination and especially in the devil, who taunted Luther endlessly and even caused his constant constipation.

Like many Augustinian-minded people, Luther had to explain how God can be freed from the charge of causing evil. First he accepted the traditional argument that what may seem evil to us may not be evil to God and may even be good for us. For example, some misfortune we encounter may be God's way of punishing us for our sins; it is thus a just act and ultimately good for us because all good people recognize that they must pay the price for their sins.

Luther also believed that God could bring good out of evil. He might let the devil roam about the world and do real harm, but he always frustrated the devil's ultimate aims.

The reformer also looked to one more explanation, the experience of the mystics. Like them, Luther often felt God's absence, and he suffered a spiritual emptiness; contrarily, he also feared God's righteousness. Luther understood these experiences as purgative, God's calling upon him to abandon all and trust in him. As the famous hymn says, Luther's God was indeed a mighty fortress, and so was Luther's faith.

The other great Reformer of the sixteenth century was the Frenchman John Calvin (1509–64). Although he himself treated predestination under the heading of redemption through Christ, his followers made it their central theme. Like Augustine and Luther, Calvin accepted original sin as the cause of human evil and he accepted the need for God's unmerited grace as the means for salvation. He differed from Luther who believed that God justified people who were *unworthy of salvation* in spite of their individual conditions; for Calvin, God graciously saves some people *irrespective* of their merits.

But Calvin's strong point as a theologian, his rigid logic, forced him to change one significant part of the Augustinian tradition. The African theologian and his Medieval successors had avoided saying that God predestined people to damnation. The explanation was thus that God chose to save some people but simply did not act in the case of others. The damned went to hell by default. Calvin considered this ridiculous. It took God out of the picture, making the fate of countless souls a consequence of divine inactivity. Calvin thought this unworthy of God, and so he opted for double predestination, to salvation and to damnation. Even some of his Protestant allies had difficulty with this, but he logically pointed out that if God does not act on someone's behalf, it is because he chooses not to act. In effect, he chooses to damn souls to hell. Why not just call it what it really is, double predestination to salvation or damnation?

Neither Luther or Calvin believed that the will was free. Following Augustine, they maintained the existence of the human will but denied that it had any power to do good, that is, it did not have any true freedom. When Luther began to deny that the will was free, Erasmus wrote a treatise against him entitled *A Diatribe or Sermon on the Free Will* (1525). The famous humanist had a fondness for Early Christian writers but was cool toward Augustine. Yet he realized how ingrained the African's theories had become, and so he stepped carefully. He used the nominalist argument that although all humans need divine grace for salvation, they can, of their own free will, cooperate with that grace. Erasmus was a great scholar but not a great theologian; he lacked the subtlety to see that both Augustine and Luther had retained the free will while denying it any power to do any good. Luther, on the other hand, was a genuinely great theologian and had little trouble demolishing his opponent's arguments. The early Protestants would stand in the Augustinian tradition.

This literary debate about free will proved that Luther and the Protestants were working within a different framework than that of the humanists. Erasmus's arguments had a genuine appeal to the humanists of his day, but Protestants and humanists were quickly going their own ways. Erasmian humanists hoped to reform the Catholic Church, not to split it, but the Protestants saw no other course. Unfortunately for the humanists, the Catholics were also moving away from them. Stung by the Protestant attacks and shocked at the rapid spread of the Reformation, the Catholic Church strove to defend its teachings, especially in their established form. Popes and bishops might personally support humanism, but doctrine would be traditional. The Catholics responded to Protestant teachings on justification and predestination, but they did not alter their view of evil: evil began when Satan sinned; evil for humans began when the first parents committed original sin; the Church and the sacraments work to save people from it.

The striving for theological precision marked just one side of the Catholic-Protestant struggle. The other side was a sleazy propaganda battle filled with accusations that opponents were in league with the devil. Since printing had come to Europe, many of these accusations appeared in scurrilous pamphlets with crude illustrations, such as the devil wearing the papal tiara or the devil with his arm around the shoulder of his good friend Martin Luther. This trash, aided and abetted by sermons and lurid accounts of martyrdoms, blanketed European cities, helping to solidify the split between Christians but also increasing the devil's perceived presence.

Any hope of easing the devil out of the understanding of evil faded quickly. How could you not believe in the devil when you see him or his minions incarnate in those heretics in the next village? A century of Protestant-Catholic hatred spawned the Wars of Religion which plagued France at the end of the sixteenth century and the aptly-named Thirty Years War from 1618 to 1648 in Germany. Once Catholicism's opponents felt secure, some of them turned to attack one another, as in England where the Puritans had to "purify" the Anglican Church of "popish" influences, a process which led to that country's civil war in the 1640s. Beset by such horrors, how could any Western Christian doubt the existence of the Evil One?

Yet, although the Reformation dominated Western history in this period, the humanists still played a critical role. They followed the lead of Erasmus by using creative works to make theological points. They may well have believed in evil spirits, but they investigated the depths of the human element, creating humans who were demonic and devils who were human. The Dutch painter Hieronymus Bosch (ca. 1450–1516) created scenes of the crucifixion of Jesus with people in modern dress, an approach which stressed the responsibility of all humans and avoided the blatant anti-Semitism of crucifixion scenes which blamed the Jews for Christ's death. Bosch portrayed faces which could scarcely exist, with features exaggerated to the point of hellish deformity. Medieval artists had used this device to portray the devil, and Bosch now turned it upon humans. Since the demons represented absolute evil and Christ represented absolute goodness, the artist portrayed a very human Jesus, saddened and accepting of what was going on about him, while the humans exhibit ferocity, vulgarity, and mocking humor. Bosch's demons reflect the same characteristics, but he broke ground with his portrayal of demonic humans.

At the end of the century William Shakespeare (1564–1616) did the same. Although he was willing to use the demonic for dramatic purposes as with the ghost of Hamlet's father and the witches of *Macbeth,* he produced villains who almost literally had no redeemable qualities and whose motivations were purely evil. Iago is perhaps the best example, a man driven by jealousy of Othello and willing to do whatever it takes to destroy him. Iago shows the traditional demonic traits, especially by his constant lying, but Shakespeare also works in other themes. Iago realizes that he can get to Othello through his wife Desdemona as, according to Medieval thinking, the serpent attacked Adam via Eve. Desdemona truly loves her husband, but Iago convinces him that she has betrayed him. Like the devil, the villain resents the love that he will never have, and he appeals to Othello's basest fears.

Iago may be driven by genuine hate, but other villains are driven by more familiar but no less evil motives. Lord and Lady Macbeth want power, and they will do whatever it takes to get it, even overturning a kingdom and killing a lawful ruler, the most serious crime of Shakespeare's day. They parallel Richard III, who would likewise harm or betray anyone in his lust for the crown. Evil characters pervert the family as well as the kingdom; Goneril and Regan betray both their father Lear and their sister Cordelia.

Portraying human villains as demonic did not challenge the notion of the devil, but it did raise questions about evil in human life. The religious bourgeoisie could safely attribute all these evil traits to the devil, yet more thoughtful people would recognize the points Bosch and Shakespeare had raised.

While some artists were portraying humans as devils, others reversed the process and brought some humanity to the evil one or at least to his demons. If, as tradition had taught, the devil was evil personified, he could not change. When we do something wrong, our conscience or the help of others can show us what we have done and how we might change. But the devil had nothing interior to help him, and all his associates were as evil as he was. Change was impossible. By giving human traits to the devil or demons some humanists challenged traditional teaching.

The English playwright Christopher Marlowe (1564–93) combined the demonic human with the humanized demon in his play *The Tragical History of Doctor Faustus*. Marlowe did not create Faust, a Medieval German professor who supposedly sold his soul to the devil for knowledge, but he did bring Faust to center stage in Western culture. Faust has been there ever since.

Like other humanists, Marlowe recognized that a new day had dawned. The play opens with a chorus, a traditional element, but the chorus proclaims an untraditional message. The play will not deal with the heroes of Greek and Roman antiquity or even with the "courts of kings," but rather with a scientist, the new man of the Renaissance whose knowledge extended to "heavenly matters of theology." The Hebrew creation myth has returned. Doctor Faustus the scientist can dominate the world around him, but, like Adam and Eve, he wants more. He cannot get it on his own, so he turns to the devil, first by consulting conjurers and wizards but then (scene 3) by summoning up the evil spirit Mephistopheles ("one who does not love the light" in Greek).

Mephistopheles differs from the traditional demons who personified evil. Marlowe put the human in the demonic. Mephistopheles has a personality.

When the demon arrives on the scene, he promptly warns Faustus about the limits of his (Faustus') power. Contrary to what he thinks, he did not summon Mephistopheles, but rather the demon came because he heard the scientist renounce God and hoped to get the man's "glorious soul." Faustus ignores this and says with remarkable arrogance, "This word 'damnation' terrifies [Faustus] not." When Mephistopheles assures him the pains of hell are real, the scientist rebukes him for his fears: "Learn thou of Faustus' manly fortitude."

When Faustus asks the demon who lives with Lucifer, he replies, "Unhappy spirits that fell with Lucifer" and who must remain in hell. To the question, "How comes in then that thou are out of hell?" Mephistopheles sadly replies:

> Why this is hell, nor am I out of it
> Think'st thou that I who saw the face of God,
> And tasted the eternal joys of Heaven,
> Am not tormented with ten thousand hells,
> In being depriv'd of everlasting bliss? (scene 3).

Mephistopheles shows genuine regret for what he has done. He remembers and regrets the lost good of heaven. Then, in sharp contrast to traditional teaching, Marlowe has the demon perform a good act—he tries to save a sinner: "O Faustus! leave these frivolous demands, / Which strike a terror to my fainting soul."

But the haughty scientist ignores the warning. The demon accepts this, and from that point on he is thoroughly evil. Faustus has had his chance.

Mephistopheles accommodates the scholar's desire to make a pact with Lucifer: Faustus will have the services of Mephistopheles for twenty-four years, after which he will die and his soul will go to Lucifer. This could have come from some Medieval saint's legend, but Marlowe transformed it into a devastating commentary on the nature of evil.

Following the Genesis account, he showed evil as unnatural. When Faustus goes to sign the devil's contract in his blood, he pricks his arm and dips his pen into the blood. Yet the blood suddenly stops flowing, a warning from Nature. "What might this staying of my blood portend? / Is it unwilling that I should write this bill?" (scene 5). But Faustus ignores this second warning (after that of Mephistopheles), and when the blood flows again, he signs the contract. At the end of the play, when the moment for him to pay the debt and go to hell has almost arrived (scene 14), he calls upon the stars to slow down the time, but they ignore him. He then calls upon the mountains to cover him and the earth to swallow him up, but they ignore him too. Like Mephistopheles, Nature had warned him once, but his pride overrode the warning and Nature could not offer help a second time.

Marlowe also emphasized the sheer stupidity of evil. Faustus genuinely believes that he can benefit from this pact. He wants Mephistopheles to get him a wife, but the demon replies, "I prithee, Faustus, talk not of a wife." A wife is someone good, and the demon can do no good. Instead he gets Faustus a succubus, a demon in the form of a woman. The scientist rejects her, so the demon, dismissing marriage as "a ceremonial toy," promises him "the fairest courtesans" or prostitutes (scene 5). Faustus actually expects to have a real relationship with a woman when evil is the basis of the relationship and a demon is the matchmaker. When, as the fatal hour approaches, Faustus considers repentance, Mephistopheles threatens to "piecemeal tear thy flesh," yet what could the demon possibly do to him that was worse than going to hell? Unable to think clearly, the scientist promptly and fearfully gives up any notion of repentance (scene 13).

Evil is unnatural and stupid because at base it is a lie, as the Hebrew creation myth taught. When Faustus has second thoughts about what he has done and regrets having lost heaven, Mephistopheles, fearing that he might repent, tells him that heaven is "not half so fair as thou, / Or any man that breathes on earth." Combining the themes of stupidity and the lie, Marlowe has Faustus believe the demon.

More than anything else, the playwright demonstrated that no good can come from evil. Faustus may have gone into the pact believing that he would gain knowledge and do monumental deeds, yet once he has made the agreement, he abandons any noble ambitions. Descending into the trivial, he discourses with the personifications of the seven deadly sins, plays infantile tricks on people, and conjures up spirits for money, but he does nothing of consequence and certainly nothing good. Augustine had written that God could bring good out of evil, but, as Adam and Eve and Faustus learned, humans have difficulty playing God.

Besides his humanism, Marlowe's Protestantism also appears in the play. When Mephistopheles appears as himself to Faustus, the scientist is repulsed and tells the demon to "return an old Franciscan friar / That holy shape becomes a devil best" (scene 3). Later in the drama, Faustus plays a vulgar joke on the pope (scene 7). The playwright's religious views appear more subtly in his attitude toward knowledge. The Medieval theologians believed that knowledge could achieve much, and the Catholic Church had relied upon this Medieval view as a response to Protestant attacks. Marlowe shared the widespread Protestant reticence about the power of knowledge and the scholastics' confidence in it (Luther had once called reason the devil's whore), yet the playwright universalizes his reticence by not making Faustus a Catholic. On the contrary, the scholar lives in Wittenberg, where the Reformation began. Marlowe presciently realized that the growing power of science, manifested in his own day by the Copernican revolution, would challenge the influence of all branches of Christianity and bring unforeseen consequences. Faustus is a scientist who rejects belief in heaven or hell and puts his faith in knowledge. A long line of great literary figures would follow him.

Chapter 8

The Devil's Last Stand

> *Better to reign in Hell than serve in Heaven.*
> —John Milton, *Paradise Lost*

In the Renaissance and the seventeenth century many intellectuals questioned the existence or at least the relevance of the devil. Yet one of the greatest intellectuals of that century not only believed firmly in the devil but wrote an epic poem about him, one which gave order to diverse traditions and which fixed the Western view of the devil. The Satan that people believe in is found not in the Bible but in *Paradise Lost*.

John Milton (1608–74) was born of a middle-class but comfortable London family. As a Puritan, he supported the parliamentary cause in the English civil war; after the restoration of the monarchy in 1660, the now blind Milton endured a brief arrest but then retired to private life. His parliamentary sympathies remained unchanged, but he moved away from strict Puritanism to a more personal view of Christianity. He wrote *Paradise Lost* in his retirement, finishing it in 1663 and publishing it in 1667. Like Dante, Milton wished to follow the ancient masters Homer and Vergil and write an epic poem on an epic topic. He chose the fall of humanity from its "godlike" status to the sinful condition into which all are born. The Puritans had a basically Augustinian/Calvinist outlook on sin, seeing it as the free choice of Adam and Eve, and they also accepted the doctrine of divine predestination, that God would save whom he chose to save. Milton recognized the difficulty of this doctrine, and in his epic poem he tried to write a theodicy, to "justify the ways of God to men" (PL i.26).

Pious people have always been disturbed at what they see as a pallid portrayal of God and a vigorous, even noble portrayal of Satan. Such concerns are misplaced. Milton really did not have much choice in his portrayal of God. Even though he was a Protestant, he could not accept the volatile, often unpredictable God of the Hebrew Scriptures. Centuries of theology had made this deity the perfect, unchangeable god of Greek thought. What can a poet do with a character who cannot change? God appears chiefly in book three where he explains to his son Messiah why he allows Satan to leave hell and to go to Eden to tempt Adam and Eve. The passage includes God's justification of his own role in humanity's fall. "Whose fault? / Whose but his own? Ingrate, he had of me / All he could have" (iii.96–8). God sounds a bit peevish and self-righteous, but Puritans would have found God's view to be sound. Yet that did not ease the poetic problem of an unchanging character, so Milton eased God into the background.

Theoretically, Satan should have been just as unchangeable as God since he was pure evil, but Milton lived after Christopher Marlowe. Satan realizes what he has done and what he has lost, and at times he regrets this as when he first sees the beauty of Eden and its inhabitants, a stark contrast to hell and its inhabitants. "Oh Hell! what do mine eyes with grief behold?" (iv.357). But, except for the occasional moment of regret, Satan is reliably evil, and the problem arises when Milton seems to give this evil being nobility. But the devil's nobility is misleading.

The poem opens when the evil angels have fallen from heaven and landed in a lake of flames. Satan immediately tries to raise their spirits with talk of revenge. His speech includes such lines as, "All is not lost— the unconquerable will" survives and "to be weak is miserable," and Milton credits him with "dauntless courage" (i.106, 157, 603). After Satan has assembled his followers, he explains his plan of getting revenge on God by destroying the deity's new little pets in the Garden of Eden. After passing through harrowing dangers, he flies through the darkness of chaos to reach earth. While at first glance such passages do make him appear noble, a second look shows the true situation. For all his courage, what Satan is really doing is destroying two completely innocent people who have done no harm to him. His noble speeches are pure bravado to mask what really happened, that he and his followers managed to get themselves expelled from heaven. This "nobility" fades as the tale progresses. Milton portrays Satan's becoming constantly more revolting and ignoble. Soon after his expulsion from heaven, he retains some of his angelic glory, but by the end of the story he will crawl like a serpent on the floor of hell. Milton used this to remind the reader that evil also looks initially attractive, but further acquaintance shows it for what it really is.

Few writers have ever portrayed the unreality of evil as well as Milton, and he dealt with it via characters who cannot face up to their real situations. Like the souls in Dante's *Inferno* who worry about their reputations back in Florence, Milton's characters lie to themselves and others about their situation. At the beginning of the tale, when Satan rouses up his followers, he uses some of the poem's most famous lines. "The mind is its own place, and in itself / Can make a Heaven of Hell, a Hell of Heaven" (i.254–5). The magnificent words provide a good insight into human nature because Satan is saying that he will somehow convince himself that he is not really in hell. He cannot acknowledge what he has done to himself. A few lines later Satan announces that it is "Better to reign in Hell than serve in Heaven" (i.263). Nobly said, but completely absurd. How can ruling ever compensate for an eternity of filth, misery, torture, and despair? Or is Satan one of those pathetic persons for whom being in charge is what counts, no matter what the misery for self and others?

Satan's followers, whom Milton named after the pagan gods mentioned in the Hebrew Bible, share his unreality. He assembles them and asks what they should do. One wants to battle God again in spite of knowing that they cannot win; another suggests that they wait in hope that God will change his mind, ignoring the obvious need for the demons first to repent for what they have done; a third suggests that if they accommodate themselves to hell, it might not seem so bad after a while. Satan's right-hand help, Beelzebub, dismisses these suggestions as "Hatching vain empires" (ii.378).

Even the physical setting helps to make Milton's point. Dante had put hell in the center of the earth, but, as Jeffrey Russell points out, Milton's hell "is nowhere. This is the beauty of Milton's conception. The place where Satan sets up his throne and with his fallen comrades seeks to raise a new empire is nowhere at all: a perfect metaphor for the absolute non-being of evil" (*Mephistopheles,* 109).

Satan's proposal, that he fly to earth and corrupt Adam and Eve, meets with demonic approval, and he sets off. Just as Milton had followed tradition in associating the demons with pagan gods mentioned in the Bible, so he follows it again by personifying evils. When Satan gets to the gates of hell, he meets Sin and Death. Sin is his daughter, born full-grown from his head when he first conceived rebellion against God, paralleling the birth of the Greek goddess Athena from the god Zeus. Athena was the virgin goddess, but Satan incestuously raped his daughter, and she gave birth to Death, a monster with an insatiable appetite. Death incestuously raped his mother and can scarcely refrain from devouring her. Although Satan first tells Sin "I know thee not, nor ever saw till now / Sight more detestable than him and thee," the paramount liar realizes that she has the key to the gates of hell and so he addresses them as "dear daughter" and "my fair son" (ii.817–8). Milton has here borrowed from Augustine, who said that the Holy Trinity of Father, Son, and Spirit co-inhere with one another in knowledge and love. Milton showed how upside down hell is with a loathsome trinity united by lust and double incest.

Satan convinces Sin and Death that they will have free reign in this new world God created if they will let him past the gates of hell, which they do. When he gets free of hell, he flies across the void where he meets the primeval forces of darkness, those mentioned in Genesis as having been banished by God's creation of light—Chaos, Night, and other spirits of the abyss. They, too, let him pass.

None of this escapes God's notice, and Milton next turned to heaven where God explains to his son Messiah why he allows Satan to tempt Adam and Eve. Messiah realizes that when the first humans sin, they cannot make it up to God and so he will have to suffer and die to atone for what they have done. The poem gives a good summation of traditional Augustinianism. "Man shall not quite be lost, but saved who will, / Yet not of will in him, but grace in me / Freely vouchsafed" (iii.173–5). Milton did, however, add to the tradition by answering a question which had been hanging fire since the third century: Why is God willing to save humans but not the demons?

> The first sort by their own suggestion fell,
> Self-tempted, self-depraved; Man falls, deceived
> By the other first: Man, therefore, shall find grace,
> The other none (iii.129–32).

Theologians had created a theodicy which argued that Adam and Eve sinned of their own free will and that the devil was not necessary for them to be tempted and fall. Milton does not deny that, but he puts some sense into the account. Maybe the first parents would have fallen even without the devil, but the devil did tempt them and that must mean something. What it meant for the poet was that, by spreading his evil to others, the devil forfeited any hope of salvation.

Satan arrives in Eden, and Milton brilliantly portrayed an unspoiled paradise and how it appeared to someone from hell.

> Beneath him with new wonder now he views,
> To all delight of human sense exposed,
> In a narrow room Nature's whole wealth, yea more
> A Heaven on Earth (iv.205–8).

Satan realizes what his evil deeds have cost him. Eden is an "eternal Spring" (iv.268), constantly coming to life, but it does him no good. Borrowing from Marlowe, Milton has Satan say, "Which way I fly is Hell; myself am Hell" (iv.75). He has lost heaven and cannot enjoy this heaven on earth.

In the midst of the garden he sees two creatures, "Godlike erect, with native honor clad / In naked majesty" (iv.289–90). Their nakedness indicates their unity with the natural world and the lack of shame before original sin. Satan realizes that he could love them, but his desire for revenge upon God soon wipes out any other thoughts.

Satan spies on Adam and Eve, until some good angels chase him away. One of the angels, Raphael, then warns Adam about Satan. The man, in turn, asks the angel about how Satan sinned. Raphael gives a long account of the evil angels' rebellion and expulsion from heaven. Next Adam asks about the creation of the world, and then he recounts to the angel his life in Eden before Eve and then their first meeting. The angel departs, but only after warning Adam again about Satan. The conversation says a few things about evil, such as Satan's ridiculous rationalizing to the fallen angels that, since they could not remember their own creation, maybe they were "self-begot, self-raised" (v.860) instead of having been made by God. Nonexisting creatures creating themselves! It says much for the unreality in hell that Satan's followers believed him.

Milton also used traditional themes, describing Satan as a giant (i.195–8) and placing his war-camp in the north of heaven (v.689), the common symbol for a region of cold and death. He added some Augustinian theology when Raphael tells Adam, "God made thee perfect, not immutable" (v.524).

The decisive ninth book starts with Satan's justification—to himself, naturally—of what he is doing. He blames God who is "Determined to advance into our room / A creature formed of earth" (ix.148–9). Since God acts unfairly by planning to put humans in the angels' place in heaven, Satan will right the situation by keeping them out. He takes over the body of a serpent and sets off in search of Adam and Eve. This all sounds like a well-planned attack, but irrationality underlies it. Satan thinks to himself, "Nor hope to be myself less miserable / By what I seek, but others to make such / As I, though thereby worse to me redound" (ix.126–8). Revenge has so overpowered Satan that he will go through with his plan, even though he will be more miserable himself.

Adam and Eve are discussing her wish to go off on her own in Eden, in spite of the angel's warning. Adam gives her a lesson on being a good wife: "for nothing lovelier can be found / In woman than to study household good" (ix.232–3), but Eve insists on going and the wearied husband gives in. It is heavy-handed patriarchal moralizing about the wife who does not know her place and the husband who is too weak to keep her in it. Unfortunately, Milton thinks this is not convincing enough, and when Satan spies Eve by herself, he rejoices. "Her husband, for I view far round, not nigh, / Whose higher intellectual more I shun" (ix.482–3). This explanation goes back to Augustine's view that the serpent attacked Eve because Adam was too intelligent to be fooled; the Anglo-Saxon poets had used it, too. But, in a moment of honesty, Milton contradicts this view. When the serpent meets the supposedly poor, foolish Eve, he does not dupe her immediately but instead must use carefully thought-out, elaborate arguments to win her over.

After Eve gets over her surprise at a talking serpent, she lets the serpent tell her how he gained the power of reason and speech by eating the fruit of a particular tree. He offers to show her the tree, so they both go to the Tree of the Knowledge of Good and Evil. She tells him she cannot eat from this tree, and then Satan tempts her in earnest. The serpent tells her that, thanks to this tree, he has a "life more perfect" than Fate decreed for him which he achieved "by venturing higher than my lot" (ix.689–90). He works the theme that Eve, as a woman, is subject to Adam and, as a human, is subject to God, and both try to keep her in her place. "Why, then, was this forbid? Why but to awe? / Why but to keep ye low and ignorant?" (ix.703–5).

Why does God need to keep them low and ignorant? To protect his own power. God lied to humans, telling them that he created them. Using the same argument he used with the evil angels, Satan says, "The Gods are first, and that advantage use / On our belief, that all from them proceeds" (ix.718–9). The irony is magnificent; the primeval liar accuses God of lying. But, Satan goes on, even if God is telling the truth about creating them, what is wrong with humans' tasting the fruit of this tree?

> Wherein lies
> The offence, that Man should thus attain to know?
> What can your knowledge hurt him, or this tree
> Impart against his will, if all be his? (ix.725–8).

Eve muses about what to do, and she does so as "the hour of noon drew on" (ix.739), the time of day when Jesus mounted the cross to redeem humanity from the sin Eve is about to commit. She concludes that eating the fruit did not hurt the serpent, but, more importantly, that God must be up to something to keep Adam and her from knowledge. "In plain, then, what forbids he but to know, / Forbids us good, forbids us to be wise? / Such prohibitions bind not" (ix.758–60). Eve eats the fruit, thus disobeying God's command but also breaking the bond between humanity and the natural world. "Earth felt the wound, and Nature from her seat, / Sighing through all her works, gave signs of woe / That all was lost" (ix.782–4). The serpent slinks away, leaving Eve to ponder what she has done. In the Hebrew Bible account, Adam takes the fruit immediately after Eve, and this emphasizes that both disobeyed God. The gap between her and his eating the fruit is microscopic. But Milton expanded this gap, realizing that no matter how small it was, there was a time when one of the first human parents had sinned and the other had not, one had lost immortality and one still had a chance to keep it. Milton used this moment to show the workings of evil.

Eve thinks she has become like God, whom she contemptuously refers to as "Our great Forbidder, safe with all his spies / About him" (ix.815–6). She wants to let Adam know about her change . . . but, maybe not.

> Shall I to him make known
> As yet my change, and give him to partake
> Full happiness with me, or rather not,
> But keep to the odds of knowledge in my power
> Without co-partner?

Why?

> so to add what wants
> In female sex, the more to draw his love,
> And render me more equal, and perhaps
> Superior—for inferior, who is free? (ix.817–25).

This is a difficult passage. On the one hand, Milton supported patriarchy, showing Eve's (and thus women's) desire for equality to be a consequence of original sin; her desire to be superior went against the patriarchal view of the natural order. On the other hand, he knew that most women and probably many socially and economically oppressed men would relate to her desire for equality. Furthermore, Milton here gave Eve one of the poem's truly immortal lines: "for inferior, who is free?" But the Puritan poet could venture just so far from his root values. Following the tradition that no human can do good from an evil base, Milton showed Eve's desires for equality degenerating immediately into something far inferior: jealousy.

> but what if God have seen,
> And death ensue? Then I shall be no more,
> And Adam, wedded to another Eve,
> Shall live with her enjoying, I extinct (ix.826–9).

Eve slides quickly down the slippery slope because she next lies to herself by saying that she will share her gift with him because of love, not jealousy. Like Satan, she needs to justify what she does. She meets Adam, who has brought her a bouquet of roses. She tells him what has happened, and he lets fall the roses which have quickly faded, the first death on earth. Adam pledges his fidelity to her ("How can I live without thee?"), although not without lamenting what she has lost. Adam also recognizes his own changed situation. He refers to Eden, the perfect garden, as "these wild woods forlorn" (ix.910). Unable to live without her, he eats the fruit, and again Nature experiences pain, symbolized by the first rain drops to fall on earth, the tears of the sky.

But Adam and Eve notice none of that; instead they notice one another's nakedness and "in lust they burn." After their lust has been satiated, the rush provided by evil promptly fades; they "Soon found their eyes how opened, and their minds / How darkened" (ix.1053–4). They experience another new feeling—guilt. Adam covers his genitalia, symbolically covering his guilt as well, but to no avail. "He covered, but his robe / Uncovered more" (ix.1058–9). Those seven words sum up what it took Augustine, Luther, Calvin, and others volumes to say.

Like Faustus, Adam turns for help to Nature, asking her to cover him up, but to no avail. Furious, he blames everything on Eve; we are back in Dante's hell where no one is personally guilty of anything and other people are always at fault. But she turns back upon him, pointing out that even if he had been with her, the same thing could have happened; it could even have happened to him! She asks Adam, "Was I to have never parted from thy side? / As good have grown there still, a lifeless rib" (ix.1153–4). But Adam does not want to hear reason, and this book ends with the two hurling recriminations at one another.

Milton believed in Satan, but even someone who does not can still appreciate the stunning portrayal of evil—the lie, the delusion, the self-justification, the resentment, the bitterness, and the sense of loss. Augustine and others had recognized the perennial weakness in the Eden story, the condemnation of the human race to death because two people ate a piece of fruit, and they had argued that the human race was naturally perfect so that even the most minor transgression had cosmic implications. Milton, on the other hand, justified the doctrine of original sin by showing what sin does to human nature, to our relationship with God, and to the world around us, but mostly what our evil does to us and those we care for.

The victorious Satan returns to hell, first passing through the gates where he meets Sin and Death. He brags of his triumph and tells Death that he will never be hungry again because he now has a world of humans to devour. In a vivid image, Death strikes the ground "with his mace petrific" and creates a bridge to earth. Milton describes the bridge with adjectives denoting size and strength—asphaltic, immense, prodigious, immovable—and then promptly contrasts these with soft words describing how simple the bridge is to use: "Smooth, easy, inoffensive, down to Hell" (x.305). Like Marlowe, he stresses the slippery slope. One evil act leads easily to another, a powerful theme then and now. In a modern drama set in the English Reformation, Robert Bolt's *A Man for All Seasons*, a royal official gets one of Thomas More's associates to betray him. The official assures the traitor that no matter how difficult betrayal was the first time, the more often he does it, the easier it will become. It does.

Milton's biblical sense of justice requires punishment for Satan and his followers, whom God turns into thirsty, hungry serpents. When the serpents slither over to a tree to snatch up fruit and assuage their appetites, they find they have been deceived and that the fruits are piles of ashes. With this irony, Milton has also completed the angels' fall from heaven. They are now no better than beasts, and the ashes symbolize their eternal death in hell. God shows the demons mercy, allowing them to assume their normal forms most of the time but still turning them into serpents once a year.

The poet's biblical sense of reconciliation finishes the tale. Adam and Eve accept their situation, and the angel Michael foretells the redemption of humanity by the history of God's people Israel and by the death of God's son Messiah. It even ends on a positive personal note for Adam and Eve who have become reconciled to one another. "They, hand in hand, with wandering steps and slow / Through Eden took their solitary way" (xii.648–9).

Not even an epic poem could stem the rising skepticism about the devil, but Milton did have considerable impact, giving the theology of the Genesis account a coherence and an immediacy it never had before. To repeat a line from the first paragraph of this chapter, the Satan that most people believe in is found not in the Bible but in *Paradise Lost*.

* * *

With the infallibility of hindsight, we can see that belief in Satan was declining in Milton's day, but many of his contemporaries would have thought just the reverse. In the sixteenth and seventeenth centuries, the devil launched his most vicious attack ever on the human race, and not with an army of demons but with an army of witches.

The European witchcraze of the sixteenth and seventeenth centuries and its North American offshoot in the Massachusetts Bay Colony have always fascinated people, not just because of the intrinsic interest of the topic but also because of our astonishment that rational, civilized societies could have legally executed more than 100,000 people in the belief that they were witches. At the time of the witchcraze, the West typically understood witches to be people, especially women, who consorted with evil spirits in order to achieve goals they could not otherwise achieve, such as wreaking vengeance upon a powerful person.

The association of women with witchcraft went back to the ancient world, for example, the witch of Endor consulted by the Israelite King Saul (1 Samuel 28). The Romans believed in the *strix,* a woman who could turn herself into a bird-like creature, fly about in the night, and suck people's blood. The ruling classes of patriarchal societies presumed that some women would resent their second-class status, but, lacking normal means of redress, they would turn to something both powerful and devious. Augustine thought they would use sexual lures, but others believed they would turn to witchcraft.

Traditionally there were both good and evil witches. Evil ones worked with the devil to harm people, while good ones offered charms and folk cures to help people, no small service in an era when most people never saw a physician. Evil witches were always in danger, but the thirteenth century turned the corner for good witches as well. Medieval Christian scholars had adopted Aristotle's scientific ideas about causality. He had no use for unseen forces which could manipulate objects or affect people at a distance. For him, causality involved some kind of physical contact or measurable process, and natural laws did not vary. But the Bible said that they could. Had not the Red Sea opened? The Medieval Christians accepted Aristotle's views about natural laws but also believed supernatural power could supersede natural laws. Supernatural power fell into two categories, divine and demonic.

The impact of this view cannot be overemphasized. For centuries most people, even scholars and church leaders, had accepted or at least tolerated the existence of good witchcraft, thinking it to be harmless, but now the theologians linked all witchcraft with the devil. The Aristotelian worldview put all witches in harm's way.

Simultaneously another ominous development threatened the witches. The High Middle Ages had witnessed the rise of heretical movements, and the orthodox response included accusing heretics of devious practices. In 1022 at the French town of Orléans the Medieval Christians first burned heretics. The charges against this group included nocturnal orgies over which the devil presided in the form of a black man and of magical transportation to the place of the orgy. There is no way to tell how much of this includes genuine practices of the heretics or just wild fantasies claimed by the interrogators, but for the first time heresy was linked with worshiping the devil and magical transportation, practices normally associated with evil witches.

As the heresies grew more widespread and threatening to Medieval society, the link between heresy and witchcraft grew, usually in the form of the heretics' being accused of witch-like practices. Around 1182, an English writer, Walter Map, wrote of heretics who worshiped the devil in the form of a huge black cat whose backside the heretics kissed—charges routinely made against witches during the witchcraze. Reflecting the prevailing anti-Semitism, Map called these meetings synagogues. Since the devil stood behind heretics, the Medieval inquisitors saw themselves in a battle against him, and the Inquisition now sought out Satan's other allies, the witches. This meant that accused witches could be interrogated under torture, a procedure that guaranteed a high percentage of confessions and convictions. The penalty for convicted witches was death by burning at the stake, a symbolic act of purification in a cleansing fire and an equally symbolic exit from this life for one who was headed to eternal flames, although sometimes the judge mitigated the penalty to long imprisonment.

Although the tools were in place for massive attacks on suspected witches, these did not occur much in the Late Middle Ages. Heresy continued to be the main problem, augmented by the divisions in the Church as well as by the threat of the Turks in Eastern Europe and the Mediterranean. When Renaissance humanism challenged scholasticism, many Italian intellectuals took an interest in the occult and dabbled in magic. Skeptics like Erasmus advocated moderation in dealing with supposed demonic activities.

But these new movements did not drive out the older views. While the humanists headed down new paths, two German Dominicans, Heinrich Institoris and Jakob Sprenger, published in 1486 the classic handbook for the detection and interrogation of witches, *Malleus Maleficarum* or "Hammer of Witches." (Significantly, the Latin form of the word "witches," *maleficarum*, ends in *arum*, the feminine plural, rather than *orum*, the masculine plural, which could also have signified both sexes.) The book did not produce anything really new, but it did organize and codify a mountain of material. *Malleus* went through many editions and was used by both Catholic and Protestant witch-hunters. Although the Protestants rejected much Roman Catholic teaching, their views about witches deviated little from those of their religious opponents.

The *Malleus Maleficarum* uses a lot of technical terminology and advocates legal procedures. It establishes the basics: "three things are necessary for the effecting of witchcraft: the devil, a witch, and the Divine permission." The authors carefully avoid making it look as if the forces of evil have free reign in the world; God permits evil beings to do what they do for purposes we do not understand. The authors discuss technical matters, such as whether a demon in form of a man (incubus) or a woman (succubus) can actually generate children (the answer was yes, but via a very complicated process). They also justify very severe punishments for witches, often by citing a variety of earlier authorities. The modern reader is also impressed by the ceaseless misogynism.

But for another three-quarters of a century, the witches generally avoided persecution, shielded partly by Renaissance skepticism but far more by the conflicts of the Reformation. If Catholics and Protestants wanted to see the devil's agents, they believed that they only had to look at one another.

The situation changed around 1560. The Reformation was forty years old. The main figures of the first generation, such as Martin Luther and King Henry VIII, had died. Europe was settling into the religious pattern which has generally persisted until today. The popes called an ecumenical council at Trent (1545–63) to reform Catholic life, while the Protestants, concerned by the continuing divisions in their ranks, turned to institutionalize their churches. Religious conflict did not cease, but leaders on both sides concentrated on strengthening the faith and morals of their own people. . Many of their efforts dealt with superstition or pagan survivals, but they also dealt with witchcraft, an old problem which now received dangerous new attention. The devil might be working openly with religious enemies, but he was also working in secret with witches.

To the zeal of the reformers can be added a constellation of other forces which became prominent from 1560 to 1700. The Catholic-Protestant polemic made the devil's presence prominent in almost everyone's mind. Few were surprised that his activity also extended to witchcraft. The European economy shifted and disrupted age-old patterns. Wealth and people migrated from the rural to urban areas and from inland agricultural regions to the seaports as sea-borne trade, especially with the Americas, grew in size and turned two seafaring nations, England and Spain, into international powers. The European exploratory voyages also changed people's views of their world; the Europeans played a lesser role in a wider world. And not just a wider world but a larger universe, thanks to astronomers like Copernicus, Kepler, and Galileo. This was an exciting but disturbing era, and people unsure of themselves might easily believe that the devil and his helpers stood behind some of the confusion.

Misogyny had been around for centuries, but now entered a new phase, largely because the fear of witch-conspiracy allowed the authorities to abuse women almost without restraint. During the craze there were approximately 10,000 trials and 100,000 executions; 80 percent of the victims were women. (These numbers include known, legal trials, and not lynchings.) All the police, prosecutors, torturers, and judges were men. Never before nor after was such a high percentage of prison inmates women. They had few rights. Jailers were free to abuse them, and torturers did their work with no restraint. If a woman died in custody or died under torture, she was thought lucky to have escaped the stake. The court was little better than the jail cell. Prosecutors could use "evidence" gained from torture and testimony given by anonymous witnesses. Charges were read in Latin to defendants who did not know the language and who had no legal counsel.

Accused men suffered as much as women from these procedures, but the system had a special treatment for women. They were believed to have intercourse with the devil, usually during some nocturnal orgy. The devil marked his mates but in a place not visible to anyone else. Since the devil's mark, as it was called, proved the defendant to be a witch, the prosecutors could arrange for the woman to be stripped and then searched, sometimes by women but usually by men, for the mark. Often the "devil's mark" turned out to be a scar of an unusual shape. Similar to this was the "witch's teat." Many people believed that a witch would keep a demon in the house, a "familiar" in the shape of a small animal like a dog or a cat. Since evil perverted what was good and since women were believed to be intended by nature to be mothers, the witch would, of course, pervert motherhood. She did this by nursing her familiar, not with her breasts but with a third appendage, the witch's teat, usually a skin growth of some kind.

The lack of restraint operated on the communal as well as the personal level. In Essex in England, 92 percent of the accused witches were women, and many of the accused men were somehow related to those women. In 1585 in southern Germany, so insanely savage were the inquisitors that by the time they had finished their work, two towns each had only one adult woman left. There was no restraint in the prosecution because there was no crime. The "crimes" existed not in reality but in the minds of the interrogators, which meant that the crimes could be whatever the interrogators wanted them to be. Surely witches practiced cannibalism, and torture elicited a confession to that. Since the witches personified the negative mother figure, they probably cannibalized their own children. Before they ate them, however, they put aside their baby fat in order to make a salve which could be rubbed on a broomstick so that they could fly on it. But many women gave their children to Satan rather than cannibalize them. Torture provided the evidence for all of these fantasies. Witches were literally guilty of anything.

Patterns emerged during the witch hunts. Although the accused included women of all ages and social status, a majority were over forty years old and came from the lower economic strata, poor but not indigent. Many were widows who had no husband and often no family to stand up for them, and frequently the charges against them included being querulous and outspoken. Since small towns experienced far more persecutions than large cities, it is likely that long-standing, familiar enmities stoked the accusations. For example, people knew and disliked a querulous old widow. When a prize mule suddenly died or when lightning struck one house but no others, the victims of these disasters wondered if she had cursed them. (Shakespeare, a contemporary of the witch-craze, included curses in many of his plays, and all the curses were effective.) A lonely woman with no financial resources made a helpless target; the accuser had no reason to fear retribution.

Social status also made a great difference. Poor people made easy targets, but when the accusations moved up the social scale, the situation changed. In 1682 Louis XIV put an end to witch-hunting in France only after his favorite mistress had been denounced as a witch. Governor William Phelps of the Massachusetts Bay Colony did not intervene in the Salem proceedings until his own wife was accused of witchcraft.

The persecution of witches also varied from country to country, but if it had national characteristics, it did not have religious ones. The worst persecutions occurred in the Catholic parts of Germany and in Calvinist Scotland. Italy persecuted less than most other countries; Spain prosecuted witches the least; Holland did not prosecute at all. Many of the prosecuting continental countries had strong monarchies and aristocracies, but England had a strong middle class. In general, local conditions seem to have been more important than national ones.

One note of sanity did appear in the midst of all this, the judicial appeals process. Local jurisdictions ordered most of the executions, and often the guilty party had no right of appeal. The German principality of Ellwangen executed four hundred people between 1611 and 1618, partly because the ruler allowed no appeal of the verdicts. In contrast, the Parlement de Paris exercised appellate jurisdiction for much of northern France, and it routinely reversed the judgments of the provincial courts. A full 36 percent of witchcraft appeals ended in the dismissal of charges. Other decisions were modified, and only 24 percent of the sentences received full confirmation. The well-trained Paris judiciary knew how valueless much of the evidence was. In late-seventeenth-century Scotland local courts had a 91 percent execution rate, but circuit courts, presided over by judges appointed by a central authority, had an execution rate of only 16 percent. In England, the circuit courts had a much lower conviction rate than was common in other countries. These justices did not act from a disbelief in witchcraft—otherwise they would have thrown out 100 percent of the cases—but because of a concern about an abusive legal process.

The witchcraze did not grow just because of fear. The authorities recognized its potential for social control, especially over women. In general, the aristocratic and wealthy classes had nothing to fear, but the peasant, the burgher, the farmer, and the housewife could never know who might be accused next. Women who were too outspoken found themselves liable to suspicion, and the accused witches' supposed sexual behavior played a great role in the trials.

No matter what theologians and philosophers and literary men thought, no matter what Catholics thought of Protestants and vice versa, no matter what Christians thought of Jews or Moslems or the inhabitants of the Americas, during the witchcraze evil wore the face of a woman.

The witchcraze seemed unstoppable, but several forces worked against it right from the beginning and others arose as time went on. On the personal level, every arrest created skeptics. It was one thing to believe that the nasty old woman down the street was a witch, but something else for people to believe that of their mothers, wives, grandmothers, aunts, sisters, or daughters. People could not safely express this skepticism publicly, but those who knew that a particular suspect simply could not be a witch inevitably came to question the whole process.

Economic and political factors played a role as well. Many princes and town counselors wanted to get rid of local witches, but they did not bargain on what could happen once the process started. The German city of Rottenburg started executing witches in 1578. By 1585, the Rottenburgers had executed forty-five witches, all women. The local magistrates called a halt to the trials because if they kept burning witches at that rate, there would be no women left in the town. (Unfortunately for the local women, five years later the Rottenburgers renewed the executions.) The deaths of many women not only caused loneliness for husbands and children, they also had grave consequences for the community. Women ran the houses while men worked in the fields and shops; a man without a wife would have trouble maintaining himself economically. Economic failure hurt not only individuals but also communities. More than one prince or town council called off or prevented a witch-hunt for fear of social or economic repercussions. Children suffered the most. Motherless children went hungry and neglected. As children of witches, they could rarely count on communal charity or even good will. No statistics survive as to how many perished. Older, more independent children, free of maternal guidance and restraint, got into trouble and often into crime. Daughters of witches had to watch their steps since they were often suspected of following in their mothers' footsteps.

Given the nature of the trials, witch-hunts invited false charges. How easy to ruin a business rival by accusing him—or, more likely, his wife—of being a witch. How easy to remove a rival in love the same way. Even if the accused avoided conviction, her reputation was often ruined as was that of her family. Many people suspected that some charges of witchcraft had baser reasons than protecting society from the devil.

Changes in the judicial system weakened the witchcraze. The differences between decisions of local and centralized courts did not go unnoticed nor did the differences in conviction rates in countries which used torture to find witches and those which did not. In the latter part of the seventeenth century, especially in France, central courts began to extend their power and procedures over regional and local courts, and the number of convictions dropped. As courts began to rely less and less on evidence obtained from torture, the number of convictions dropped even more. In fact, the witchcraze partly spurred on this judicial development.

Religious elements also entered in. Witches were in league with the devil, and the prevalence of witches magnified the devil's power. All of

Western Christendom seemed threatened by it. Inevitably some people began to wonder where God had gone. Had he simply turned the world over to the devil? Satan seemed to have broken all boundaries, and many religious people wondered if his power, manifested by the ubiquitous witches, had been overestimated and misunderstood.

Another religious element was a general cynicism with violence in religion, particularly after the Wars of Religion in France (1562–98), the Thirty Years War (1618–48) in Germany, and the English Civil War (1642–48). It was no coincidence that the religious wars petered out at the same time people were rethinking the witch trials.

Protestantism opposed Catholic institutionalism and emphasized the role of the individual in religious life, yet many important Catholic figures of the period, such as Ignatius Loyola (1491–1556), founder of the Jesuits, and Theresa of Avila (1515–82), a famous mystic, also emphasized individualized piety. To this religious individualism can be combined emerging capitalism, when talented, non-ennobled entrepreneurs such as the Italian Medici and German Fugger families built financial empires. Parliament and the middle class rose to power in England. People generally felt more and more able to free themselves from oppressive forces. The Medieval devil, the oppressive aristocrat par excellence, seemed increasingly out of place.

Perhaps most importantly, people's attitudes toward the natural world had changed enormously between 1560 and 1700. Copernicus and Kepler had provided the mathematical foundations for understanding the cosmos; Galileo had provided telescopic observations to support these theories; Newton had provided a new physics which not only complimented the Copernican cosmos but overthrew Aristotelian physics as well. The peasant farmer knew little of this, but educated, professional people came more and more to view the world scientifically, to explain the world by natural forces. They increasingly found it impossible to believe that by uttering spells someone could cause a hail storm or kill cattle.

The rise of science also affected religious understanding, especially since many great scientists, like Newton, were religious. Christians maintained the notion of God the creator and sustainer of the universe, and the scientists demonstrated just how complex that universe was. Many religious intellectuals followed natural theology, the attempt to understand God from the natural world. For these intellectuals, a supreme intelligence stood behind the incredibly intricate laws of nature, and these laws were more and more considered to be rational or scientific proofs of God's existence and providence. As these ideas caught on among the educated, it became increasingly difficult to believe in witches for religious as well as scientific reasons. How could a witch rub a salve made of baby fat on a broomstick and then violate the divinely established laws of nature?

It made more sense to disbelieve in witches than to believe they could subvert the harmony which God established in creation.

Although the occasional trial and the more frequent lynching still occurred after 1700, the witchcraze had essentially ended by then. Folk customs and practices, including "good" witchcraft, continued, but the authorities considered their practitioners harmless and their adherents superstitious, the attitude which prevails today. The general situation of women did not improve significantly; they continued to be second-class citizens in virtually every respect. Religious leaders supported this, continuing to see the man as the head of the household and to insist, as in the old marriage vow, that women obey their husbands. But Christian leaders stopped talking about the devil's gateway or identifying women as prime and easy targets for demonic temptation. No longer would evil be personified as woman.

Alongside the notion of the demonic woman, another traditional Western idea of evil lay in the wreckage of the witchcraze. Supposedly the witches had aligned themselves with the devil in the most powerful assault ever on Christendom, which had to struggle by desperate and severe means to defeat it. But now people realized that this frightful demonic assault had simply never occurred, and 100,000 direct victims, and no one knew how many indirect victims, had suffered or died for no reason. But if there were no witches, what about their erstwhile ally? If witches did not exist, did the devil?

Belief in Satan among the educated had been declining in the Late Middle Ages and the Renaissance. The Reformation and the witchcraze had propped it up again; educated people like monarchs and judges believed in the devil and witches strongly enough to commit people to the flames. But when such people stopped believing in witches, they largely stopped believing in the devil. There is no reason why someone cannot believe in the devil and yet not believe in witches, as many religious people do today, and in 1700, most people did believe in the devil. Among the politically and socially influential, however, such belief declined.

The rising disbelief in the devil probably had more than an intellectual base. Society persecuted the witches because they were servants and allies and even lovers of Satan. Yet if no one had believed in Satan, then no one would have believed in witches. Regardless of the intellectual arguments for and against Satan, it was an undisputed fact that belief in Satan lay behind the judicial murder of 100,000 people and the suffering of untold others. While the social consequences of an idea do not necessarily justify its intellectual rejection, they do give people pause.

If not with the devil, then where was evil to be found?

Chapter 9

Rationalizing Evil

> *There are those who think God could have done better.*
> —Leibniz, *Theodicy*

Well into the seventeenth century, most Westerners looked to the Bible, tradition, and reason as guides for knowledge. Reason usually played the role of explicator of the other two, especially the first. No one could really use reason completely on its own because Scripture came with divine inspiration, and human reason corrupted by original sin might err but the Bible could not. Science changed all of that because it dealt with matters on which the Bible and tradition had little to say. The condemnation of Galileo in 1633 was less a setback to science than a manifestation of how desperate his opponents had become. By the end of the seventeenth century virtually all major scientists had abandoned the Medieval world view in favor of the new one created by science. Many scientists, including Copernicus, Galileo, and Newton, were personally religious. Newton routinely investigated theological questions and wrote a commentary on the book of Revelation. But when they did their scientific work, scientists relied upon reason.

The rise of science completely changed how the West viewed the world. It taught people to consider problems first with reason and only later via authority or tradition. Its awesome impact had economic, social, and political consequences as well as religious ones because the use of reason cut across all boundaries. In France brilliant middle-class strivers like Voltaire and Rousseau had more influence than aristocrats with antique titles, while the sharp-minded entrepreneurs who created the Industrial Revolution in England made that country more powerful than any monarch could have dreamt. Inevitably reason, independent of revelation, also came to bear on the problem of evil.

The Briton Isaac Newton (1642–1727) made science triumphant because of the completeness of his system, both physical and mathematical. Since his day, scientists have challenged many of his conclusions, but in his day his impact was as great as Aristotle's had been in the twelfth and thirteenth centuries. All of a sudden, the world looked different, but it made more sense. His impact can best be gauged by a couplet written by an admirer, the British poet Alexander Pope: "Nature and Nature's laws lay hid in night: / God said, Let Newton be! and all was light." Except for his apocalyptic speculations, Newton did not write about evil, but philosophically he accepted the argument from design, that the universe could not have become an ordered whole without a creator. "This most beautiful system of the sun, planets, and comets could only proceed from the counsel and dominion of an intelligent and powerful Being," he once wrote. Occasionally he speculated that divine power lay behind some forces he could not explain, but he did not use the deity only to fill in the scientific blanks. He truly believed that only an intelligent creator could have produced a Newtonian cosmos. Significantly, he also believed the converse. If the cosmos needed God, the deity needed the cosmos: "and a god without dominion, providence, and final causes is nothing else but Fate and Nature." Both quotations come not from one of Newton's religious works but from the second edition (1713) of his scientific masterpiece, the *Principia Mathematica* (Book III) (quoted in *Newton's Philosophy of Nature*, ed. H. S. Thayer, 42, 44).

Such views made natural theology possible. The natural theologians did not abandon the Bible, but they acknowledged its deficiencies when it discussed the physical world, at least in comparison to the new scientific views. Newton himself recognized this. He accepted Moses' authorship of Genesis. He did not want to question the truth of the Bible, but he disagreed with the inspired author in several places. He concluded that Moses did indeed know the correct science, but he could not write about it because simple believers would reject his views. On the surface, this argument sounds specious, an unworthy attempt to save the authority of the Bible, but Newton has made a considerable advance here. He was wrong to believe that Moses knew the correct science, but he anticipated a fundamental principle of modern biblical study when he acknowledged that the scriptural writing style reflected the historical situation of the writer and audience. Even more importantly, he subjected the text of the Bible to the findings of modern science. He did not allow the literal interpretation of the Genesis creation account to take precedence over what science told him the world was like.

Later religious thinkers would recognize the latent threat in this approach, that they would have to constantly fine tune their interpretations to keep up with new scientific discoveries, but the natural theologians saw no difficulty. They recognized the inadequacies of the literal interpretation. Preferring scientific and rationalist approaches, they wanted to work without revealed religion whenever they could, to tone down the miraculous, and to outlaw the superstitious. They believed they could make religion rational, at least to the educated for whom that was necessary. (The natural theologians patronizingly assumed that the uneducated would continue to rely upon religious authority rather than upon reason.) The more one knew about the complexity of the cosmos, the more one had to recognize the hand of a creator behind it.

But if the cosmos reflected the creator, what role did evil play? It clearly did not reflect the creator, but it was as much a part of creation as the orderly revolution of planets and moons. Was evil the fly in the ointment?

No, said Gottfried Wilhelm, Baron von Leibniz (1646–1716), German aristocrat, diplomat, philosopher, scientist, and believing Protestant. For Leibniz, how God and evil could coexist became a major question because it challenged God's righteousness, so he wrote a book about the problem in 1710. Combining the Greek words for God, *theos,* and righteousness, *dike,* he created a neologism, *theodicy.*

Like Newton, Leibniz wished to preserve what he could of traditional Christianity. In his *Theodicy,* he quoted the Bible, made a brief reference to the devil and, like Newton, suggested that the Bible was written so that uneducated people could understand God's teaching. Leibniz defended the traditional Lutheran understanding of grace, free will, and predestination, although he investigated all of those concepts. He also demonstrated the openness that characterized natural theology. Leibniz cited and occasionally praised the Medieval scholastic theologians, long despised by Protestants for being both outdated and Roman Catholic. He also cited contemporary Catholic authors and acknowledged a personal acquaintance with some Jesuits, whom many Protestants demonized.

Leibniz started with a simple but fundamental premise: God exists and is a perfectly good being. Therefore, he always does what is best, including creating the world. In spite of evil, this world is the best one God could have created—the best of all possible worlds. This is a familiar phrase because the French writer Voltaire parodied it mercilessly in his book *Candide,* in which Dr. Pangloss (from the Greek *pan,* meaning "all," and *glossa,* meaning "tongue") fatuously writes off every disaster as unimportant because this is the best of all possible worlds and thus nothing really can go wrong. But parody is only parody, and Leibniz's theory deserves consideration on its own.

Yet even people who want to be open-minded recoil at that celebrated (infamous?) phrase. How can a world contaminated by so many evils be the best of all possible worlds? All humans have suffered from evil and can easily conceive of a better world than this one. Leibniz did not say that this is the best of all *conceivable* worlds, but rather the best of all *possible* ones. Like Newton, he saw God as a creator, and he saw in the complexity of the cosmos a proof of God's existence. But deity could not do anything he wanted. God has to follow his nature. He used this approach extensively to establish an explanation for evil.

God created the human race in his image and likeness, which means he gave humans intelligence and free will. God must respect his own handiwork. To make humans any less than what he did would be to demean his own creation. But since only the deity can be infallible, there is the chance that a fallible creature with intelligence and free will might choose something other than the good.

But could not God have created humans so that we would always freely choose not to sin? Theoretically yes, but factually no, because, if he could have, he would have. That he created us as we are was proof to Leibniz that God could not simultaneously respect his creation and produce beings who were incapable of sin. This is hardly a consoling argument. After all, what good is free will if we use it to sin our way into damnation? Would it not have been preferable for God to make us to be automatons or moral robots if that way we could avoid damnation? Again, the answer is theoretically yes but factually no, because automatons would not be in the divine image. God has to be God; he has to give us the free choice. Moral evil resulted from our free choice. As Leibniz observed, "To wish that God should not give free will to rational creatures is to wish that there be none of those creatures" (*Theodicy* 119.iv; 192).

Along with moral evil, Leibniz recognized metaphysical and natural evil. He interpreted metaphysical evil not in the usual spirit-over-matter form but rather as imperfectability of the cosmos. This imperfectability resulted from the cosmos' being a creation and thus incapable of the perfection of the deity. He considered metaphysical evil theoretically and actually unavoidable because he could not conceive of a perfect cosmos.

Natural evil represented a different sort of problem. People had traditionally pictured God as the lord of creation, but science had firmly placed him within the workings of the cosmos. So how could these smoothly functioning natural laws produce earthquakes, floods, and hurricanes, which harm so many people? Leibniz replied that God can only do what is best, and so if he permits a natural disaster to occur, this cannot mean that he is acting evilly toward us. Following Augustine, Leibniz believed that God could bring good out of evil, that every act was part of a divine plan. He matched this with the book of Job, arguing that we simply cannot understand why God does what he does. If humans could see the whole—which we cannot—we would understand the role which natural disasters play in the universe, "the general plan of the universe, chosen by God for superior reasons," that is, reasons superior to our understanding (*Theodicy* 105; 180). Leibniz sadly recognized that the average person "feels an inclination to believe that what is the best in the whole is also the best possible in each part" (*Theodicy* 212; 260).

Leibniz realized how hard his teaching sounded. He acknowledged that there were those who thought that God could have done better, but he insisted that just because humans can conceive of a better world, that does not mean God has to create it. Why not? One answer centers on limited human knowledge: How do we know what we conceive of is indeed a better world? Many myths and folktales deal with people like Midas of the golden touch, who regretted that his wish was fulfilled. A second, more Leibnizian answer, centers on the nature of God. Flood victims may conceive a world without floods which seems to be a better place, but, if they can, so can God. If he chose not to create such a world, then he must have had a reason, one which the flood victims cannot comprehend. God always does the good, so if he created this world, he knew that it was the best possible one, if not the best conceivable one. This world contained evil but no more than was consistent with its being the best of all possible ones.

But if this world is the best possible one, why, critics asked, has God "interfered" in its operations with miracles? Leibniz replied that when God envisioned the creation of the cosmos, he included miracles among the infinite possibilities which could occur in that world. Miracles do not interfere with the order of creation because that order existed first in the divine mind, which allowed for miracles.

For the first time since Augustine someone had produced a theory of evil which related to the understanding of the cosmos as a whole. The belief in the best of all possible worlds earned for this theory the name "optimism," an appropriate name since Leibniz insisted that God's justice does indeed prevail. The theory was easy to mock (as *Candide* did) or to cheapen (by allowing theists to retreat behind "it's God's will" whenever evil occurred), and its completeness did not guarantee its correctness. But Leibniz had updated the theist approach to evil to meet the needs of the new world created by science and reason. The questions he raised persist—for theists, at least—into the modern world. After all, if one believes in a good God who acts in this world, does he not always act for the best?

One of optimism's most fervent supporters was the British poet Alexander Pope (1688–1744), who presented his views most clearly in the philosophic poem "An Essay on Man," written in 1733–34. Whereas Leibniz had derived his views of evil from the nature of God, Pope started with cosmology of his hero Newton. The complex universe created by God and described by the great scientist could only be good. "Whatever is, is right" he wrote in the "Essay" (i.294). He envisioned a universe filled with beings, all occupying their appointed places, a "Vast chain of being!" (i.237), "A mighty maze! but not without a plan" (i.6). As God's work, this is the best of all possible worlds: "Of systems possible, if 'tis confessed / That wisdom infinite must form the best" (i.43–4). And it functions well: "The general order, since the whole began, / Is kept by Nature, and is kept by man" (i.171–2).

Humans, in their pride, resent their place in the cosmos. Like their first parents, they want more, but they do not understand the divine plan. They consider themselves the wonders of creation, yet they paradoxically know they are fallible—they sin, become ill, and die. They see only themselves and believe they deserve better. Wrong, said Pope.

> Presumptuous man! the reason wouldst thou find
> Why formed so weak, so little and so blind?
> First, if thou canst, the hard reason guess,
> Why formed no weaker, blinder, and no less (i.35–8).

Pope is right on target: humans wonder why they are not better, but in their limited view they do not wonder why they are not worse.

But is it not intrinsically good to strive for more? No, said Pope, because that would mean that God had failed us. "Then say not man's imperfect, Heaven in fault; / Say rather, man's as perfect as he ought." "The bliss of man (could pride that blessing find) / Is not to think or act beyond mankind." Besides, if we assert our right to push higher, we will upset the balance of nature and could pay a price ourselves, something which we in our pride do not realize. "On superior powers / Were we to press, inferior might on ours." The consequences? "In the full creation leave a void, / Where, one step broken, the great scale's destroyed" (i.69–70, 189, 241–4). In *Paradise Lost,* Adam and Eve did not care about the effect of their sin on the natural world, but people living in an age of science had to consider it.

Then why, in this so well-ordered world, does evil exist? Since Pope had put his emphasis on the Newtonian harmony of the physical world, he did not deal with moral evil but instead with natural evil.

> But errs not Nature from this gracious end,
> From burning suns when livid deaths descend,
> When earthquakes swallow, or when tempests sweep
> Towns to one grave, whole nations to the deep?
> "No" ('tis replied) "the first Almighty Cause
> Acts not by partial, but by general laws" (i.141–6).

Pope did not deny the reality of evil but insisted that it has a place in the divine scheme and that God can somehow bring goodness out of it. He reached through Leibniz and Augustine back to Job. We cannot always understand what God is doing, but we must trust that God is doing what is good for the creation as a whole, no matter how much individuals may suffer:

> All Nature is but art, unknown to thee;
> All chance, direction, which thou canst not see;
> All discord, harmony not understood;
> All partial evil, universal good (i.289–92).

Optimism deserved its name.

Newton, Leibniz, and Pope were not alone in trying to relate evil to the new world created by science and reason. The French philosopher René Descartes (1596–1650) had explained evil by the imperfectability of the cosmos because God could not create something as perfect as himself. The British theologian William King (1650–1729) tried to explain evil rationally, while the French Protestant Pierre Bayle (1647–1706) took a skeptical approach to revealed religion. The tendency was unmistakable. Adherents of natural theology avoided the supernatural wherever possible. They definitely felt uncomfortable using the devil to explain evil; those who kept him did so because of his presence in the Bible. Yet as more and more intellectuals preferred the supposed clarity of science and reason to the supposed obscurity of the Bible, the devil was doomed, and, if that trend persisted, the Bible would not be far behind him. The Bible's moral principles kept their hold on people, but for Western intellectuals biblical teachings now had to pass muster with reason. Since so much of the Bible presumed a now-outdated world view, its teachings seemed less and less relevant and more and more necessary of explanation. Most problematic was the intervention of God in human affairs, particularly miracles. The smoothly-flowing Newtonian cosmos did not need such intervention or at least not nearly on the scale presented by the Bible. But while natural theology, or natural religion as it was often called, had difficulty with the Bible, a second intellectual movement, deism, simply abandoned it.

Deists believed in a deity who had created the world but who then withdrew and now had little to do with it. They differed from natural theologians who saw the Newtonian cosmos as a proof of God's existence, who acknowledged but wanted to limit divine intervention in human affairs, and who hoped to reconcile the Bible to the new scientific views. The deists, by contrast, gave no authority to supernatural revelation, considered dogma to be obfuscation, and said that prayer or any other attempt to contact the deity was fruitless. While the natural theologians could explain the existence of evil as part of a divine plan, the deists did not feel comfortable with a divine plan since they could not accept its ultimate biblical base. The Irishman John Toland (1670–1722) was an early deist; his book *Christianity Not Mysterious* (1696) claimed that Christianity was a perfectly logical religion and its mysterious elements resulted from the influence of paganism and "priestcraft." He accepted no communication with the supernatural, including divine revelation. Another deist, the Englishman Matthew Tindal (1655–1733), believed that the religion of nature was all anyone needed since it was available to all, perfect and unchangeable. The best Scripture could do was to reinforce this teaching.

The deists found less and less to learn from the Bible, which soon became a pale source of ethical teaching, provided, of course, it met the ethical standards of the deists. The most prominent American deist, Thomas Jefferson (1743–1826), went through the Gospels, chose the passages he considered most reasonable, and then created a personal gospel which he called "The Philosophy of Jesus" (1804); he later went over the material again and produced "The Life and Morals of Jesus" (1819). The Bible could not indefinitely sustain such patronizing and still retain any of its authority.

Deists could accept the "doctrine" of creation only because they considered it rational, but they rejected a deity who was active in the world. Instead they favored the image of the divine clockmaker: God created the world, which now runs on its own, but on very rare occasions he has to step in to keep it working properly. As time went on, the deists found that they not only needed the biblical creator less and less, but also they needed the god of natural theology less and less. If God were God, why does he need to intervene at all in creation, once it is up and running? The later deists had trouble finding something for the divine clockmaker to do. The shallowness of this approach to God provoked pungent criticisms. Biblical theists asked, who cares about a deity who has nothing to do with world? Picture Moses standing on the shore of the Red Sea, waiting for a deist god! A sharper criticism came from the secularist French intellectual Denis Diderot (1713–84), who snidely observed that a deist was someone who had not lived long enough to become an atheist.

Traditional religious thinkers did not mount an effective resistance to what the natural theologians, optimists, and deists were doing. But they did not have to. Intellectuals skeptical of religion, both revealed and natural, went to the attack. For the rest of this chapter, we will see how they attacked deism, natural theology, and optimism; in the next chapter, we will see how they treated revealed religion.

François Marie Arouet (1694–1778) wrote under the name Voltaire. A well-educated commoner, he fought a lifelong battle for freedom and against injustice. He personified the French and European Enlightenment, the intellectual movement which claimed to abolish superstition and harmful, unquestioned traditions, and to replace them with the clarity of reason. In France, the Enlightenment intellectuals called themselves *les philosophes*, literally, "the philosophers," but they did not consider themselves philosophers in the formal sense. The term rather referred to their love of wisdom and the works of the intellect. They believed the enemy of reason was organized religion, and they feared that optimism, technically a philosophy, gave it aid and comfort.

In spite of a Jesuit education, Voltaire loathed organized religion because he found it irrational and believed it fostered superstition on the people to keep them under control of both Church and state. He feared that religious authorities who could make people believe absurdities had the power to get people to commit atrocities. Anticipating Marx, he considered religion the opiate of the people. Voltaire rejected optimism as a support for Christianity because optimism could be used to justify any evil, human or natural, and this attitude of it's-all-part-of-God's-plan would rob people of a just indignation at their oppression and suffering. Yet it was not human evil but a natural one which engendered his most scathing attack on optimism.

On November 1, 1755, a tremendous earthquake shook the Portuguese city of Lisbon, and between thirty and forty thousand people lost their lives. A believer in God, Voltaire reacted against the facile, optimist explanations for the earthquake, and so he wrote a poem about it: "The Lisbon Earthquake," subtitled "An Inquiry into the Maxim 'Whatever Is, Is Right.'" In spite of disclaimers about his professed admiration for Alexander Pope, Voltaire attacked the now deceased poet and herald of optimism. He concentrated on the theme of individual suffering's relation to the overall good. He recognized that much theorizing about this theme was of the armchair variety and did not affect the theorist, so, instead of framing individual suffering against a philosophical backdrop, he personalized it. He invited the optimists to come to Lisbon and see

> Women and children heaped up mountain high,
> Limbs crushed which under ponderous marble lie;
> Wretches unnumbered in the pangs of death,
> Who mangled, torn, and panting for their breath,
> Buried beneath their sinking roofs expire,
> And end their wretched days in torments dire (*Portable Voltaire*, 560).

But this suffering somehow fits into the theme of universal good, does it not? Voltaire contemptuously pointed out how such a theory portrays God: "Say, will you then eternal laws maintain, / Which God to cruelties like this maintain?" Could the optimists not realize what they were saying about God? Yet their theory left no choice: as Voltaire correctly pointed out, optimism forced God to be responsible for such a cruel act in order to maintain "eternal laws."

Voltaire stayed with the particulars. Why did Lisbon suffer? Was it any worse than London or Paris? And he focused on the quantitative element: Why so much suffering? And what do the optimists say to people who cry out to God for help?

> . . . mortals cry
> "Heav'n, on our sufferings cast a pitying eye."
> All's right, you answer, the eternal cause
> Rules not by partial, but by general laws (ibid., 561).

Pope had written that humans are dissatisfied with their condition because their pride makes them want more. He had dealt with the question intellectually, showing how all beings fit into their place in the vast chain of being. However, Voltaire dealt not with people who through pride theorized and wished for a better world but rather with people who were actually suffering now. "When man groans under such a load of woe, / He is not proud, he only feels the blow." If optimism is correct, then why does it say nothing to those who suffer? When armchair philosophers say, "general good from partial ills must flow," they do not realize, "No comfort could such shocking words impart, / But deeper wound the sad, afflicted heart." Isn't it bad enough that these people are suffering so much? Is it really necessary to tell them that the deity whom they are beseeching for help actually caused this disaster as part of his overall divine plan?

Voltaire went on to discuss the extent of human suffering, and he railed against a theology which "enchained" God by forcing him to follow such precepts. If God is good, "God should His will to human kind explain. / He alone can illume the human soul, / Instruct the wise man, and the weak console."

The voice sounds familiar. Voltaire spoke with the modern voice, with an impatience for the kind of theorizing which ignores reality, with a concern for the individual, and with a theist's indignation with a belief system which justifies suffering to the point of claiming not only that the God allows it but even wills it. He returned to the theme in *Candide*, including having the characters go to Lisbon during the earthquake, but the satiric novella never surpassed the passion of this poem.

Voltaire criticized well, but what did he offer in return? He did not create a theodicy to replace the one he attacked so effectively; he simply did not have an answer to the problem of evil. A deist and a dedicated Newtonian who placed much faith in science, this *philosophe* did not create a philosophy to replace that of Leibniz. Yet almost single-handedly he struck optimism with a fatal wound. After him, many people continued to try to reconcile God's universal will for the good with cases of individual suffering, but they did so under constraint. They recognized the difficulty of the problem and, in spite of Leibniz' insistence on a rational approach to the problem, they avoided any talk about "the best of all possible worlds" which had been reduced to a joke in *Candide*.

But theists of all varieties worried less about Voltaire than about another Enlightenment figure who denied God any place in serious intellectual life.

David Hume (1711–76) came from a Calvinist, well-to-do Scottish family. He acquired an early distaste for Christianity, which he considered irrational, and he tried to construct a theory of knowledge which would have no dependence upon divine revelation and which would use only proven knowledge. Hume was seventeen years younger than Voltaire (who actually outlived him by two years), and he represented the next generation of Enlightenment thinkers. Hume favored empiricism, the theory that all knowledge comes to us from our senses or by devices which extend the power of those senses, such as a microscope. People can theorize on the basis of empirical evidence, but empiricists deny innate knowledge or knowledge of general truths arrived at solely by reason. This put Hume at odds with Leibniz who started with the idea of God and reasoned his way to his theodicy. Empiricism also put Hume at odds with Christians, deists, and natural theologians, especially on the question of evil.

Like Voltaire, Hume believed that organized religion led people astray. He primarily opposed Christianity, which he considered superstitious, but he also considered Judaism narrow and Islam intolerant. Having grown up in a conservative Protestant environment, Hume knew about biblical miracles, and he believed that if he could destroy the rational foundation for miracles, he could destroy the biblical religions' claims to authenticity. Deists applauded his first steps.

Since he accepted only empirical evidence, Hume had little difficulty in dismissing miracles. By definition, miracles transcended the laws of nature. Leibniz may have fitted them into his system, but Hume points out that they cannot be verified scientifically. Belief in miracles relied upon the testimony of others, which is inherently suspect. He pointedly asked if any intelligent person would believe that Queen Elizabeth had risen from the dead, no matter how many people insisted they had seen her. He did not have any explanation for why people claimed to have seen miracles; he simply dismissed the notion of miracles for lack of scientific evidence. Many people did not need scientific proof for miracles but rather accepted them as a matter of faith. But that, too, Hume found irrational. In a brilliantly ironic passage he wrote, "And whoever is moved by faith to assent to [a miracle], is conscious of a continued miracle in his own person, which subverts all the principles of his understanding, and gives him a determination to believe what is most contrary to custom and experience" (*An Enquiry Concerning Human Understanding,* 10).

Deists and natural theologians no doubt chuckled at this rout of the simple believers, but their time had also come.

In *Dialogues Concerning Natural Religion* (published posthumously in 1779), Hume focused on a theism based upon the complex and intricate workings of the cosmos, clearly the product of a divine intellect for the deists and natural theologians. But, he asked, how valid is it to make a conclusion about the existence of a supernatural being when all we have is natural evidence? And what role does evil play?

In his discussion of evil in chapters 10 and 11 of *Dialogues,* Hume concentrated on methodology. For him, the only knowledge we have comes from empirical observations. We deduce that God exists from the creation which we observe. And that is precisely the problem: What do we observe? "Labor and poverty, so abhorred by everyone, are the certain lot of the greater number; and those few privileged persons who enjoy ease and opulence never reach contentment or true felicity. . . . Why have all men . . . in all ages complained incessantly about the miseries of life?" If God exists, these miseries must be explained in reference to him. "Is he willing to prevent evil, but not able? then he is impotent. Is he able, but not willing? then he is malevolent. Is he both able and willing? whence then is evil?" (*Dialogues* 10). Hume succinctly stated the fundamental problem which evil presents to all theists.

What of the traditional argument, that we do not understand how God acts? Hume responded, if "our common measures of truth and falsehood are not applicable" in this discussion, then we do not know what we are talking about. How can we speak intelligently about something which we admit we cannot understand? Hume acknowledged that suffering might be compatible with a benevolent deity, but first the existence of that deity has to be established, and innocent suffering works against that.

Natural theologians and deists wanted to go from the existence of a harmonious cosmos to the existence of God, but Hume insisted that empirical evidence shows a world which includes evil as well as good. This clearly points to an imperfect universe. Here is the crux of the matter: since we all can empirically observe an imperfect, evil-infested universe, how can we use that to prove the existence of a perfect and good God? People can *believe* in a good deity if they wish, but they cannot *prove* such a deity exists. "There is no view of human life or of the condition of mankind from which, without the greatest violence, we can infer the moral attributes or learn that infinite benevolence, conjoined with infinite power and infinite wisdom, which we must discover by the eyes of faith alone" (*Dialogues* 10).

Hume went on to argue that because people believe beforehand that God exists, they can find him in the universe. He asked:

> But supposing . . . that this creature [a being unacquainted with our universe] is not antecedently convinced of a supreme intelligence, benevolent, and powerful, but is left to gather such a belief from the appearance of things—this entirely alters the case, nor will he ever find any reason for such a conclusion (*Dialogues* 11).

He next went after the classic deist contention, that God respects his creation and intervenes only to keep it running well. He should have intervened more frequently, Hume taunted the deists: "One wave, a little higher than the rest, by burying Caesar and his fortune in the bottom of the ocean, might have restored liberty to a considerable part of mankind." For that matter, the divine clockmaker did not do such a good job in the first place; we can observe

> the inaccurate workmanship of all the springs and principles of the great machine of nature. . . . One would imagine that this grand production had not received the last hand of the maker—so little finished is every part, and so coarse are the strokes with which it is executed (*Dialogues* 11).

He finished by returning to the central point, methodology. The only knowledge we have in any discussion, the only proof we can offer in any discussion, must come from empirically observable phenomena. We can see an imperfect world; we can see a world wracked by evil and suffering; we can see no other world. From such evidence, how can we infer the existence of a good God? We cannot.

The *Dialogues* fell like a bombshell upon the natural theologians and deists. Deism floundered and never recovered; natural theology did not disappear but it declined precipitously. Hume had hit his opponents where it hurt. They wanted to use science to prove God existed; thanks to Hume, this tool had been turned against them.

The greatest continental philosopher of the age, Immanuel Kant (1724–1804), worked to save knowledge from Humean skepticism, but he, too, argued against any theodicy based on reason alone in a brief work appropriately titled "On the Miscarriage of All Philosophical Trials in Theodicy." He claimed that one could accept theodicy only by understanding the mind of what he called "the world-author" and grasping how that being works in the sensible world. Since no human being can do that, no one can create a philosophical theodicy.

The eighteenth century proved that Western intellectuals could no longer be satisfied with traditional religious teaching about evil. Natural theologians tried to maintain the traditional teaching but to rationalize it as much as possible. Deists went a step further, reducing the deity's participation in a harmonious cosmos. Voltaire attacked the optimism of the natural theologians, while Hume destroyed the notion of a harmonious cosmos and thus of the rationalized God who stood behind it. Yet most Westerners accepted the authority of the Bible, stood by traditional teachings, and remained untouched by much of this speculation. But in much of the West, *les philosophes* also strove to destroy not only natural religion but also traditional Christianity.

Chapter 10

The Attack on Christianity

The triumph of barbarism and religion.
—Edward Gibbon, *The Decline and Fall of the Roman Empire*

Hume once patronizingly observed that outside the boundaries of his enlightened friends and colleagues lay a vast region afflicted with "stupidity, Christianity, and ignorance." Hume's disgust with Christianity did not lead to social action by him, but French intellectuals, the *philosophes,* routinely attacked the Catholic Church as an enemy of learning and of the people. Contrary to these polemics, not all French ecclesiastics were power-hungry aristocratic bishops; many sincere priests worked to eliminate superstition and especially social abuses. But the *philosophes* overlooked the particulars to attack the institution, which they did with relish and with talent. More than one Catholic ecclesiastic lamented that all the literary skill lay with the Church's opponents.

The *philosophes* charged that the Church gained and maintained power by frightening the people with tales of demons and hellfire and by seducing them with promises of miracles and salvation. The *philosophes* created one of the great intellectual achievements of the eighteenth century, the *Encyclopedia* (1751–76), a collection of books which made available to educated people all the newest advances, especially in science and geography, and which offered superb illustrations to make the books more attractive. With the enormous popular support the *Encyclopedia* gained, the *philosophes* could vent their views on religion and still escape censorship.

Paul-Henri Thiry, Baron d'Holbach (1723–89), a militant atheist, wrote the encyclopedia entry on "Priests." Supposedly discussing ancient pagan priests, he caricatured the priests of his day:

It is sweet to domineer over one's fellow men. The priests knew how to make profitable the high opinion which they cultivated in the minds of their fellow countrymen. They claimed that the gods appeared to them; they announced their decrees; . . . they determined what pleased or displeased the divinity; . . . they made [people] tremble for fear of the punishments with which the angry gods menaced rash people. . . . They introduced ceremonies, initiations, and mysteries . . . so favorable to the empire of fanaticism. . . . People submitted to a multitude of frivolous and revolting practices that were, however, useful to the priests, and the most absurd of superstitions finally extended and consolidated their power. . . . To resist [the priests] was a revolt against heaven; to touch their rights was a sacrilege; to want to limit their power was to sap the foundations of religion (*The Encyclopedia,* trans. S. J. Gendizer, 200–1).

Since d'Holbach was discussing pagan priests, what could the censor say?

But for the *philosophes*, religion not only oppressed the people, it also stifled intellectual life. Denis Diderot, the atheist editor of the *Encyclopedia,* believed that philosophy, that is, secular learning, could advance only if religion retreated. He intended the *Encyclopedia* to be a triumph of scientific, secular, free inquiry, an instrument which would force educated people to realize how much progress can be made without or in spite of the Church. Diderot had plenty of support. Voltaire did not worry about belief in a deity because belief was superfluous. Natural theology relied only upon knowledge gained from the scientific observance of nature, knowledge available to all and not the province of the priests. His real concern was the power of organized religion. Voltaire correctly insisted that intellectually progressive societies always acknowledge freedom of religion as a basic human right.

Hume also weakened Christianity by his incessant attacks upon it. He claimed that, for all its silliness of lascivious gods and vindictive goddesses, polytheism allowed for diversity of views and thus for tolerance, whereas Christianity, insisting that there is only one deity, paved the way for intolerance. That is hardly an irresistible conclusion, but many Enlightenment intellectuals supported it.

The English historian Edward Gibbon (1737–94) furthered this trend with his multi-volume *Decline and Fall of the Roman Empire* (1776–88). Church historians had often included the pious and miraculous in their narratives, but Gibbon treated Christianity as just one more force, albeit a decisive one, in Rome's decline and fall. In superb prose, he accused the Christians of weakening Roman virility, of introducing intolerance into society, and of discarding all the classical values which had made Rome great. He questioned Christian virtues, such as asceticism, and portrayed its practitioners, the monks, as fanatics. Traditional Christian heroes, such as the great theologians of antiquity, appear in his history as mindless fools, debating minor and irrelevant points of doctrine, which they then imposed on a superstitious populace. Gibbon did not blame Christianity alone for Rome's fall; the empire's vast size, inefficient government, ambitious usurpers all aided the Christians in weakening Rome and making it a prey for the northern barbarians. But Gibbon gave his true view in a famous summary; the fall of Rome was "the triumph of barbarism and religion" (*Decline and Fall,* ch. 71). In an era which worshiped classical antiquity, this was a serious charge, and Gibbon knew it, but he was the authority on Rome, and no traditionally-minded Christian historian could refute him.

Attacks made on Christianity by such great intellectuals impacted the Western understanding of evil. Since its origins, Christianity had presented itself as the bulwark against evil. The Christians understood their faith to be the only antidote to the consequences of original sin and to the machinations of the evil one. Enlightenment intellectuals had no use for the latter, dismissing the devil as a fable foisted upon ignorant people so that Church officials could control them. They routinely discussed evil with simply no reference to the devil. But original sin was another matter.

The traditional, Augustinian approach to original sin is doctrine repugnant even to many Christians. It teaches that humans are born sinful, so sinful that they deserve to be damned to hell for eternity, even though they have personally committed no sin. Even the method of salvation, freely given divine grace, is repugnant to many Christians because humans do not do anything to deserve that either; God just chooses to give or not give it to them and thus either to save or damn them. This human helplessness is linked to yet one more repugnant doctrine, predestination, which teaches that God planned this horrible scenario before the world came into being, a scenario which portrays God as a capricious tyrant. Why did Christians not disown such a teaching? The *philosophes* had two answers: ignorance and power. Most Christians blindly accepted a doctrine which demeaned them. Since the Church controlled the means of salvation, the doctrine of original sin gave the Church great power, a power Voltaire tried to weaken by ridiculing baptism, the sin's antidote: "What a strange idea, that a pot of water should wash away all crimes" (*Philosophical Dictionary* i.110).

It was in the interests of the *philosophes* to overstate the case and cast Christianity in the worst possible light. In fact, the doctrine of original sin involved more than just ignorance and power. As the book of Job proved, explaining the coexistence of God and evil is a formidable task. Augustine had labored lifelong on the question of evil, and original sin was the only coherent explanation he could find, one which both explained evil and protected God's goodness and which did so while maintaining fidelity to the Bible. The Christian thinkers who followed his lead found themselves in the same bind, unable to find an alternative but conscious of the difficulties of the traditional approach.

Yet original sin commanded more than just theological assent. It was central to the practices of most churches. Freely-given divine grace which saved humans from the effects of original sin formed the basis of most Protestant theology. The Catholic Church had established, both theologically and pastorally, its sacramental system to provide grace to its members, thus offsetting some of the worst of Augustine's theories. That some unworthy ecclesiastics used original sin to advance their own power is unquestionable, but most Christians simply could not conceive of a Church without that doctrine.

The Enlightenment *philosophes* approached original sin like the Gordian Knot. They did not try to unravel; they simply cut through it. They pointed out that their idolized Greeks and Romans knew no such teaching but simply treated human nature on its own. The villainous Christians had introduced this pernicious doctrine and then burdened it with superstition.

The *philosophes* claimed to liberate the people by denying the existence of original sin and proclaiming the goodness of human nature. The European discovery of the Americas and the Pacific islands seemed to support the *philosophes* because the Europeans came in contact with numerous peoples untouched by Western values and who, on the surface at least, appeared happier and more noble than the Europeans and who had no knowledge of original sin or any belief that humans are intrinsically evil. The intellectuals quickly rushed to take advantage of this new "evidence." The British poet John Dryden (1631–1700) coined the phrase "the noble savage" who was "as free as nature first made man," an implied criticism of the doctrine of original sin which taught that all humans are descended from the first parents and therefore carry the guilt of Eden.

In 1772 Denis Diderot wrote a scathing attack on Western society and Christianity via a story in which a native elder gives a speech as French explorers depart from Tahiti. The Tahitian contrasts how honorably he has treated the Europeans and how dishonorably they have treated the Tahitians and even one another. The French have no values, not even their chaplain who abused native women. The Christians' very presence corrupts Tahiti. "You had hardly come among our people than they became thieves. You had scarcely landed on our soil, than it reeked with blood." The French should recognize that they and the Tahitians are "both children of nature." In contrast to the visitors, the Tahitians "respected our likeness in you. Leave us to our ways; they are wiser and more honest than yours. We do not want to barter what you call our ignorance for your useless civilization" (*Supplement to the Voyage of Bougainville,* in *The Portable Enlightenment Reader,* 641). Untainted by belief in original sin, by Christianity, and by the European civilization which Christianity had corrupted, the Tahitians lived a natural and, therefore, a free life. Diderot himself had never been to Tahiti, but his imaginary native elder met his propaganda needs.

Powerful as Diderot's attack was, the chief apostle of this new teaching was Jean-Jacques Rousseau (1712–78). Freedom was a major theme of his writing. He equated being human with being free, including being free from the guilt imposed by original sin.

Rousseau remained for life a believing if somewhat unorthodox Christian (he was a Protestant, then a Catholic, and then a Protestant again). A native of Geneva, he made his career and reputation in France. He had a difficult life, largely because of his difficult personality, but he championed a variety of Enlightenment causes, often with a personal passion which offended more reserved writers. He began his book *The Social Contract* with the startling and unforgettable words, "Humanity is born free but is everywhere in chains." That book dealt with practical politics, but it related to his other works on philosophy and education. In another vivid opening sentence, this time of *Émile,* an educational treatise in the form of a novel, he wrote, "All is good as it leaves the hands of the Author of things, all degenerates in the hands of men."

Having grown up in Calvinist Geneva, Rousseau knew well the power of original sin. Wisely, he did not risk a frontal, theological assault, but simply proclaimed human goodness. (In asserting people's right to "life, liberty, and the pursuit of happiness," Thomas Jefferson did likewise, proclaiming that "we hold these truths to be self-evident," that is, not requiring the proof Jefferson would never have been able to provide to someone like Hume.)

Rousseau had a genuine veneration for the natural human. Voltaire once asked him if he wanted people to walk on all fours, but the witticism missed the point. Rousseau believed that what is natural is good, and humanity is good insofar as people can live within nature or in harmony with nature. People become corrupt when they come in contact with human values. In social life, human desires exceed human strengths and people fall out of balance, a sort of secularized version of Alexander Pope who attributed such desires to pride. Since people are imitative animals, we can do more than other animals, but we can also do much harm. Humans should therefore try to live as harmoniously with nature as possible.

Rousseau recognized that if we believe that we are inherently sinful, we look at the world differently than if we do not. Without original sin, we would look at the world the way that ancient Greeks and Romans, the American natives, and the Tahitians did. He also recognized that advancing Enlightenment views depended upon belief in human goodness. If humans are naturally good, then a good, free society, however ideal or seemingly impractical, is possible. On the contrary, if they are born sinful, a good, free society is impossible, period. Augustine had accepted the latter consequence and envisioned the state as little more than a bulwark against chaos. Calvin had also accepted it and created a tyrannical theocracy in Geneva where the self-identified good people strictly regulated the behavior of "libertines." The prevailing view was that if society gave people freedom, they would use it to sin.

The notion of natural human goodness, so widespread in modern democracies, was a revolutionary concept in the eighteenth century. It represented a completely different way of looking at human nature, and it had serious social and political consequences, especially for Christians. Although it may have mattered little to uneducated Christian believers, this notion stunned religious thinkers who also had reservations about original sin but were stuck with a literal interpretation of Genesis and thus with a primeval sin. The educated West was moving in a different direction, and they were unable to move with it: If people are naturally good, why does the Church teach them that they are evil? Is the Genesis creation account even true? And are not the supposed consequences of original sin, such as death, just part of the natural cycle of the world? There were also consequences outside the Church. If we are all naturally good, then why are we not all equal? And if inequality is a product of society and not of sin, then why not change society?

Most *philosophes* rejected Leibnizian optimism, but they created an optimism of their own, emphasizing inherent goodness instead of inherent human fallibility. But Rousseau and the *philosophes* had a problem. If original sin did not cause evil, what did? Ironically, the *philosophes* avoided philosophy in looking for the answer. Instead they chose to look at society as it actually existed; why theorize about evil when the evidence was right there?

Voltaire accepted good and evil as part of life, rising from nature and curable by natural rather than supernatural solutions. Diderot cited more specific targets as the causes of evil, such as education and legislation which worked against the human good; he even added bad models of behavior. Rousseau's egalitarianism rose to the question; he found the origin of evil in the first person who marked off a piece of land and claimed it for himself and somehow managed to convince other people to accept his claim. All disharmony in the world arises from our wanting what others have and our unwillingness to share with all. Yet he did not explain what made this first person want land of his own.

The theme of societal corruption was hardly new. Augustine's opponent Pelagius had suggested that humans sin by example, not by any inherited guilt from their first parents. But the *philosophes* were not interested in the history of the question. They made an end run around original sin not just to reject the basis of Christian claims to offer salvation but also to advance their own social views.

The Enlightenment intellectuals knew that everyone, even primitive people, did evil things; banishing original sin would not change that. But Rousseau believed that society could also be made moral so that the individual need not be corrupted by it. Humans should not be enchained by an oppressive government, but they could accept restrictions of their behavior via a social contract by which free citizens voluntarily agreed to limit some of their individual desires so that the group could live peacefully and morally. A precondition of this was social and economic equality or at least social and economic balance. Rousseau did not anticipate a perfect society but one based upon principles of justice and equality, two major themes of the *philosophes*. The doctrine of original sin was itself evil because it taught people that they could not become better. By believing that people are inherently good but become evil via society, the *philosophes* could make people good by making society good—by better education, just laws, fair treatment.

For some Christians, this Enlightenment attempt to raise the status of human nature actually pulled it down. The Bible teaches that humans are made in God's image, a statement with little meaning for the *philosophes*. Furthermore, Christian teaching claimed that original sin required the son of God to become human in the person of Jesus Christ and, by so doing, he raised human nature to a status it did not have even before the Fall. But the *philosophes* rejected this as sophistry intended to keep people in poverty and misery by convincing them that they were not as badly off as they thought.

Secularist intellectuals then and now believe that only by getting rid of the divine can one view the human as human and not against an infallible background, but even theistic intellectuals like Voltaire and Rousseau believed that humans had a dignity natural to them and not dependent upon sacraments or grace or any other divine gift. In Peter Gay's words, "the point of Christian anthropology was that man is a son, dependent upon God. . . . The point of the Enlightenment's anthropology is that man is an adult, dependent on himself" (*The Enlightenment,* ii.174). To which Enlightenment thinkers would add, not just independent of Father God but also of Mother Church. Even ecclesiastical officials recognized, however reluctantly, what had happened. To quote Gay again, "Finally, priests less and less emphasized the rigorous Christian teaching of sin: the old grim story of Adam's fall had become less persuasive, and even those who attended Mass without fail were no longer inclined to feel guilty simply because they were human" (ibid., i.354).

But while the Enlightenment intellectuals enjoyed palpable victories, their overall triumph was far from complete. Most obviously, Christianity did not disappear. It remained strong among the rural populations, for whom all the ferment in London and Paris meant little, and it kept the allegiance of most urbanites as well. For many believers, atheism made little sense because they could not explain the existence and order of the world without a creator. This was not Newtonian natural theology with its argument from design; the believers simply could not imagine how else the world could have come into being. To believing Christians deism appeared as a half-way house: God exists but does not do anything. Who cares about a god like that? If God exists, then divine intervention in human affairs seems plausible and even necessary—why pray to a God who does not act in human lives? As for evil, everyone knew that the devil caused that. Theodicy was the province of the intellectuals; simple believers knew that the ancient enemy had not changed his ways since the Garden of Eden. But Christianity's continued success did not rest solely with the uneducated.

Educated Christians successfully resisted much of the Enlightenment, including the attacks of David Hume. His empirical method was hardly all-conquering. Strange as it may sound, many people in the organized, biblical religions applauded Hume. They knew what he thought of them, but their real concern was with deism and natural theology which claimed that faith and thus revelation and organized religion were unnecessary. Religious leaders argued that acknowledging a divine creator of the Newtonian cosmos hardly led to the conclusion that the creator had intervened in the history of Israel. As the French Catholic intellectual Blaise Pascal (1623–62) had observed, the god of the philosophers was not the God of Abraham, Isaac, and Jacob. It took faith to accept the biblical God. By demolishing natural theology and deism, Hume had simultaneously demonstrated faith was necessary for religious people.

Hume considered faith irrational, but believers did not. "Irrational" means contrary to reason. While the existence of God cannot be proven empirically, likewise the nonexistence of God cannot be proved empirically, as Hume's method would demand, and it is thus possible in Humean terms that God exists. It is not contrary to reason to believe in the divine existence, although the believer must acknowledge that this belief is a matter of faith and not a consequence of an irrefutable proof. Believers could even argue that, in Hume's terms, atheism is irrational since one cannot prove that God does not exist, even though atheists claim it to be so. (Hume never denied God's existence and may even have been a theist; for him, atheism, like faith, was too certain of itself.) Believers, and all of Hume's critics for that matter, could go one step further and ask him to prove empirically that empirical knowledge is the only reliable kind. After all, many distinguished thinkers who were not Christian theologians (Plato, Descartes, Spinoza) had accepted the existence of knowledge not completely gained from empiricism. Hume, of course, would reject such knowledge, but believers could easily demonstrate that several great philosophers had rejected strict empiricism.

Many Christians of the Enlightenment era accepted that faith was something interior, something which moved the individual, and something which involved mystery—a process called fideism. Empiricists could consider such an approach irrational and self-delusional, but fideists simply denied that empiricism was the final criterion. Fideism had an internal logic, arguing that it is irrational to claim that humanity can understand the divine, and therefore humble faith is the only way to know the divine. This simplistic approach often ignored theological problems, but fideists had little use for theology. In the nineteenth century fideism declined into genuine irrationality and was attacked even by Christian theologians.

Pietism, a seventeenth-century German Protestant movement with Reformation roots, spread its influence in the eighteenth century, partly in reaction to the Enlightenment. The pietists believed that not just deism or natural theology but also organized religion put too much emphasis upon reason, creating vast dogmatic structures and external observations. These obscured the practice of piety which was essentially internal, recognized by experience and manifested by personal commitment and good works. Pietism had an anti-intellectual element, and it joined fideism in demonstrating that, for many believers, God lay beyond human knowledge and that Enlightenment emphasis on proving everything simply missed the point.

Some Christians openly accepted the validity of the Enlightenment criticisms. A German Protestant theologian, Friedrich Schleiermacher (1768–1834), wrote *Religion: Speeches to Its Cultivated Despisers* (1799). The title says it all; Schleiermacher hoped to convince educated people that they could still be religious. He himself had rejected Pietism and had adopted many Enlightenment views, especially about original sin. God can only create fallible beings, and original sin symbolizes that fallibility. The Bible remains central to Christian faith, but only if it is understood in its historical context. The devil is a myth; he appears in the Bible because the ancient Jews and Christians were people of their age and believed in evil spirits. True religion derives from a sense of the infinite and a consequent sense of dependence upon the infinite, which is most logically a single being. Schleiermacher tremendously influenced

German Protestant theology, but the "cultivated despisers" did not return to the fold in great numbers.

The Enlightenment had another tremendous effect upon the question of evil—and many other questions—by separating many intellectuals from religion. Religion continued to attract some brilliant people, but many who moved Western intellectual history, such as Darwin, Marx, Nietzsche, and Freud, were often atheists and almost as often genuinely hostile to religion. Even some theist intellectuals, especially scientists, perform their work without reference to revelation, tradition, and church authority, all of which were taken for granted as sources of knowledge by the pre-Enlightenment intellectual. Christian intellectuals continued to use those sources but looked at them more critically.

The Enlightenment also had a sinister side. For all their insistence upon liberty and equality, Enlightenment intellectuals never shook off an older, irrational view, the demonization of Others. We may not be surprised to find Cotton Matther in Massachusetts or the missionaries in the Pacific identifying the natives' religion with devil worship, but we might expect more from so-called "enlightened" thinkers. Yet Hume could write:

> There never was a civilized nation of any other complexion than white.
> . . . Not to mention our colonies, there are negro slaves dispersed all over Europe, of which none ever discovered any symptoms of ingenuity. . . . I am apt to suspect the negroes and in general all the other species of men, for there are four or five different kinds, to be naturally inferior to the whites (*Essays, Moral and Political*).

Thomas Jefferson was willing to grant some nobility to Native Americans but almost none to blacks. He pointed out that slaves had all the advantages of contact with white civilization yet produced little from it. "The Indians, with no advantages of this kind, will often carve figures on their pipes not destitute of design and merit," whereas the slaves did not do so. Jefferson considered that perhaps slavery prevented blacks from achieving, but he believed that the real reason was race. Some slaves could advance culturally, but he had little hope for *black* slaves: "Epictetus, Terence, and Phaedrus [ancient Greek and Roman writers] were slaves. But they were of the white race. It is not [the blacks'] condition then, but nature, which has produced the distinction" (*Notes on the State of Virginia*).

The *philosophes* patronized Judaism as a religion and therefore a repository of mindless superstition, but they did not realize, or did not care, that such attacks on Judaism helped to justify anti-Semitism. Even Voltaire, who defended French Protestants, could not rise above his anti-Semitism.

The Enlightenment followed the century of the Witch Craze, and one might think that the *philosophes* would be concerned about the status of women. Familiar images of eighteenth-century Parisian society picture cultivated, sophisticated women gathering intellectuals in their salons for an evening of brilliant conversation. But however much the intellectuals enjoyed the company of particular women, their view of women as a gender remained appalling. Hume could claim that nature had established equality between the sexes but could simultaneously believe that women were more religious than men simply because they were more credulous and superstitious.

For admirers of the Enlightenment, the greatest surprise and disappointment is Rousseau. He believed that humans were best in the state of nature and that nature had created women inferior to men. He railed against social customs which required women to put up with offensive or silly social customs, yet he believed that their subjection to men was natural. These views do not appear in a remote corner of his writings but in his major educational treatise, *Émile*. He sounded like an apologist for the old order: "Though swayed by these passions man is endowed with reason by which to control them. Woman is also endowed with boundless passions; God has given her modesty to restrain them." "Women do wrong to complain of the inequality of man-made laws; this inequality is not of man's making, or at any rate it is not the result of mere prejudice, but of reason." That nature has destined women for one occupation is proved by childhood play, that is, before society forms our roles: "The doll is the girl's special plaything; this shows her instinctive bent towards her life's work."

The *philosophes'* redefinition did not touch the Other. But at least one contemporary took seriously their admonitions to subject all customs to the scrutiny of reason, and she concluded that women should be recognized as equals. In 1792, Mary Wollstonecraft (1759–97) published *A Vindication of the Rights of Women*. She brilliantly used Enlightenment themes and even refuted Rousseau by name. He had written that true humanity requires freedom; she wrote, "It is vain to expect virtue from women till they are in some degree independent of men." Freedom gave birth to virtue, "for how can a being be . . . virtuous, who is not free?" (*Vindication* ix; 145), echoing Eve in *Paradise Lost:* "For inferior, who is free." Wollstonecraft recognized that a society which values women solely for their appearance effectively alienates them from their true being. "What can be a more melancholy sight to a thinking mind, than to look into the numerous carriages that drive helter-skelter about this metropolis [London] . . . full of pale-faced creatures who are flying from themselves!" (ibid., 151). People thought women incapable of doing anything other than being pretty or taking care of a home, but, if they had the chance, "Women might certainly study the art of healing and be physicians as well as nurses. . . . They might also study politics. . . . Business of various kinds, they might likewise pursue, if they were educated in a more orderly manner" (ibid., 152). The *philosophes* had liberated more than they knew.

The eighteenth century had forever changed the understanding of evil, and virtually all subsequent developments flowed from it. Reason and its stepchild science would judge all theories, and Christian teaching would automatically be intellectually suspect. But, however triumphant, the Enlightenment, too, faced the pendulum of history. Dissident voices questioned its values.

Chapter 11

Dissident Voices

> *Culture, which shapes the whole world*
> *Has overtaken the devil, too.*
> —Goethe, *Faust, Part One*

The Enlightenment had challenged superstition, despotism, and censorship, while elevating reason and its child science to new heights. Yet for all its greatness, the Enlightenment harbored significant problems, and it did not take long before someone exposed the greatest of these.

Donatien Alphonse Françoise de Sade (1740–1814), better known as the Marquis de Sade, gave his name to sadism, taking enjoyment by imposing sufferings upon others. A pornographer and a criminal, de Sade frequently expressed his delight in inflicting pain on women and children. He practiced what he preached and in consequence spent long years in prison. At first glance, he does not seem to belong in a book with Dante and Newton, but de Sade demonstrated, as no one after him has, the weakness of an understanding of good and evil based solely upon human values.

The *philosophes* had liberated the world—or at least themselves and their readers—from original sin; humans were no longer born evil. Atheist intellectuals argued that all of our values, including notions of evil, have a base in human activity; some theist intellectuals had pushed the divine so far out of the world that they, too, had to insist that many human values derive from human activity. Since humans are born naturally good, we have to create a society which allows that goodness to flourish as much as possible. This view always held some danger, and no less than Voltaire patronizingly suggested that, for the good of society, perhaps the uneducated classes should keep their religiously-based morality. But this would not work forever because the intellectuals believed that their values would eventually supersede religious ones. At some point someone had to posit a theory which explained evil in terms of purely human values. De Sade did.

De Sade defined goodness as doing what you wanted to do and evil as the frustration of that goodness. He was that rarest of people, a pure relativist. He genuinely believed that good and evil lay solely in the eyes of the beholder. He expressed his views in his novels which were banned for a long time because of their pornographic content. In these surprisingly tedious pieces, de Sade attacked the *philosophes*.

He did not do it incidentally. His novel *Justine* (1791) parodies *Candide* by having the central character go on an endless series of adventures. Justine believes in God and in justice and that God will make all things right in the end. She repeatedly finds herself kidnapped and abused by men mostly who justify their views for what she perceives as mistreatment but which they perceive as their right. She knows that God will pay them back for their crimes, but instead her tormentors go on to achieve wealth and power. When she finally escapes from these predators, lightning comes from a clear sky to strike her dead, de Sade's way of showing that in this world, the only one which exists, there is no God who can right our wrongs.

The very title *Philosophy in the Bedroom* (1795) tweaked the *philosophes*. It recounts the licentious adventures of a group of aristocrats. This parodies Plato's philosopher-king because these perverts put their philosophy into practice. One of them, Dolmance, gives a long account of his (and de Sade's) views; he turns upside down much of what Rousseau and others had written and believed. Dolmance starts his lengthy soliloquy with an attack on religion, stressing the relation between religion with absolutism, mocking the Eucharist (flour dough best left to mice), and asserting that only atheism is consonant with reason. Even if the institutionalized version were not so corrupt, Christianity would still offer us nothing since the fear of hell has never deterred evil; on the contrary people commit crimes in the name of religion. Like a good disciple of Hume, de Sade scoffed at belief in a being undetectable by any of our senses; religion bases itself upon ignorance and fear.

De Sade used religion as a Trojan Horse. He demonstrated his solidarity with the Enlightenment intellectuals, but then he turned to his real concern, personal behavior. He stole a march from Rousseau, claiming that, according to Nature, no one loves one's neighbor as one's self, but rather Nature, *the only voice which we must follow,* insists we love others as friends. This sounds like a mild adjustment, but de Sade has established his methodological base: we should only do what is natural.

But suppose we differ on what is natural? Precisely, declared de Sade, and that is why we cannot have universal laws. People differ so much naturally that the same law cannot govern all. De Sade recognized that people will want laws anyway, but these should be very flexible and never harsh, especially because many "crimes" are misunderstood, and four particularly: calumny, theft, impurity, and murder. Invoking Nature and mocking Rousseau, de Sade cleverly insisted that he arrived at his rather unusual ideas while still a child, that is, before society had a chance to corrupt him.

His mouthpiece Dolmance briefly dismisses calumny since evil people deserve it and good people are always vindicated. As for theft, that is merely the redistribution of wealth, and any blame should adhere to those who stupidly fail to guard their property.

On the subject of sex Dolmance does not demand just that religion withdraw its strictures but goes on to explain how liberating de Sade's views are, especially for women. Women are born lusty, but religion imposes modesty upon them. So does society. If only, Dolmance sighs, women would do what Nature intended for them and subject themselves to all the sexual whims of men. After all, Dolmance observes, are men not endowed by Nature with the physical strength to make women do what they want? Besides, women benefit from this, being liberated from all the constraints of religion and civilization and enjoying the role carved out for them by Nature. But suppose a man forces himself upon a woman? Surely rape is still a crime. Absolutely not. Rape is a crime only if a man has no right to force a woman to have sex with him; Nature gave man the right to any woman, so rape simply cannot exist.

Dolmance finishes this disquisition with a defense of murder, arguing that the manly races of the world always allowed the practice of killing others, but with the understanding that the killer might be subject to vengeance by relatives of the deceased.

This remarkable view of the world has many ancient and traditional precedents, but it also contains much that is new. Theism preserved the traditional views of evil, that a deity would determine what was good and evil and would then inform his servants (Moses, Jesus, Muhammad), who passed the divine revelation along to the people. But with God out of the equation, then humans and humans alone determined what was good and evil. In fact, not much would be different in the daily life of a society guided by theistic or atheistic norms. Religious believers might insist that God wishes us not to harm others while secularists might insist that we as humans owe it to other humans not to harm them. But de Sade realized that the claims of secular society could be used to justify his own views. He offered a simple syllogism: all values are those of humans, his values are those of a human, therefore his values are as valid as anyone else's.

This is not as trite as it initially appears. Rousseau and others had insisted that humans are born naturally good, only to be corrupted by society. De Sade agreed, and said he merely advocated that we do what Nature allows. If men naturally have greater physical strength than women, then Nature clearly permits them to subject women, and women should act naturally and be subjected. De Sade pushed natural goodness even further. If we free ourselves of the imposed values of society—which he certainly did—then no idea which such a free person has can be unnatural, including even murder.

De Sade was a loathsome person, but he must be credited for seeing where Enlightenment thinking about good and evil could lead. If all values are human, what right does any human have to determine what another human should think or do? A lot of counter arguments come to mind, the most obvious being, what would de Sade think if someone did to him what he did to others? He would recognize that people do what they want to do if they are strong enough to do it, and if someone can overpower him, then that is simply too bad for him. But suppose the majority rejects his values? So what. They have the numbers and strength to prevent him from following Nature's dictates (recall that he had been imprisoned), but that did not privilege their views over his. Just because at one time most people rejected what he thought did not mean he was wrong. After all, numbers and strength shift. To use a modern example, suppose the majority voted to reopen Auschwitz or the Gulag? Would it now be moral to have death camps because the majority approved? And was slavery moral in those eras when a majority of people thought there was nothing wrong with it? De Sade stands on very firm ground in rejecting the morality of the majority.

But wouldn't de Sade's views cause chaos if everyone simply did what he or she wanted? Nonsense, de Sade, would reply. How can society be harmed if we all act naturally? After all, he asked (again tweaking Rousseau), isn't living according to Nature the desired goal?

De Sade was a pervert but not a fool. He found the Catch-22 in the goodness-of-Nature argument, and he exploited it. Yet he was not taken seriously in his day. He wrote after the deaths of most of the great *philosophes,* and contemporary philosophers such as Kant worried more about what Hume's skepticism and empiricism had done to good and evil than about the fantasies of a pornographic criminal. Literary people admired de Sade for his investigation of the shadow side of the personality, and he influenced European Romantic literature in the nineteenth century. A watered-down version of his relativism would become popular in the twentieth century, and one of that century's great intellectuals, Jean-Paul Sartre (1905–80), had to concede that "everything is permissible if God does not exist" ("Humanism," 70–1).

Quite a different critic of the Enlightenment was the German poet and scientist Johann Wolfgang von Goethe (1749–1832), whose long life stretched from the heart of the eighteenth century into the first phase of the Romantic movement. Like most young Europeans, he saw the Enlightenment as the force which would drive back ignorance, super-stition, clericalism, and the entire host of retrograde demons. But as the great movement wore on and frayed at the fringes, Goethe took a hard but not unappreciative second look, especially at the question of good and evil. His musings resulted in two dramas, *Faust, Part One* (1808) and *Faust, Part Two* (1832).

Faust, Part One opens in the heavenly court as did the book of Job. Mephistopheles is there, implying that evil is a part of the divine plan. God even acknowledges that he has never hated Mephistopheles (which is orthodox since God must love all his creatures), but then he adds that this rogue never bores him, unlike the other upright beings who come to the court. God points with pride to Faust who, like a good *philosophe,* strives always for knowledge. Mephistopheles says that he can turn Faust away from his pursuit. God accepts the challenge, although quali-fying it by limiting the demon's power over Faust to the time that he lives. Agreeing to this condition, Mephistopheles heads off to earth.

Goethe's pen quickly turns satiric as Faust, alone and unheard, admits that although he is smarter than all the academic charlatans, all his ef-forts at knowledge have produced nothing except to lead students around by the nose (scene 1). He despairs of knowledge—a reversal of Enlighten-ment values—and looks toward magic. He temporarily despairs and even laments his own and society's loss of faith, when he hears some believers singing Easter hymns. With his pedantic assistant Wagner, he bemoans his life and his inability to reconcile his desires to master this world and his aspirations for a higher one. He envies the simple townsfolk who cele-brate Easter and Christ's salvation of the human race. At that moment, Mephistopheles arrives not to save but to destroy.

Goethe has some fun here since the demon first appears as a black dog which trails fire behind him. But soon Mephistopheles appears as an urbane, well-dressed, sophisticated traveler from another place and time, a devil created by Goethe and widely imitated after him. In Russell's words, the demon "has the ironic, aloof, critical, cold, judg-mental qualities of the academics Goethe despised" (*Mephistopheles,* 159). He challenges not Faust's goodness as Satan did with Job but rather his striving to know, which was accepted by both Faust and the Enlighten-ment as the highest virtue. Here the Easter background enters in. Goethe was not personally religious, but he held up Christ as one who died because he himself loved people and urged people to love one an-other. The dry, rationalist Faust was no Christ-figure.

Faust will lose his soul if he ceases to strive for knowledge. Mephistopheles warns Faust that he is a spirit which negates everything, but the scholar is confident that he can handle this spirit. Mephistopheles then offers him new worlds of knowledge beyond those open to the academician, the same promise Satan made to Adam and Eve. Evil has not ceased to be attractive. But Faust soon learns that evil, the nothing of the philosophers, produces nothing.

Mephistopheles takes him to a witches' kitchen to meet his friends, witches and apes, and he convinces Faust to drink a potion which will cause him to fall in love with the first woman he sees. Goethe cleverly shows how naive the supposedly brilliant Faust is about people and how evil uses the human need for love as a tool to destroy. He also uses this scene to set one of the classic lines of the tragedy. When a witch who has known Mephistopheles for centuries sees him dressed as a dandy, she asks what happened to his cloven hooves. The demon responds, "Culture, which shapes the whole world / Has overtaken the devil, too" (scene 6). Evil keeps pace with the changing world.

Influenced by the potion Mephistopheles gave him, Faust meets and becomes enraptured with an innocent young woman named Margaret. Normally love can redeem, but this relationship began with a demon's potion and continues with Faust's asking for the demon's help. The aging scholar, unfamiliar with love, does not know what to do, and he foolishly relies on Mephistopheles' advice. Faust sends Margaret a casket of diamonds, but her mother won't let her keep it. Margaret's mother has become an obstacle, so Faust turns to the demon for assistance. Mephistopheles gives him a sleeping draught, which Faust convinces Margaret to give to her mother so that they can have some time alone. The sleeping draught is poison.

Faust soon seduces Margaret, who becomes pregnant. In a poignant scene, she prays at a statue of the Virgin Mary, who was also pregnant and unwed, but whereas Mary had Joseph who recognized God's hand in her pregnancy, Margaret has Faust—and Mephistopheles. Goethe contrasts Margaret's goodness to the demon's evil. She tells Faust that she hates Mephistopheles, but Faust cannot give him up, he cannot turn from evil to love. The situation worsens. Margaret's brother Valentine, knowing what has happened, seeks out Faust to avenge his sister's honor, but Mephistopheles helps Faust to kill him. Having lost her mother and brother, Margaret becomes deranged, gives birth to the baby, and then kills it. The authorities arrest, try, and condemn her to execution.

Margaret provides the counter to Faust. When he uses the demon's power to rescue her, she refuses him. In her jail cell she acknowledges her responsibility for her actions and rejects any help provided by Mephistopheles. A heavenly voice announces her salvation, while Faust laments that he had ever been born, echoing Jesus' words about Judas: "It would have been better for that one not to have been born" (Mark 14:21).

Goethe's indictment of knowledge without love, of the pursuit of learning without the pursuit of wisdom, and of the refusal to recognize the nature of evil did not always take on so serious a form. Just before the attempted rescue of Margaret, Mephistopheles takes Faust to a Witches' Sabbath on Walpurgis Night. In attendance are parodies of intellectuals and social leaders—a minister, a general—as well as representatives of philosophical schools—an idealist, a realist, a skeptic. Earlier in the book, Mephistopheles pretends to be a professor and gives an unsuspecting student appallingly pedantic advice. Aging Enlightenment types would have not found a devil recommending the study of philosophy to be amusing.

On the surface, *Faust, Part One* could be an intellectual's satire of academic life, but Goethe wanted to warn about an unrestrained faith in the power of reason and the naive assumption that it would solve all problems, a warning that carried weight because, like Faust, Goethe was a scientist. Faust needed knowledge but he also needed true love.

When he returned to the topic a quarter of a century later with *Faust, Part Two,* Goethe made great use of allegories and allusions but again took up the central points of Part One. Once more the reader encounters a collection of prominent fools—politicians, poets, philosophers—but now Mephistopheles has moved up in the world. He has become a financial advisor to the emperor, and he recommends inflationary policies which ruin the country and provoke a civil war (in which the incompetent Faust gets to be a general). Following the demon's advice, the emperor embarks on schemes which engender poverty and death on a vast scale. When Faust points this out to Mephistopheles, his response is that the "human ants" amuse him, and he really does not care whether there is war or peace. He, and therefore evil, will continue to do their traditional work. Like Dante and others, Goethe stressed the sheer stupidity of evil but a stupidity with dangerous consequences.

Faust's former student Wagner has kept up his scientific work and in the laboratory has created Homunculus, or "little man," who must live a phial. The Enlightenment *philosophes* had hoped to create a new humanity, freed from the fears and superstitions of the religion and tradition, but now it is the visionless Wagner who achieves this. Homunculus can reason and talk, so Mephistopheles convinces him to come away with him—as he once lured Faust. Wagner wants to come too, but Homunculus tells him to stay home and read some books. The scholar has created this being but cannot control it. Goethe also uses Homunculus to poke fun at the Enlightenment obsession with classical antiquity. When the Greek philosopher Thales meets Homunculus, he admits that he cannot understand him; the modern world, for better or worse, is outstripping the ancient one. Faust next has a series of adventures and still foolishly listens to Mephistopheles, but at the end of his life he asserts the importance of constant striving for wisdom, from childhood to old age. Ultimately, he did not succumb to sensual pleasures such as wealth, sex, and power, and when Mephistopheles claims his soul, a host of angels rebuke the demon. They carry him off to heaven where he meets Margaret. Shrewdly, Goethe does not show Mephistopheles lamenting this turn of events. Evil is never at a loss, and Mephistopheles exits the story fantasizing about the boy angels.

Faust's Christianized salvation has only a symbolic value; Christian virtues do not save him but rather his recognition of the power of love, of striving, and of avoiding "the antiphonal errors of sensuality and arid intellectualism" (Russell, *Mephistopheles,* 167).

Perhaps the most dissident voice of all disagreed, however unintentionally, with both Christianity and the Enlightenment. In 1798 a British clergyman named Thomas Malthus (1766–1834) anonymously published his *Essay on the Principle of Population*. This brief book warned that the world's population was outgrowing its food supply. Malthus suggested a variety of remedies, including abstinence and birth control, but he is best known for his list of three checks on the population: famine, pestilence, and war. Subsequent research has questioned and dismissed many of his conclusions. Modern demographers would warn about war over resources rather than only food, but our concern is how Malthus impacted the notion of evil with his explanation of war.

Many believers thought that of all the evils the devil could provoke, none was worse than war, the deliberate attempt by humans to kill other humans in large numbers. Both theists and secularists knew that most wars began over things like border disputes, dynastic succession, land hunger, or some generations-old offense. Yet Malthus said that war is not *necessarily* a consequence of evil, human or demonic. He knew that most wars had little to do with food, but his point was that, even if all other factors would be eliminated, war would still be an inevitable consequence of the population's outstripping the food supply. People would go to war for food, and the deaths caused by war would diminish the gap between the population and the food supply. At some point, a fact of nature would demand war to reconcile the crisis caused by the size of the population and the availability of food.

War, as well as famine and pestilence, was not inevitable in Malthus' scheme. If population growth were limited and/or the food supply increased, war could be avoided, at least as a consequence of hunger. One could even argue that people can avoid war by working to restrain population growth and increase the food supply, and thus bring this evil under human control. But if some blight or drought or excessive rains were to ruin food crops and cause a shortage, people could do nothing.

Malthus' ideas did not influence the West until decades after his death, via Charles Darwin and other writers of the late nineteenth century, but the effects of his views were far-reaching. War, one of the worst of evils, could occur whether there was a devil or not. War could occur in spite of any Enlightenment-encouraged schemes to eliminate social and economic equality. In the form of droughts, locust plagues, floods or anything which diminished the food supply, blind Nature would drive humans to this worst of moral evils.

Malthus had introduced a jarring note into the discussion of evil. At least one serious manifestation of evil could be independent of demonic devices or human intentions.

The eighteenth century had considerably broadened the Western understanding of evil. The nineteenth century would have to deal with that legacy.

Chapter 12

Human Evil in the Nineteenth Century

The Romantic and Gothic writers may have reacted against what they considered the excesses of the Enlightenment, but they did not return to traditional values. The new intellectuals had little use for religion, at least for the traditional kind. The British poet Percy Bysshe Shelley (1792–1822) was expelled from Oxford University in 1811 for his pamphlet "On the Necessity of Atheism." Yet the Romantics also offer the first example of what has since become a widespread phenomenon—a rejection of organized Christianity but an adherence to some of its basic doctrines and an admiration for Jesus.

This can be seen in an early Romantic work, "The Rime of the Ancient Mariner," published in 1798. Samuel Taylor Coleridge (1772–1834) had his Mariner twice invoke the Virgin Mary and once acknowledge a patron saint, had a hermit as a major character, and used sin and redemption as a central theme. He created a world of spirits and alluded several times to Milton's *Paradise Lost*. Coleridge also introduced themes important to the Romantics, such as a oneness with creation. The Mariner commits the sin not of violating God's commandments as given in the Bible but of killing a naturally good creature, the albatross. The spirits of the sea force him to do penance, after which the Mariner learns how to be naturally religious. The Mariner tells his listener, a wedding guest (a wedding being a major church event), that:

> He prayeth well, who loveth well
> Both man and bird and beast.

He prayeth best, who loveth best
All things both great and small;
For the dear God who loveth us,
He made and loveth all.

Coleridge rejects both the Augustinian and Enlightenment traditions. With the Enlightenment and against Augustine, he believed in a good world and a God who loves and can forgive everyone without the necessity of grace and predestination. But with the Christians and against the Enlightenment, his central character is saved not by rejecting religious tradition for scientific knowledge but by accepting God's forgiveness and love. Furthermore, the forgiveness entailed penance, a righteous suffering for a good end.

The Romantics have a deserved reputation for rebelliousness, sometimes in their lifestyles which violated contemporary social mores and sometimes for participation in actual revolutions. To some Romantics, no power appeared more tyrannical than that of God, the supreme ruler whose adherents said he made no mistakes and whose judgments were final. In the early part of the nineteenth century, some writers celebrated the devil as a revolutionary against that most awesome of powers, but this nonsense did not last long. The revolutionaries hoped to better society, and they could not seriously invoke as a symbol a being whose whole existence was devoted to harming people.

Romantic portrayals of evil are eclectic, drawing from the Enlightenment, biblical and Christian tradition, Greco-Roman Antiquity, non-European religion and philosophy (which were just becoming known in the West), and their own idiosyncratic views. Romantic writers were found in most of the West, but we will concentrate on English-speaking authors who represent the views of the era and who are most accessible to the readers of this book.

William Blake (1757–1827) gave currency to an old idea, the coincidence of opposites. In his richly-illustrated poem *The Marriage of Heaven and Hell,* he portrayed God as a good figure but one moved by reason and law and unsympathetic to many primal forces. "Without Contraries is no progression. Attraction and Repulsion, Reason and Energy, Love and Hate, are necessary to Human Existence. From these contraries spring what the religious call Good & Evil. Good is the passive that obeys Reason. Evil is active springing from Energy" (Plate 3). "That Energy, call'd Evil, is alone from the Body, & that Reason, call'd Good, is alone from the Soul" (Plate 4).

He believed that religion had established the dominance of the soul over the body, and this distorted people's view of human nature, which consists of both. He further believed that organized religion had established the dominance of reason (one shudders to think how Hume would have responded to that!), but human nature requires energy to break the bounds set by reason. Rejecting both Eden and Faust, he claimed that humans cannot be fulfilled by living within the bounds set by reason and religion: "You never know what is enough unless you know what is more than enough" (Plate 9). He attempted to show that this view does not go completely against established tradition by citing Milton and the prophet Isaiah, but he had to insist Milton was "of the Devils [*sic*] party without knowing it" (Plate 6) and he had to reinterpret the monotheist prophet Isaiah practically as a pantheist (Plate 12) who sees the divine in everything.

Blake feared that Enlightenment rationalism would snuff out the spirit and devalue the emotions. He recognized that reason had its limits and that humans have to accept some degree of mystery in their lives, including the mystery of evil. His solution, "Without Contraries is no progression," set evil within creation and thus avoided the very difficult idea that evil is ultimately nothing. God creates all things, including those most humans perceive as evil, but when we recognize that evil is actually a progressive force, the energy, the desire we have to break boundaries, then we will simultaneously recognize the unity of all creation and transcend evil. Blake's optimism exceeded that of the optimist philosophers.

The poet Lord Byron (1788–1824) shared Blake's view to some extent. He set his poetic drama, *Cain,* outside the Garden of Paradise as Adam, Eve, their two sons, Cain and Abel, and their two daughters, Adah and Zillah, try to define their relationship with God. The rest of the family wishes to venerate God and thank him for his gifts, but Cain asks some revolutionary questions which many believers of Byron's day also probably asked. Why must Cain suffer for his parents' sins? Why did God put this tempting tree in the garden in the first place? And why is God silent when his people need him so much? Like Mephistopheles in Marlowe's *Dr. Faustus,* Lucifer hears the questions of a doubter and rushes in to take advantage. Cain recognizes a kindred spirit: "never till / Now met I aught to sympathize with me." Lucifer strikes hard: "Did *I* plant things prohibited within / The reach of beings innocent, and curious / By their own innocence?" (I.i.189–90, 200–2).

Although Lucifer self-righteously denounces "the Omnipotent tyrant," Byron still represented the devil as an evil being. Lucifer always misrepresents himself and responds evasively to Cain's questions. He so turns Cain against God that when Abel urges Cain to offer sacrifice and make peace with the deity, in a rage Cain kills his brother. Cain has made Zillah a widow, devastated his parents, and ruined his relationship with Adah, whom he truly loves.

On the other hand, Byron gave both Cain and Lucifer the chance to voice the poet's own opposition to the Christian God and to raise the question about what exactly evil is.

> He [God] as a conqueror will call the conquer'd
> *Evil;* but what will be the *good* he gives?
> Were I the victor, *his* works would be deem'd
> The evil ones (II.ii.443–6).

Byron here used clever ambiguity. The question is a good one, but it is found in the mouth of a liar. Is evil nothing more than what the victor says it is? Has the Christian establishment clothed its own views in the divine robe and imposed them a gullible populace? Or is Lucifer demeaning the good for his own purposes? Byron did not know, and he believed that no one else could be sure either. Cain's murder of Abel was wrong, but many conflicting elements, including God's treatment of his people and his silence, contributed to what Cain did.

Percy Shelley discussed evil in a frontal assault on Christianity in an essay entitled "On the Devil, and Devils." He accused the Christians of being Manichean dualists by creating good and evil deities, and he further accused them of fantasizing about spirits to explain a simple human phenomenon.

> To suppose that the world was created and is superintended by two spirits of a balanced power and opposite direction, is simply a personification of the struggle which we experience within ourselves, and which we perceive in the operations of external things as they affect us, between good and evil.

And such an approach is a mask for a shallow relativism:

> To give that which [is] most pleasing to us, a perpetual or an ultimate superiority, with all epithets of honourable addition; and to brand that which is displeasing, with epithets ludicrous and horrible, predicting its ultimate defeat, is to pursue the process by which the vulgar arrive at the familiar notions of God and Devil (*Complete Works,* vii. 87).

God and Devil are merely names we give to the opposing forces within us, "God" for those forces we consider positive and "Devil" for those we find negative. Shelley claimed to have found the origins of the notion in the ancient Near East, a notion which slipped into the Bible. He blamed the Christians for not learning from the Greek philosophers to center the discussion of evil in the person and activity of the divine. He flippantly observed that Samuel Johnson (1709–84) was "the last man of considerable talents who shewed any serious attachment to the antient faith" (ibid., 93).

The Christians of his day provided endless targets, such as his "pious friend Miss _____" who told him that "about nineteen in twenty will be damned." He also poked fun at the Christian unwillingness to defend the basic doctrines.

> Formerly it was supposed that all those who were not Christians, and even all those who were not of a particular sect of Christians, would be damned. At present this doctrine seems abandoned or confined to a few. . . . Christians, indeed, will not admit the substantive presence of Devils upon Earth in modern times, or they suppose their agency to be obscure and surreptitious, in proportion as any histories of them approach to the present epoch, or indeed any epoch in which there has been a considerable progress in historical criticism or natural science (ibid., 96, 98).

Shelley was correct. Trapped by a literal interpretation of the Bible, most Christians shrank from science and historical criticism. They simply could not explain evil biblically, and even most theologians had to include the devil in their systems. Yet the Shelley with whom we associate evil is not Percy but his wife Mary (1797–1851), daughter of Mary Wollstonecraft and author of the Gothic classic *Frankenstein*.

Gothic literature contributed to the understanding of evil by stressing the shadow side of the human personality, the side which socially upright people did not wish to see or be seen. Literary critics have seen in caves and tunnels and dungeons an expedition into the unconscious and in the demons and monsters a fascination and fear of what is different. The central characters of Gothic literature go beyond the borders of religion, of social mores, and of nature; like the primeval couple in Eden, they want more than convention allows. This Faustian device became a staple of Gothic literature and helps to explain its unending popularity. Every human being has had that desire, even if we know we will pay a price for it, and sometimes we believe the price will be worth it. As Blake put it, "You never know what is enough unless you know what is more than enough."

But the Gothic dealt with more than just the desire to be free of convention. Following, perhaps not always consciously, the Marquis de Sade, the Gothic writers recognized that we are not necessarily appalled to find a shadow side to our personality. But they also followed Dante and Milton, and Gothic works include many Christian themes such as sin, repentance, redemption through love, and damnation.

Initially dismissed by critics as a facile horror tale, Mary Shelley's *Frankenstein* has won recognition as a masterpiece. The teenage daughter of an early feminist, she ran off to live with the married Romantic poet Percy Bysshe Shelley in foreign Switzerland. She wrote *Frankenstein* in

1816 when she was only nineteen. She used the device of a story within a story within a story. The book opens with Robert Walton, an Englishman seeking a sailing route near the North Pole. He was doing that for the good of humanity but simultaneously for his own glory. In the northern ice his crew saw in the distance a gigantic creature driving a dog sled; then the crew found Victor Frankenstein with just one dog floating on an ice fragment. After being rescued, Victor told Walton his story.

He grew up in a socially prominent family in Geneva, Switzerland, and he loved and eventually married Elizabeth, an orphan whom his family took in. He went off to a foreign university to study medicine and became obsessed with the power of science. He wanted to do research into the creation of a human being, only to find that science could not carry him the distance. He turned to earlier writers who dabbled in alchemy and other practices which Victor's fellow scientists considered either foolish or demonic. His interest in such writers was the first step down the slippery slope.

This sounds a great deal like Marlowe's *Doctor Faustus,* but Shelley is more original than she first appears. When Marlowe wrote, scientists were one step ahead of magicians; even the great astronomer Kepler used to pay his way by doing horoscopes for Polish and German nobles. But Shelley wrote after the Enlightenment had turned science into the intellectual icon, the force which would defeat ignorance, superstition, and religion. The educated reader would initially identify with Victor and would not like to be told, even in a work of fiction, that scientific knowledge had limits and the scientist, the archetypal seeker after truth, could be dangerous.

But Shelley did more than challenge the Enlightenment icon. She emphasized that there is no knowledge without the humans who have that knowledge, and flawed humans often do not know what to do with their knowledge. For example, she had Victor pursue his researches so intently that he completely ignored his family, not visiting or even writing to them for years. His passion for knowledge cut him off from human love, a very ominous foreshadowing.

Eventually Victor succeeded in creating a male human being, a work previously done only by God. The creature was eight feet tall, which reminded the reader of the old tradition that the devil was a giant. This showed Victor's pride or *hubris;* he created a being larger than God did. Like Adam and Eve, Victor wanted to be like God; also like Adam and Eve, he found out that it was not so easy. When the creature opened its eyes and, later, smiled at its creator, Victor could not accept what he had done. He ran from his laboratory into the rain, symbolizing that he sought redemption for what he had done, but blood, not baptism, would have to wash this sin away. When Adam and Eve disobeyed God, he did not cease loving them, but Victor, who had the technical ability to create, did not have the ability to love. He first turned from his family and now he turned from his "newborn child." Although it is common to speak of the "monster," the creature was socially, psychologically, and intellectually a baby, desperately in need of a parent.

In fear, Victor returned home, assuming the creature would die from neglect. Miraculously it survived. Scorned by humans, it headed into the wild, eventually coming upon a cottage with three inhabitants, a blind man, his daughter, and his son. Her name was Agatha, the Greek word for good, and the son's name was Felix, the Latin word for happy, as well as being the names of two prominent Catholic saints. Poor and deprived as they were, the children led a good and happy life because their father, unlike Victor, loved his children. Hiding from the cottagers but listening to their conversation, the creature learned about the world; he even learned to read. The cottagers welcomed a guest, Safie, a young Turkish woman who loved Felix and who was a refugee from the French government. In a touching scene, Safie inside the cottage and the creature outside both wept when they heard of the destruction of the native Americans, innocent people demonized by European society, just as the creature was. The creature wanted love, and he entered the cabin when the children were away. In a touching scene the blind father, who could not see the creature's monstrous exterior, saw his interior goodness, but the children returned and fearfully forced the creature to leave the cottage. Soon after this, when he saw his reflection in water, the creature knew that he would never be accepted by humans and decided to revenge himself upon Victor.

Just as Milton's Satan revenged himself upon God by attacking Adam and Eve, so the creature did not kill Victor but instead his family members and best friend. The irony is frightful. Victor cut himself off from the love of his family to play God, and now his creation would cut him off once again from his family's love, but this time permanently. At one point, before the creature has completed his work, he and Victor met and talked, and the creature recounted the story of his survival. Shelley used the conversation to give her views of evil.

The creature, who had read *Paradise Lost,* told Victor, "I ought to be thy Adam, but I am rather the fallen angel." The apostle Paul in the Epistle to the Romans (5:12-14) identified Christ as the New Adam. Furthermore, Adam was born without original sin. Christian theology linked original sin with descent from the primal couple, but the creature did not descend from them. He had the potential to be good because he was free from original sin. What destroyed him was not an ancient taint on the soul but the intolerance of humans. "I was benevolent and good; misery made me a fiend," said the creature, "Make me happy, and I shall again be virtuous" (69).

But a fatal corner had been turned. The creature, like the native Americans he wept for, had been corrupted by Western society, represented foremost by Victor the scientist. The creature did not know of his damnation and still hoped to be happy. He demanded that Victor create a mate for him, a new Eve. Victor, fearful for his family, agreed to do so, but as he was completing fabrication of the woman, a vestige of goodness made him fear that the two creatures would generate a race of monsters. He destroyed the woman before she could come to life, unaware that the creature was watching him. It groaned at the loss of its hoped-for companion and swore to Victor, "I shall be with you on your wedding-night" (123). Victor's overriding *hubris* led him to think the creature would try to kill him and thus on his wedding night he ignored Elizabeth's safety. The creature instead killed Elizabeth, thus paying Victor back in kind for destroying his intended spouse. Creature and creator both now fell into despair, the unforgivable sin (Luke 12:10) because someone who cannot hope cannot accept redemption. Victor set out to kill the creature, who deliberately led him to the northern ice, an echo of Dante's frozen bottom circle of hell and the place where Walton encountered Victor. Borrowing from Milton, Shelley described Victor as a demon; he lamented to Walton, "if you had known me as I once was, you would not recognize me in this state of degradation" (157). Like Satan in *Paradise Lost,* Victor steadily deteriorated after his fall. The creature boarded the ship to see Victor, who had already died. It talked to Walton and then announced that it would destroy itself in a funeral pyre. Walton, deciding not to seek glory with the lives of his crew, turned his ship around.

Like Goethe, Shelley recognized the danger of knowledge without love, of reason without emotion. She further recognized that reason, which celebrated the light, could not penetrate to the shadow side of the personality where different values resided. Victor acted irrationally, trying to play God, and reason could not recall him from that dangerous path—only love could, but the scientist cut himself off from love, thus ensuring his damnation. Yet Shelley stopped short of condemning science and knowledge. She knew that knowledge had pushed back the frontiers of ignorance and that this was all to the good. She did not promote ignorance but insisted that knowledge must be tempered by love and that those who seek knowledge must be aware that it—and they—have limits.

Ecologists can count themselves among Shelley's many descendants. She sees Nature as good and human *hubris* as evil. Frankenstein cannot live in harmony with the world around him but instead must dominate it. Victor must win a victory over Nature. He ignores other persons and even love itself in his quest for dominance, a quest which led to disaster. The creature could have been good, but humans would not let it be. And once its nature had been corrupted, it could not return to primal innocence.

Shelley's variation of the Faustian theme resonated with later writers. Nathaniel Hawthorne (1804–64) set his short story "Rappacini's Daughter" in Renaissance Italy. The young student Giovanni goes to Padua to study. He gets a room in "an old edifice" and sees on the wall the coat of arms of a nobleman whom Dante had placed in Hell. This supernatural foreboding is supplemented by warnings from his landlady and by a local professor named Baglioni about the mysterious man who owns the adjacent garden which Giovanni can see from his room. The man is the renegade scientist, Rappacini, who has perverted nature by growing all sorts of poisonous plants, including ones created by him. Another of his creations, his daughter Beatrice, lives in the garden and is, in her own words, a sister to the plants.

Just as nature is inverted, so are the humans. Dante's Beatrice guided him to heaven, but this Beatrice will guide Giovanni to hell. God had created the Garden of Eden, but the demonic Rappacini has created this garden; *all* the trees in this garden are forbidden. Giovanni is taken by Beatrice's beauty and contrives to meet her, only to be warned by her about staying too long in the garden. By living in the garden and inhaling its fragrances, Beatrice has become inured to the plants' poisons, but she cannot live outside the garden. Giovanni ignores the good wishes of those warning him and returns regularly to the garden, until he realizes to his horror that he, too, has become acclimated to it. Unknown to Giovanni, Rappacini has planned all of this so that his daughter and the young student might propagate a new race. Professor Baglioni, who has warned Giovanni, prepares what he claims is an antidote. Beatrice takes it, but her poisoned body cannot accept it and she dies. Her redemptive death gets her to heaven, while Giovanni is stuck in Rappacini's hell.

Traditional Gothic elements are there—a foreign environment, a historical setting, a man of mystery, a garden which replaces the deep woods of other stories—but Hawthorne also deals primarily with evil in a biblical way. Rappacini is a corrupt figure, manipulating nature and using his own daughter, whom he should love, to do so. The garden motif suggests that Rappacini, like Victor Frankenstein, is playing God but, like Victor, he lacks the love which God has for his creatures. On a lesser scale, Giovanni also represents evil. In his arrogance, he ignores the warnings he receives, the conventional ones (from his landlady and Baglioni) and even the unconventional one (the coat of arms). His arrogance does not match Rappacini's, but it is there. Both Rappacini and Giovanni have Faustian characteristics.

Another variation on the Faustian theme is *The Strange Case of Dr. Jeckyll and Mr. Hyde* by the Scottish writer Robert Louis Stevenson (1850–94). Once again the main character is a scientist and once again he wishes to play God by creating a human being. But, this time, the creation is literally in the image of the creator. Frankenstein had created a child, and Rappacini had used his own daughter for his experiments, but Dr. Jeckyll turned to the other side of his own personality.

Henry Jeckyll is a successful London physician who wants to know more than science could tell him. He wonders why humans do evil deeds. He reasons that evil represents a distinct part of the personality which could be separated from the good part. Through a series of experiments, he succeeds in separating the two parts with Jeckyll as the good one while the evil one takes the form of Edward Hyde, a play on words since he represents the shadow side of the personality which we "hide" in daily life.

Paralleling Frankenstein and Rappacini, Jeckyll conducts his research in secret, cutting himself off from his friends. His chemical formula, which he ingests, turns him into Hyde, a demonic figure, both physically and psychologically. Like the devil, Hyde is completely evil. He has no good traits, and he is very cunning. Jeckyll once refers to him as a "familiar," the name for the devil in the form of a small animal which the witches had been accused of keeping around the house. Hyde leaves Jeckyll's house and wanders about London at night, returning before morning to take a second dose of the formula which restores Jeckyll's body and personality. Stevenson used the slippery slope. Initially Hyde is physically small, commits minor brutal acts, and is willing to return to Jeckyll's form. But as time goes on, Hyde commits a murder; Jeckyll notices that Hyde is becoming physically larger; and Hyde becomes increasingly reluctant to turn back into Jeckyll—all indications that the newly released evil is overtaking the good.

Jeckyll realizes that he must do something, but, like all Faustian figures, he foolishly assumes that he will remain in control of the situation. He soon discovers a horrible problem. He has run out of the ingredients to make the formula which returns Hyde to Jeckyll, and he cannot find new ingredients. In terror, he realizes that Hyde will soon take over, once and for all. Falling into despair, Jeckyll commits suicide, but only after writing an account of what he had done. When a friend breaks into his laboratory in search of him, he finds the body not of Jeckyll but of Hyde.

Jeckyll has done what no one else had, but he is doomed. Jeckyll wishes to play God by imitating divine power, but he never recognizes that playing God requires more than just power. The Faustian stories have the same theme of humans who think that knowledge and power are enough, only to find that they have unleashed forces beyond their comprehension.

This theme has lasted well beyond the nineteenth century. It is a staple of modern science fiction movies to show some scientist, such as an archaeologist or anthropologist, ignoring the warnings of native people about opening a sacred tomb or deciphering a sacred text and thus unleashing forces beyond her or his control.

It would be unfair to the Gothic writers to expect them to have discussed evil in the same way that Leibniz or Hume did, but, as the Medieval treatment of the Other showed, the understanding of evil was always more than just the theoretical one. Shelley, Hawthorne, and Stevenson turned the Enlightenment hero, the scientist, into a villain. The *philosophes* wished to banish all ignorance, but the Gothic writers showed that all that is not knowledge is not necessarily ignorance. They stubbornly insisted that there are some places where the lights of reason and knowledge should not shine. The shadow side of the personality is not inherently evil; it can also represent the unknown, but it must be accepted and respected as the unknown. Frankenstein, Rappacini, and Jeckyll fell precisely because they wanted to shine the light into a natural darkness and because they had the Enlightenment arrogance of subjecting all things to reason.

The Gothic writers did not specify where the investigation of Nature should stop—who could? But they did revise the Enlightenment view of humanity. The *philosophes* emphasized the human to free it from what they perceived as the tyranny of religion; although rejecting conventional religion, the Gothic writers realized that the human must include some mystery and that something beyond the human ken must remain central to our existence.

* * *

In the late nineteenth century another group of writers took a long, hard look at human evil, but they did not use Gothic devices or Romantic themes, nor did they rely upon theistic explanations. Instead they investigated, sometimes in brutal detail, purely human motives and drives. Yet the person who most mercilessly scrutinized human evil was himself a believer and a devout member of the Russian Orthodox Church.

The Russian Fyodor Dostoyevsky (1821–81) began his public life as an antireligious revolutionary who was arrested by the czarist government. After four years of imprisonment in Siberia, he returned to civilization and eventually to religion. He believed in the importance of spiritual redemption, and he had little use for the liberal Westernizing views gaining currency among Russian intellectuals. In his novel *The Possessed,* he scathingly portrayed supposedly enlightened writers and poets as hopeless pedants. In his classic *The Brothers Karamazov,* the vulgar but clever old man Fyodor Karamazov makes a fool of a Westernized Russian who is contemptuous of both Russian culture and religion. Dostoyevsky, who had frequent fits of despondency, saw little in the world to justify the optimistic views of Western liberals.

In *Crime and Punishment,* he portrays evil as the great lie. The central character, the student Raskolnikov, believes that humanity consists of two kinds of persons, the harmless drudges who will do nothing in life except replace themselves and those gifted few who will contribute something new to the world. Naturally, Raskolnikov sees himself as one of the latter, but his aspiring greatness is retarded by his poverty. This is intolerable, and, as a man of destiny, he has the right to do what is necessary to get out of poverty. The moral law observed by the harmless drudges does not apply to him. He murders his landlady, a loathsome greedy woman whom Raskolnikov considers to be vermin and deserving of her miserable death. But during the crime, the woman's semi-retarded sister stumbles on the scene, and the student, to protect himself, kills her too, even though she has done him no harm.

After the act, Raskolnikov sees himself in a different light. He is not a great man but a murderer. The truth of what he has done haunts him, and a shrewd police inspector, convinced that the student is the killer, provokes him constantly, feeding on his guilt. Some of the most powerful chapters in the book trace the power of guilt wearing away at Raskolnikov, until he finally breaks down and admits to the inspector what he has done. He not only admits what he has done but also what he is, comparing himself to vermin, the designation he had used for the landlady. He goes to prison, but not before he finds redemption through the love of Sonia, an impoverished young woman and a Mary Magdalene figure, who prostitutes herself to feed her family. She too violates the moral code, but she does it for food and not for some imaginary greatness.

In *The Brothers Karamazov,* the skeptic Ivan confronts his half-brother, Alyosha, a devout young man who personifies the values Dostoyevsky believed that the world needed. Alyosha takes his religion seriously and tries to love everyone. But Ivan considers Alyosha to be naïve, especially on the topic of evil. In the novel's fourth section, "Pro and Contra," Ivan asks Alyosha about a series of true and contemporary crimes, especially against children. Ivan wants to know how Alyosha can believe in God in the face of such atrocities. Anticipating one traditional Western argument, that such evils are just a small part of the divine plan and do not negatively impact that plan, Ivan asks Alyosha if the creation of the entire cosmos required the torture and death of only one infant, would he consent to it? Alyosha replies that he would not, but he goes on to insist that any act, no matter how barbarous, can be forgiven by the God who sent his only son to suffer and die for humans. Ivan responds that he has been waiting for Alyosha to bring Christ into the discussion and begins his famous tale of "The Grand Inquisitor."

The Grand Inquisitor is an elderly Spanish cardinal, a representative of the Roman Catholic Church and thus of Western culture and attitudes. The cardinal and his associates rule like dictators because they have figured out that people really do not want freedom but instead want to be told what to do. The inquisitor acts in the name of Christ, but he is actually in league with the devil. To the churchman's horror, Christ returns to earth and is venerated by the people. The cardinal has him arrested and brought to trial.

The inquisitor explains to Jesus that times have changed since he last came to earth. The organization founded in his name has matured and come to terms with the world. It wants to make people happy, which it can do only by deluding them. The inquisitor is an atheist. He warns Jesus that he should not trouble people with ideas of freedom and responsibility—better to let the Church tell them what to do. The inquisitor threatens Jesus with death, but, perhaps realizing that Jesus can do little in a world dominated by the Church, he decides to let him go with just a warning. Christ was as silent before the inquisitor as he was before the Roman governor Pontius Pilate (and as Alyosha was before Ivan) but, before leaving the inquisitor's presence, Jesus kisses him. Ivan assures Alyosha that although the kiss glows in the cardinal's breast, he does not change his views.

In a later chapter Ivan has another conversation, this time with the devil. Ivan does not believe that the devil exists, except in his own disturbed mind. Significantly, Dostoyevsky never makes it clear whether the reader is supposed to agree with Ivan or not. Like Goethe's devil, this one makes it clear that he no longer uses horns and claws but rather works in people's minds. The devil dresses like a slightly impoverished country gentleman, someone not to be taken too seriously but impossible to avoid. The devil tells Ivan a story which Ivan himself had invented. The man accuses the devil of cheating, but the devil mocks him, claiming that he does not even know who speaks within him— Ivan or Satan. The devil quotes a fictional Jesuit who claims that God has a great plan which mortals do not understand, an argument which the atheist Ivan cannot accept but which, by claiming God has a plan, derides Ivan's attempts to make sense of a godless world. Dostoyevsky had little use for Russians who adopted Western European secularist values without thinking through the consequences of such values and without looking at what Russia and its church offered them. Ivan's hallucination of Satan is no passing fancy in the story. This symbol of the new Russian intellectual is, in fact, going mad.

For Dostoyevsky, there was no answer to the question of evil which he examined so minutely. But if there was no answer, there was redemption, won for humans through the goodness of people like Alyosha. Although Dostoyevsky believed in God and the devil and although some of his characters believed in one or both, he did not use either to explain evil, choosing instead to examine its workings in the human psyche. Others followed his lead, although none has matched him. Catholics and Protestants join the Orthodox in seeing Dostoyevsky as one of the great Christian writers of any epoch.

His younger contemporary, Leo Tolstoy (1828–1910), took on the question of human evil most directly in his novella *The Kreuzer Sonata* (1891). The main character, Pozdnischeff, has murdered his wife. To the unnamed narrator, he recounts how it happened. Although Tolstoy slips in criticisms of the mores of aristocratic Russian life, the novella deals primarily with jealousy and hatred. Pozdnischeff, a rural aristocrat, has a very low opinion of women and believes that he had done his wife a favor by marrying beneath his social station. They tried for a while to maintain the semblance of a marriage, but both soon lost any love or trust for one another. Since social mores demanded that they have children, they did, but the children brought them no joy. The two slowly succumbed to mutual hatred and distrust; they even used their children to get at one another. The cynical Pozdnischeff has no use for the Church whose marriage ceremony did nothing more than authorize him to take a wife. He likewise has no use for society which demanded that he and his wife maintain this loathsome charade. When his wife had finally had enough and begun an affair with another man, Pozdnischeff killed her, but only after the excruciating self-torture of jealousy, fomented not by love but by an anger that someone who belonged to him could turn to another man. Like few other books, this one deserves to be called difficult to read, yet it is difficult to put down as Tolstoy pulls the reader more and more into the appalling barrenness of the couple's lives. These two needed no supernatural temptation to be evil.

In the United States, Dostoyevsky's contemporary Herman Melville (1821–91) examined human evil in his novel *Moby Dick* (1851), focusing on Ahab, captain of the American whaling ship *Pequod*. The Hebrew Bible recounts the story of Ahab, an Israelite king who marries a pagan princess named Jezebel and who introduces the worship of pagan deities into Israel. Ahab not only practices idolatry but even descends to human sacrifice, permitting the offering of children victims to pagan gods. Melville's Ahab practices an idolatry of his own. His goal in life is not happiness or reconciliation with his fellow humans but rather the destruction of Moby Dick, the white whale who, on a previous voyage, had robbed Ahab of one of his legs. Ahab's hatred drives him on, and it replaces all other values for him. He cheats his employers who expect that he will hunt whales and bring back as much whale oil as possible, rather than scour the oceans in pursuit of one beast. More importantly, Ahab betrays his crew. The ship's captain had almost absolute power on his ship, but this father figure, like his biblical namesake, was willing to sacrifice children for his own ends. The Bible gives a brief account of Ahab's actions, but Melville goes into great depth. Like Tolstoy, Melville shows us a character being eaten away by his own hatred. This new Ahab kills his children not immediately but slowly, spreading his hate among them, so that they share his mania to get the whale. Moby Dick becomes the Other, the being on whom humans focus the blame for their own shortcomings. Melville uses some traditional demonic images—Moby Dick is the sea monster, Ahab is an idolator—but the evil he portrays is purely human.

Toward the end of his life the American author Mark Twain (1835–1910) wrote a very bleak story entitled "The Mysterious Stranger." He set the tale in sixteenth-century Austria. His central character was a young boy, Theodor, and the mysterious stranger of the title was the devil. Yet Twain had no interest in demonic evil but rather in how the devil could bring out the worst in humans. He used some traditional themes. Theodor and his friends try to use the devil's power for positive ends, only to find that the mysterious stranger thwarts all their good intentions. As Marlowe, Milton, and so many others had taught, no good can come from evil.

But Twain's real interest lay in how the human characters dealt with one another. The people of the village believed in witches and were ready to burn them; they showed little pity for the poor; they hypocritically abused the hospitality of a family they loathed but to whom Satan had given material prosperity. Satan is a liar, but his lies serve to bring out the truth about people. If Satan does speak the truth, it is to convict humans of their crimes. "Monarchies, aristocracies, and religions are all based upon that large defect in your race—the individual's distrust of his neighbor, and his desire, for safety's or comfort's sake, to stand well in his neighbor's eye." When Satan has finished disillusioning Theodor about his neighbors and about his society, he then disillusions the boy about the whole of creation. He tells Theodor that "life itself is only a vision, a dream," and that "nothing exists," not even the boy himself.

Twain closed the story with a bitter denunciation of God by Satan:

> A God who could make good children as easily as bad, yet preferred to make bad ones; who could have made every one of them happy, yet never made a single happy one; who made them prize their bitter life, yet stingily cut it short; . . . who mouths justice and invented hell—mouths mercy and invented hell . . . who mouths morals to other people and has none himself; who frowns upon crimes and commits them all; . . . and, finally, with altogether divine obtuseness, invites this poor, abused slave to worship him ("Mysterious Stranger," 121).

"The Mysterious Stranger" presents Twain's views in the starkest terms: God does not exist and human life has no purpose since all existence is an illusion.

Although not an author of fiction, the German philosopher Friedrich Nietzsche (1844–1900) wrote in a vivid style which still catches the imagination of the reader. He is famous for his aphorisms ("There was only one Christian, and he died on the cross"), but these barbed one-liners should not detract from his greater significance as the writer who forced the West to consider the consequences of the Enlightenment, of science, and of the growing emphasis upon the material rather than the spiritual in Western life.

Nietzsche believed that the God of the West had died. For Nietzsche, God had never existed, but now the deity had died for all those who used to rely upon him and who based their idea of goodness upon obedience to his commandments. Since ordinary people did not wish to face up to that, they hid behind conventional ideas and morality. But Nietzsche, a personally lonely man, insisted that humans had to face the fact that they are alone in the cosmos and that there was no supernatural being to make things right or to justify ills.

He used themes familiar from the Enlightenment. The Greeks lived before the Christians convinced people that they were born corrupted by original sin, and so the Greeks appreciated humanity. Furthermore, all believers frame humanity against a divine backdrop and thus automatically devalue humanity. But Nietzsche took up these themes with a new vigor and a new urgency. During the Enlightenment, many Western intellectuals were theists, and the established churches played a great role in daily life. Nietzsche recognized that in his day few intellectuals were theists, especially after the rise of socialism and capitalism, both practically if not theoretically godless, and the widespread acceptance of the theory of evolution. Nietzsche believed that the West was spiritually bankrupt and in need of a new message.

He employed an apt literary device, the prophet Zarathustra, who achieved wisdom on top of a mountain, thus paralleling Moses and Jesus, and who came down to bring the message to people who did not want to hear it. Zarathustra taught the people that God was dead and that they must learn to live in a world without him. Few received the message, Nietzsche believed, not only because of its strangeness and the difficult demands it would make, but also because entrenched institutions hypocritically fought it. The leaders of the churches were not fools. They knew they preached an empty message, but, like Dostoyevsky's inquisitor, they believed that people wanted that message. (The endlessly critical Nietzsche admired the Russian novelist.) Christianity preached a herd mentality and a herd morality. Christian virtues, such as humility and obedience, urged people to deny their true selves and take up negative attitudes toward normal human desires. The greatest crime for a Christian was to rise above the herd, and the few who dared to do it were put down by the establishment and by the rest of the herd who feared any challenge to their own values. Son and grandson of Lutheran pastors, Nietzsche made the Reformer an especial target, believing that Luther's obsession with his imagined guilt prevented the Renaissance from turning European culture away from Christianity.

Nietzsche had a gift for choosing titles for his books, and one of the most striking is *Beyond Good and Evil,* written in 1887. The title says it all. True humans must rise above what society has labeled good and evil because those labels reflect the herd mentality of the churches and of the weak. In a world of false values, the true human must exercise a will to power, the drive to be fully human regardless of the costs. Nietzsche used a daring term, the overman *(der Übermensch),* to describe the ideal person of this godless era.

The overman rises above the passions (echoing Nietzsche's love for ancient Greece) and the trivia of daily life. The overman exercises creativity; Nietzsche repeatedly emphasized that the artist, not the tyrant, is the true overman. Most important of all, the overman could look into the void of a meaningless world and still affirm the goodness of humanity. He knows who he is, and he rejoices in that. The overman does not fear evil but rather incorporates it into his own being because he has risen above the petty divisions which plague the herd. But does he not experience loneliness and even depression when his will to power cuts him off from others? Yes, but it is the loneliness of authenticity. The overman is, to use another of Nietzsche's book titles, *Human, All Too Human.* Better to face the world as it is and affirm one's humanity than to hide in the herd and pretend that all is fine. Besides, the herd mentality ultimately fails since all people, sooner or later, will encounter some situation which will reveal their hollow values for what they are. Yet the overman also surpasses the human. A perfect blend of being and instinct, he represents what humans can aspire to, if they could only first recognize their true humanity and free themselves of stultifying chains of religion, fear, and weakness.

For Nietzsche, as for so many other earlier thinkers, evil is false, hollow, and untrue to human nature. Yet many of those thinkers saw human nature as a creation of God and believed that humans are most true to their real nature when they obey him and when they live with him in a blessed afterlife. Nietzsche insisted that humanity had to grow up, to abandon the myth of a beneficent deity, and to recognize that this life is all that there is. Only when we do that can we be true to human nature. Evil is that which distracts us from being fully human in a godless world. It was a small step from Evil to the greatest evil. For Nietzsche, Christianity is evil because it deludes people into thinking that the world has meaning outside the individual, that a kindly divine being presides over creation, that this being has a secret plan which justifies all the horrors humans experience, and that a life of self-negation, of denying those drives which make us truly human, is the only life which is good. The philosopher had to dispel such illusions. What for so many people had been the chief if not the only antidote to evil he now proclaimed to be itself evil.

* * *

The nineteenth century had taken notions of evil a long way. The Romantic and especially the Gothic writers had attacked the Enlightenment icon, the scientist, and had claimed that all humans, regardless of their exalted profession, still have to question and recognize the forces which push them on. Led by Dostoyevsky, writers in the second half of the century had examined in detail how human, not supernatural, evil corrupts us. Dostoyevsky considered Christianity an antidote to evil, but Nietzsche set up a new ideal, the human who affirms humanity in a godless world, and defined evil as that which threatens to hold humans back. Enlightenment values had suffered a setback, but Christianity had suffered a greater one. The Enlightenment had been able to deal with the human in treating of evil, but nineteenth-century Christianity still had to affirm original sin as evil's ultimate cause.

Ironically, science, the great Enlightenment weapon against Christianity, was finally to free it from an Augustinian conception of original sin and allow it to pursue new understandings of evil, while simultaneously changing secular concepts of evil.

Chapter 13

Science, Evil, and Original Sin

> *The survival of the fittest.*
> —Herbert Spencer, *Principles of Biology*

In the nineteenth century scientific work had significant impact on the question of evil, largely because Western Christians held to the doctrine of original sin in a basically Augustinian format: Adam and Eve, parents of the human race, had committed an actual sin in an actual garden. As long as Genesis kept its historicity, original sin, the classic Christian explanation of evil, remained viable.

Belief in the physical reality of the Garden of Eden had important scientific consequences. The book of Genesis had traced the succession of patriarchs from Adam to Noah and had even given their ages. After the Flood, it was not a long jump to Abraham and thus into history, however obscure the tales of the Hebrew patriarchs might have been. The creation was not that distant in time. Conscientious historians, using the Bible along with Greek and Roman evidence, had tried to determine how old the world was. James Ussher (1581–1656), an Anglican bishop, placed the creation in 4004 B.C.E., a date which won wide acceptance in his day and which many conservative Christians still accept. (Many bibles published as late as 1900 have the marginal notation, "4004 B.C." next to Genesis 1:1.) This biblical chronology meant that, circa 1800, the world was less than six thousand years old, and when scientists wished to examine the natural history of the planet, they had to work within that framework. Any evidence pointing to an older world simply could not be reliable or had been interpreted incorrectly.

The historicity of Genesis had another important consequence: the fixity of species. Plant and animal species came into existence when

God created them during the six-day creation, and they had remained unchanged ever since. Although even in 1800 people knew that some species could be modified, such as horses bred for speed, they considered these minor variations that did not represent any real change.

But Genesis contains the religious traditions of an ancient people, not physical accounts of how the world began, and inevitably a crisis arose between the literal interpretation of Genesis and scientific advances, particularly in geology.

Everyone knew that the physical world had changed over time. Many people had wondered how the fossilized sea shells could be found embedded in mountains. Scientists offered several explanations, with catastrophism being the one most in harmony with Genesis. This theory taught that major catastrophes, such as volcanic eruptions and earthquakes, had altered the earth's surface over the centuries. The greatest catastrophe was the Genesis Flood, when water high enough to cover mountains surged and flooded across the entire planet, ravaging as it went.

In the late eighteenth and early nineteenth centuries scientists observed both the distribution of fossils in exposed ancient strata and the forces constantly at work in nature, such as wind and rain. Some concluded that the earth had changed not from occasional catastrophes but from the uniform workings of nature and that the world had to be older than 5800 years. The Englishman Charles Lyell (1797–1885) completely discredited catastrophism, and established uniformitarianism, the theory that uniform, observable processes determined the physical condition of the earth. Significantly, Lyell, a devout Christian, insisted that geologists had to rely upon the evidence gained from investigation and could not let other nonscientific considerations influence what they did. Genesis would not determine their conclusions.

Modern geologists speak of billions of years of natural history, a sharp contrast to the earliest geologists who wondered about tens of thousands of years, but it was no small task to break through the biblical chronology. Once that was done, however, no limit prevented geologists from pushing back the age of the earth.

Geologic investigation challenged not only the age of the earth but also the fixity of species. The fossil evidence made it clear that some species had become extinct, which threatened the notion that all species survived from Eden until the modern world. The same evidence further suggested that some species had come into being later than others, contradicting the notion that all species came into being simultaneously at the creation. Finally, the fossil evidence also suggested that some species had changed. Scientists discovered animal remains which looked like modern species but which also differed from them. As the evidence piled up, it looked more and more as if some species had altered through the ages, but that was impossible. How could two dogs mate and produce an animal which was not as much a dog as its parents? Furthermore, the great Swedish taxonomist Carl Linneaus (1707–78) had classified natural life according to genus and species, and all life fit into one of those categories. Fixity of species would be far more difficult to displace than the biblical chronology had been.

We know today that evolution held the answer and that Charles Darwin (1809–82) made evolution scientifically feasible. Earlier scholars like the Frenchman Jean Baptiste Lamarck (1744–1829) and Darwin's own grandfather Erasmus Darwin (1731–1802) had argued for the evolution of species, but they had neither the mechanism to explain it nor the time for it to happen. Charles Darwin certainly had the latter. Lyell influenced Darwin more than any other scientist did, and evolution's founder took the geologist's most important book, *Principles of Geology,* on his momentous voyage on the *Beagle* (1831–36). Darwin recognized that evolutionary change would occur slowly, and the constantly increasing age of the earth meant that there had indeed been enough time for evolution to occur. Darwin also determined the mechanism for evolution, natural selection. Darwin's 1859 book *The Origin of Species* provided massive evidence for it.

Many people, including important scientists as well as clerics, had reservations about some specifics of Darwin's theories or even rejected the theory outright, but by the end of the nineteenth century no educated person could doubt that species had changed. Evolution and uniformitarian geology had demonstrated that the opening chapters of Genesis did not contain an account of the physical creation of the world and its inhabitants. Some Christian apologists contended that the seven days of creation actually symbolized seven geological epochs. Since humanity appears last in the story of creation, Genesis parallels the notion that humans appeared last in evolution. But these were obviously attempts to save Genesis and not credible scientific theories. They did not even make sense within the biblical context. For example, if the Hebrew word for "day" means a geological epoch in Genesis, does it also mean that if King David traveled for two "days" that he actually traveled for two geological epochs? That "day" meant epoch was simply special pleading.

The consequences of evolution were enormous for all Christians for the understanding of evil. If the Genesis creation account was not historical, then clearly Adam and Eve did not exist as actual persons and so they could not have committed the sin of eating the forbidden fruit. Evil in the world did not arise from a prehistoric sin. Original sin could not refer to an actual event.

Natural selection, as distinct from evolution, reinforced this notion. Species survived because they were able to adapt to their environment.

This often meant that they had to edge out other species for space and food. The result was, in the memorable phrase of the English philosopher Herbert Spencer (1820–1903), "the survival of the fittest." The survival of some species often meant the decline or even extinction of others. This endless struggle had gone on since the first appearance of life. Augustinian Christians believed that all of nature had lived in harmony until original sin; violence, illness, and death had all entered the world as a consequence of that. But fossil evidence had proved that animals and plants had been competing with one another for food and space long before humanity made its appearance on the planet, and theory of natural selection meant that they would continue to do so. It was also clear that carnivorous animals had always fed upon other animals; violence and death did not enter the world with some human sin. Contrary to biblical literalism, the lion had never lain down with the lamb.

Just as the cosmological revolution had removed the earth from its special place in the center of the universe and set it among the planets which revolved around the sun, the biological revolution of the nineteenth century placed humanity firmly within the sphere of living beings and no longer at its apex. No one could deny the unique place of humanity in the world, but neither could anyone deny that humans are subject to the same forces which act upon other living beings. Humanity as we know it did not emerge fully formed from the hand of God but evolved along with the other creatures of earth. This was more than just one more nail in the coffin for the historicity of Genesis; it had tremendous if temporary impact even on the secular understanding of evil.

Genesis described an ideal human community, at least before the Fall. No one needed Malthus or Darwin to prove that life was a struggle for survival, but theists taught that this struggle was a perversion of what should be, that God intended humans to live in harmony. Yet some nineteenth-century social thinkers suggested that since survival of the fittest was natural, it was the way life *should* be. That primitive indigenous peoples could not resist European imperialists simply proved that they could not compete. This was a scientific fact of life, something to be accepted as natural rather than deplored as evil. This kind of thinking acquired the name Social Darwinism. It has a familiar ring—what is natural is good—but Rousseau intended nothing like imperialism. Amazingly, such thinking could go well beyond imperialism. In nature, since only the fittest would survive, only they propagate offspring, thus guaranteeing the survival of the species. Nature would not allow a slow rabbit or a blind bird to live. Yet one species did allow the weak to survive, and in so doing jeopardized its own survival. While such thinking never reached recommendations to kill off people with disabilities, it did stand partly behind theories of eugenics as well as questions about the value of helping society's marginalized whose unfortunate condition could be cited as proof that they were not among the fittest.

This attitude still survives in some social and political circles, but it has never won over large numbers of people because of its sheer harshness. Furthermore, people can legitimately ask, should humans adopt survival of the fittest as their ethos? In one sense, we are part of the natural world, but in another, we are distinct. We lament that distinction when we see a polluted stream, but we rejoice in it when modern medical science saves us from natural debilities such as poor eyesight or hearing. Social Darwinism had its fifteen minutes of fame, but it too passed.

Darwinism also dealt a serious blow to nineteenth-century natural theology. Some important Christian thinkers, especially in England, had simply ignored Hume, and the Anglican William Paley (1743–1805) continued to insist that the harmony of nature reflected a divine plan. But natural selection argued against a divine plan. Darwin said that there was selection, but no rational being was making it. Nature marched indifferently through the millennia, and a natural world filled with mortal competition for food and living space was hardly harmonious. Trying to explain earthquakes and predatory animals as negative elements which still fit into a beneficent divine plan interested few people. A previously important theory of evil faded away. Some Christian thinkers tried to revive natural theology in the twentieth century, but it does not figure largely even in theistic explanations of evil.

Darwin considered himself a biologist, but he knew that his researches would have a wider impact, especially upon religious thinking. We cannot consider the manifold impact of Darwinism upon religion, but we can sum up its impact on the notion of evil. Combined with geology, it killed off the classical notion of original sin. Adam, Eve, the Garden, and the fruit never existed, nor did the serpentine tempter. The origin of evil in the world could not be blamed on the devil, who is not mentioned in Genesis but who had been identified with the serpent for generations. Violence, illness, and death did not enter the world because of a prehistoric human sin but had been around long before humans existed; these sad phenomena occur naturally in the world and can be independent of human action. Evil did not cause disharmony in the world; that, too, had always existed.

Augustine had been wrong; the perfect cosmos had not been broken; it had never existed. After 1400 years, the Augustinian version of original sin had ceased to be credible.

Not all Christian denominations reacted against Darwin. Philosophically-oriented Roman Catholics responded more easily than evangelical Protestants did, while more liberal Protestant sects did not defend biblical literalism. Some Christians simply refused to accept the consequences of evolution for biblical literalism and evolved into modern fundamentalists. Most others were deeply shaken, devastated at the loss of biblical certainty yet fearful of challenging the new science. This was a new world for them; natural theology had insisted that science aided religion. Many Christians did not like how natural theologians avoided the Bible in order to find God in the natural world, but at least they had not attacked the Scriptures. On the contrary, they had insisted that science supported the Bible, even if not always explicitly. Nineteenth-century Christians had grown up trusting science, and now science had turned against them. Or had it?

Some liberal Christians simply baptized evolution, claiming that God used that method to create and act in the world, and this has become the view of most modern Christians whose scientific education convinces them that evolution occurs and whose faith convinces them that God still acts somehow in the world. But the liberals jumped on board the evolutionary bandwagon a bit too quickly. There was still the problem of Genesis. Christians and Jews could not simply discard the Bible; they had to explain it. Many nineteenth-century theists acknowledged that the *philosophes* had scored some heavy points in their criticism of the Bible in general and the opening chapters of Genesis in particular. When geology and evolution made disbelief in the historicity of Genesis 1–11 intellectually acceptable, religious scholars successfully reworked their understanding of those chapters, and they did so using other new sciences.

Because religion requires faith and because so much of religion deals with the spiritual, the study of religion is not always taken seriously by secularist scholars, yet, when done well, it is just as demanding as any science. In order to study the book of Genesis, scholars had to learn paleography, archaeology, history, as well as Hebrew and Greek. From the nineteenth century onward, they have had to learn other ancient languages as well. As anyone who has studied these languages and disciplines knows, faith and spirituality play no role in learning them.

The rationalism of the seventeenth and eighteenth centuries had affected biblical studies. The Dutch Jewish scholar Baruch de Spinoza (1632–77) shocked both Jewish and Christian opinion by suggesting that scholars should study the Bible as they would any other piece of ancient literature. Since no one studied Homer or Aeschylus from a theological point of view, this meant that the Bible should be studied without reference to any religious tradition, Jewish or Christian. Not surprisingly, Spinoza published his views anonymously at first. A century later, at the height of the Enlightenment, Edward Gibbon could do with ease what Spinoza could do only with difficulty. In *The Decline and Fall of the Roman Empire,* he used Christian literature as just one more source for understanding Roman history. Conservative clerics objected, but soon Christian scholars began adopting these methods themselves. Other Enlightenment thinkers besides Gibbon took the same approach and applied it to the Bible. The German poet J. G. Herder (1744–1803) declared that the Bible was a book written by men for men and that the Bible should be studied in the same manner as any literary work.

Modern biblical scholarship started in Germany, and it first centered upon the New Testament and especially upon the Gospels. The *philosophes* had made belief in miracles intellectually outdated. Natural theologians discreetly avoided them, but since Christianity is founded upon Christ who is known primarily through the miracle-laden Gospels, the German biblical scholars rightly recognized that they had to interpret the Gospels somehow. Initially they succumbed to facile rationalizing. Schleiermacher suggested that the resurrection was actually Jesus' awakening from a kind of lethargy. In 1828 his contemporary, H. E. Paulus, theorized that the angels of the nativity story were actually phosphorescence. The next generation eschewed rationalizing the text in favor of understanding what its authors intended. Ferdinand Baur (1792–1860) claimed in 1847 that the Gospels emerged from struggles between various early Christian groups, while David Strauss (1808–74) argued that Jesus was a country wise man whose followers had turned him into a wonderworker.

These views offended public opinion, but they also prepared for a scholarly if not a popular acceptance of what geology and evolution would do to the literal meaning of Genesis. Jewish and Christian scholars continued to believe that God had inspired the Bible's first book, but the scientific discoveries confirmed for them that they had to find another way besides traditional literalism to interpret its meaning.

W.M.L. de Wette (1780–1849) focused on a historical question—how did the Bible develop in the history of Israel? Julius Wellhausen (1844–1918) created the documentary hypothesis, that is, that Genesis (and other books) preserve documents from different traditions, and this phenomenon explains why some verses contradict each other on the literal level. Hermann Gunkel (1862–1932) contended that the Hebrew creation myth and other material in Genesis derived at least partially from parallel pagan accounts. He also tried to look behind the text to trace the development of oral traditions. There were many other writers and theories, and later scholarship modified or discarded most of them, but clearly biblical exegetes were discarding literalism in favor of understanding Genesis in its historical environment and literary forms, the path exegesis has followed ever since.

Another solution to the problem of understanding Genesis lay not in the text but in the earth. The nineteenth century saw the first great age of Middle Eastern archaeology. The archaeologists discovered texts, written with symbols such as animals and plants (hieroglyphics) or with wedged-shaped impressions originally made in wet clay (cuneiform). At first scholars could only stare in wonder at them, but soon they moved toward decipherment, thanks ultimately not to another scholar but to an ambitious general, Napoleon Bonaparte. Scholars on his Egyptian campaign discovered the Rosetta Stone, a plaque with three ancient languages, one Greek and the other two native Egyptian ones. In 1822, a French scholar, Jean-François Champollion, used the famous stone to decipher Egyptian hieroglyphics and open up a whole new world to biblical scholars and ancient historians. In 1837 the English scholar Henry Rawlinson had deciphered Old Persian, and by 1852 Rawlinson had begun translating Babylonian texts. Assyrian texts were next to fall to the interpreters, and in 1872 another English scholar, George Smith, astounded the world by announcing he found a pagan text, older than Genesis, which recounted the story of the Great Flood. The pagan text was a version of the *Epic of Gilgamesh,* the ancient Semitic hero myth.

Ancient pagan literature filled in the background of biblical history, explained biblical customs, demonstrated how the other ancient nations viewed the people Israel, and aided in the decipherment of obscure Hebrew words. Most importantly, by its many parallels to biblical passages, it made it clear that the ancient Israelites were very much products of their era and geography. Biblical scholars stressed then and now that Israel could still be God's chosen people because this was a matter of faith, but as a matter of history, Israel had to be understood in context.

The *Epic of Gilgamesh* broke the back of Genesis literalism for mainline Jews and Christians. Fundamentalists inevitably claimed that the pagan author had stolen material from the Bible and corrupted it with false belief, but scholars knew better. Abraham and his tribe had emerged from a pagan Semitic milieu, and they had kept much of their culture even after they migrated to the land of Canaan. The *Epic of Gilgamesh* had parallels to Eden via a serpent and a plant. It had a character named Enkidu, a wild man who lived in harmony with the animals until he met a woman, and so even the patriarchal values matched. The Flood account in *Gilgamesh* paralleled Genesis even more strongly: the gods decide to destroy the world with a flood but one of the gods warns a good man, Utnapishtim, who builds a boat and brings on board his family and animals; the flood destroys the earth; when the waters subside, the boat lands upon a mountain top, and the grateful Utnapishtim offers a sacrifice to the gods. Significant differences exist between Genesis and the Gilgamesh accounts, but no one can doubt the basic similarities. Discovery and decipherment of the Babylonian creation epic with its account of Tiamat and Marduk and its many parallels to passages in the psalms, prophets, and Job filled in the picture even more. It was not always possible to determine if the pagan text influenced the biblical one or vice versa or whether both were influenced by a yet unknown third source, but no one could doubt that the ancient Israelites interacted heavily with the nations and cultures around them.

But biblical scholars discovered more than facts; they discovered a firm religious attitude. Rationalists use the word "myth" to mean something untrue or a flimsy story about gods and humans, but for ancient peoples a myth opened up to humans a window into the real, into the world of the gods by recounting the deeds of the gods. Myths had great power and deserved reverence. When scholars speak of the opening chapters of Genesis as the Hebrew creation myth, they do not demean it; on the contrary, they recognize its supreme importance in the life of Israel. In that myth can be found the basic beliefs (one god, the goodness of the physical world, humanity in the divine image) of a remarkable ancient people. Scholars also claim that, when properly understood, Genesis can still speak to modern Jews and Christians. But ideas like that sink in slowly. In the nineteenth century only scholars recognized the significance of the decipherment of the ancient pagan texts for understanding the Bible.

Nineteenth-century biblical scholars also profited from an increasing knowledge of religions in Asia and Africa. Many Europeans and Americans went to those continents as imperialists or missionaries, but inevitably some people came to appreciate the traditions of the indigenous peoples. As Christians and Jews learned of other societies with, among other things, primeval couples, flood stories, and sacred plants, they recognized that some elements are simply common to creation myths. They could not say finally whether these similarities are psychological or cultural, but that was not important initially. The parallels to other traditions helped to prove that the ancient Israelites, like all ancient peoples, could only be understood in the context of their age and place. There was nothing wrong with saying that Israel had used myths because every ancient and primitive people did.

A crucial corner had been turned. Biblical theists had finally been freed from the literalism of the creation account. To an extent they had been pushed to that status by the scientists and to a greater extent they had liberated themselves, but liberated they were. At first glance they benefited most from not having to fight a losing battle with evolutionary scientists, a battle which they could not win and which made them look like obscurantists, but they also benefited from no longer having to defend the traditional interpretation of original sin. Evil remained a problem, but at least Christian scholars did not have to tell people that they were all born damned because two prehistoric people had been tempted by a talking snake into taking a bite out of a piece of fruit. To this day their sighs of relief are almost audible.

These new views did not catch on immediately with all scholars, but their impact is clear. In a technical theological treatise, *Institutiones Theologicae Dogmaticae Specialis: De Deo Creatore* (1871), the German Catholic scholar Bernard Jungmann wrote a great deal about original sin. He accepts the historicity of Genesis and defends the seriousness of eating the fruit (*propter perfectionem status primoparentum*—"on account of the perfection of the status of the first parents," 247). Yet the historicity of the Fall is clearly less important than the understanding of human nature and the effects of sin upon it. The treatise makes heavy use of Thomas Aquinas and other earlier writers to explicate the biblical passage so that it fit Catholic tradition. This book is important because it was a typical theological handbook of the late nineteenth century.

Prominent Protestant theologian Isaak Dorner (1809–84), professor at the University of Berlin, took a different approach. In his *A System of Christian Doctrine, ii* (English translation 1883), he wrote much about the nature of sin in the Old Testament but little about Adam and Eve. He believed that sin was not innate in human nature but is derived from human sin—thus following Augustine—but he also discussed philosophical theories of evil, such as human imperfectability, quoting Schleiermacher. It would take a while for mainstream theologians to adopt the new understanding of the Bible into their systems, but its effects were felt before being openly acknowledged.

Gospel scholarship also changed the understanding of evil, although not as dramatically as Genesis scholarship. Since the Enlightenment, religious thinkers had been embarrassed by the devil. The natural theologians and deists had simply ignored him, but many nineteenth-century biblical scholars aggressively attacked his existence. They did so by emphasizing the historical background of the Gospels. Both Jesus and the evangelists lived in an era when people believed in evil spirits, and so the early Christians also believed in evil spirits. Just as moderns do not accept the biblical, geocentric cosmos, why should they accept belief in a devil? The heart of Jesus' teaching must be excerpted from the crude and dated worldview from which it emerged. Naturally, the heart of Jesus' teaching corresponded to the views of nineteenth-century, socially conscious, liberal European Protestants, and thus it did not contradict the findings of modern science. Rosy as this sounded, it overlooked a huge problem: if the Gospel writers believed in the devil, what would be left of the Gospels themselves when demonic stories were exorcised from them? Yet theist intellectuals could not turn back. They were free of the devil and would not yoke themselves to him again, even if much of the Gospels had to be explained away. Conservative Protestants did not always exaggerate when they accused their co-religionists of throwing the baby out with the bath water. But even conservatives felt awkward talking about evil spirits in an age of science.

The Rise of the Social Sciences

The scientific method had been applied successfully to the physical world, and at the end of the nineteenth century scholars applied it to the study of the human race, creating what are commonly called the social sciences: anthropology, sociology, and psychology. These would significantly alter the Western understanding of evil. Their practitioners did not set out to do so, but the result was inevitable. These disciplines have developed considerably since their founding, but their initial impact on evil has had deep and long lasting consequences.

Anthropology literally means the study of human beings, and it has several branches, but we will focus upon social-cultural anthropology, which studies primitive peoples. Modern anthropology was founded by Franz Boas (1858–1942), who trained many famous scholars such as Margaret Mead (1901–78). Technologically advanced peoples had studied primitive peoples for centuries, but not always for scholarly purposes. Diderot wrote about the Tahitians to prove their native nobility and to contrast it with the low morals of the French. But Boas and his school insisted that researchers must eschew any motives other than scholarship. They must especially avoid ethnocentrism, the judging of one group by the standards of another, a very common practice among virtually every people. [Even Darwin could describe the natives of Tierra del Fuego as savages and less close to civilized people than some apes were.]

Anthropologists returned from their field work among primitive peoples with objective reports of their behavior, much of which differed from accepted European and American moral norms. Some of it was not surprising, such as polygamy and polyandry, long known from missionaries' reports. Some of it was also easily understandable, such as public nudity among people living in tropical areas. But other practices included infanticide, self-mutilation, and suttee (the killing of the wife upon the husband's funeral pyre by the husband's relatives). Two centuries before Westerners would have rejected these as the barbarous practices of sinful pagans who ought to be evangelized, but by 1900 their reaction was less religious than scientific. Inevitably, some kept the older view, but others recognized a more serious problem. Westerners could certainly feel revulsion at these practices and even hope that the primitive peoples could be induced to change them, but, regardless of what one thought of such practices, it was obvious that views of good and evil differed considerably in different parts of the world. Such views were more relative than had previously been suspected.

Anthropology did not turn Westerners to relativism, but it did demonstrate that many moral values previously thought to be essentially human or "natural" were in part culturally conditioned.

The French social theorist Auguste Comte (1798–1857) first used the term sociology, and another Frenchman, Emile Durkheim (1858–1917), helped to make the study of social structures and groups a scientific discipline. Sociologists studied social grouping with a depth and reliability unknown before. They proved that humans grow up in a web of relationships, such as family, work, neighborhood, or school, and these relationships impact how we understand our world, including our moral and ethical values. It did not take long before sociology influenced the Western understanding of evil.

The initiation ritual of some urban teenage gangs in the United States requires a boy to endure a beating from other gang members and a girl to have sexual relations with several gang members. "Initiation ritual" sounds like a euphemism or even an excuse for battery and gang rape. This clearly sounds like an evil act, involving the deliberate imposition of suffering upon another sentient being. Or so it seems to those who live outside this environment. If someone grew up in a dangerous neighborhood, membership in a gang could provide protection and a sense of community. For poor children who are despoiled of their humanity by relentless materialism which tells them that they are worth only as much as they possess, gang membership provides an alternative to consumerist culture. It provides a sense of accomplishment, of having made it, of being someone. What outsiders would consider immoral brutality, the gang members would consider the price for admission, a price that many young people from the streets are willing to pay. Their willingness to subject themselves to such acts does not make those acts morally viable, but it does demonstrate that the understanding of good and evil can be affected by social status and group interaction. (In *Monster: The Autobiography of an L. A. Gang Member,* Sanyika Shakur describes such an initiation and his own willingness to endure it in order to "be someone" by belonging to a gang.)

Examples of the importance of the group upon values need not be criminal ones. One member of the country club may be willing to vote for admission for a black person but knows that most other members are opposed, and so he or she votes against admission rather than risk social ostracization. The act may be less brutal than gang violence, but it illustrates the same point: we all grow up with the ethos of our group and accept much of it for life. Even people who turn away from the group they grew up with will usually join another group, sometimes one proclaiming itself alternative or counter-cultural, and they accept the values of that group.

No one doubts today that social background impacts moral judgment. Like anthropology, sociology had demonstrated that the understanding of evil is rarely objective.

Psychology is the disciplined study of human behavior. The history of psychology can legitimately begin with Augustine, whose scathing examination of his desires and failings and hopes appears in such detail in his *Confessions*. Modern psychology began in the nineteenth century, and its best-known practitioner was Sigmund Freud (1856–1939), founder of psychoanalysis. Many modern psychologists have questioned or even rejected much of Freud's and other nineteenth-century theories, but the rise of scientific psychology significantly influenced the Western understanding of evil.

Traditional theories of evil had portrayed people considering good and evil and then opting for one. Anthropology and sociology had made it clear that cultural and social elements affected that decision. Psychology now made it equally clear that a person's immediate background and upbringing had equal if not stronger effects. Psychology also brought into the discussion the concepts of repression and of the unconscious. Any discussion of evil now had to include how people are moved by forces of which they were not even aware, at least not without training or therapy.

The importance of psychology in understanding evil can be seen in many areas; let us choose just one. In recent years the public has become very aware of the appalling phenomenon of spousal and child abuse. As scholars have studied it, one factor has stood out beyond all others. Abusers are very likely to have been abused themselves, usually when they were children. This factor is neither universal nor determinative. Some abusers do not come from that background, and many abused children grow up to be caring adults. Yet the statistics make it clear that an abusive childhood stands behind many incidents of abuse by adults.

These statistics impact the notion of evil because they prove that an abusive childhood has diminished the ability of many people to make a moral judgment, to see abuse as something evil, and to realize that understanding rather than violence is the way to deal with problems. Some people make an immoral judgment to abuse, but others make an amoral judgment; they simply think that violence is an acceptable method of handling marital or family difficulties. Recognizing the psychological background of the abuser does not make child or spousal abuse acceptable or even morally neutral, but it does make it clear that the choice between good and evil acts is almost never an objective one of deciding between two clear alternatives.

To abuse can be added a long list of other evils which people cannot recognize for what they are because their background and upbringing have affected their understanding. This is now largely accepted in society. Media stories routinely point out how the teenage prostitute was seduced by her father or the teenage thief was neglected by his mother. Knowing this background does not cause us to ignore the crimes, but it does explain, at least partially, why they occurred. It will also often mitigate society's view of the offender. No one today would discuss someone's evil acts without considering the psychological factors involved.

Psychology also took aim at sexual concupiscence, for Augustine a major consequence of original sin. Freud particularly was convinced that many psychological problems arose from sexual repression which in turn arose from society's unwillingness to accept full human sexuality. As an atheist, he had no use for original sin; for him, sexual desire was natural to humans and not a consequence of sin. And since sexual desire is natural, trying to repress it is harmful. No one rises above sexual desire, and it was both foolish and abnormal even to try. But there was more. Not only did repression not get rid of sexual desire, it actually channeled it someplace else. Freud's clinical experience convinced him that many problems such as a man's impotence or a mother's inability to nurse a child arose from sexual repression.

Another part of the broken cosmos had been mended. Sexual desire (sexual concupiscence) was not sinful but normal and natural. Freud generally avoided using terms like "good" and "evil," but the implications were clear to others. If sexual desire is natural, sexual repression could not be good. This did not mean that there should be no restrictions on sexual activity—Freud was not de Sade—but it did mean that sexuality no longer had to be hidden in the pages of contraband novels.

Psychology also affected evil by killing off the devil, definitely for most educated people and practically for anyone else, because it explained or, rather, explained away, the last bastion of belief in the devil, human experience. Scientists had no use for the devil in understanding the natural world. The witchcraze proved that belief in him was dangerous. The natural theologians and deists ignored him, and the liberal theists dismissed him as a historical relic. But many people had claimed that Satan had appeared to them. Elitists could dismiss the witness of uneducated people, but the witnesses included such major figures as Martin Luther and the Spanish Catholic mystic Teresa of Avila (1515–82). No one could call them simpletons or fools. But psychologists, especially Freudians, explained such apparitions as consequences of sexual or some other form of repression. They insisted that repressed thoughts do not really go away, they can manifest themselves in a number of ways, such as dreams or impotence. Luther's musings about the devil's causing his constipation, previously considered either earthy (by Protestants) or gross (by Catholics), now led people to wonder about his anal obsession. For Freudians, Teresa's celibacy proved in advance that she was sexually repressed, a view reinforced by her claims that the devil had appeared to her in her cell where her bed was. This was rather rough treatment of famous people, but the psychologists did not shrink from it. Since a nonexistent devil could not have appeared to these people, what else could the explanation have been?

In fact, no one had actually proven the devil did not exist. Providing a psychological explanation for demonic apparitions was one thing, and proving conclusively that a supernatural evil being did not exist was something else. But, conclusive proof or not, the devil disappeared as an actual being among the educated. He remained a symbol of evil but also became a comic figure. Few religious scholars use him to explain either primal or continuing evil; indeed, few even believe in him.

But is this not just a scholarly attitude? What about those polls which show that many people still believe in the devil? Does not the devil continue to live among the believers if not in the university? Maybe, but repeated anecdotal evidence has made me question the sincerity of the interviewees who form the basis of these statistics. Percy Shelley contended that people claim to believe in the devil but will never acknowledge any specific instance of his work. I have lectured about evil to many church groups in the Cleveland area. When we get to psychology and the devil, I ask a simple question of the audience: "If someone told you that the devil was appearing to him or her, how many of you would tell that person to see a minister or rabbi or priest? Please raise your hands." Usually no hands go up; at most, one or two. "Thank you. Now, how many of you would tell that person to seek psychiatric help? Please raise your hands." Usually all or all but one or two hands go up. And these are church audiences.

Admittedly, anecdotal evidence is not strong, and I wish I had more formal evidence. But if my lecture audiences in greater Cleveland are typical of modern believers, and there is no reason to think they are not, then many people who say they believe in the devil do not know what to do when confronted with supposedly specific demonic acts. People can believe in the devil and hesitate to say that he acted in a particular situation, but at some point they have got to believe that he did something specific. Possibly the high percentages of believers in Satan (63 percent of Americans—cf. p. 2) reflect a reluctance of the interviewees to disagree with the Bible or their church's teaching. I simply cannot explain the statistics. (No doubt the figures also include Satanists who supposedly worship the devil, but they are few and would be statistically marginal.)

The social sciences did not solve the question of evil although they did help people to understand many evils. They diminished belief in the devil and they also diminished any lingering belief that when someone chose between a good or evil act, that this person rationally considered two alternatives and made a choice for one. We now know that our culture, social grouping, and personal background impact that choice.

[It is essential to note that modern ministers, rabbis, and priests not only utilize the social sciences but are routinely trained in them, especially psychology.]

Except for biblical scholars, the scientists of the nineteenth century set out to do science and not to deal with religious questions, although they recognized that their work might impact religion. They did not investigate evil per se, but their work demolished the most widespread Christian explanation of it, a literal original sin. Their work also drove the devil largely out of the discussion.

Thanks to the social sciences, the study of evil would fall more and more upon human explanations rather than supernatural ones. We have arrived at the contemporary world.

Chapter 14

Modern Literary Approaches to Evil

> *The candles of the churches are out.*
> —Archibald MacLeish, *J.B.*

The modern explosion of printed books has included literally millions of works of fiction. Many short stories and novels deal with evils, such as murder or betrayal, but far fewer deal with Evil, the force which stands behind the individual evils. Many modern writers have taken pessimistic and even nihilistic views, but their concerns often mirror those of traditional theistic writers. They were also greatly affected by two world wars.

Some early treatments of evil appeared after the First World War, expressing the meaninglessness which life presented for many in the aftermath of the war which destroyed what had been the European order and the enforced international innocence of the United States. In *The Great Gatsby* (1925), F. Scott Fitzgerald portrayed a world of amoral people, anesthetizing themselves nightly at Gatsby's parties, trapped in loveless marriages, and amusing themselves by trying to figure out just who this mysterious man is. Gatsby's funeral attracts few mourners. The "great" man has simply passed into eternal night, and those still living simply go on without him. Ernest Hemingway's *The Sun Also Rises* (1926) portrays much the same thing. Jake, the main character, is an American journalist who lives in Paris. He fought in the Great War. His idealism ended in a wound which left him impotent, a striking symbol of his generation for Hemingway. Jake and some friends go to Spain on vacation to see the bullfights, along with Lady Brett Ashley, an unhappy American with a British title she gained through marriage. Her meaningless title echoes the meaninglessness of the society that gave it to her. She and Jake had once been lovers, and after some sterile affairs with other men, she finds herself again with Jake at the end of the book, traveling in a taxi, carried about by a stranger, lamenting what might have been.

Literary approaches to evil become even more negative after World War II with its frighteningly large involvement of noncombatants. Air power opened up for attack cities which were well behind the front lines and made innocent people of every age and both genders "acceptable" targets. To this can be added the attempts by some nations to destroy entire races of people, the renewal of centuries-old ethnic conflicts, and the appalling treatment of prisoners of war, while Hiroshima had ensured that the world would now have to live forever in fear of a nuclear conflict. The war had defeated fascism, but Westerners had to explain to themselves how the supposedly "civilized" nations had produced Auschwitz and Hiroshima. Not surprisingly, many intellectuals found little to be optimistic about as evil seemed everywhere triumphant. As the American philosopher Gordon Kaufman put it, "Exploration of the varieties, subtleties, and enormities of evil has become perhaps the principal of literature, art, and drama since World War II" (*God: The Problem,* 171–2).

Before World War II had even ended, the Northern Irish writer Clive Staples (C. S.) Lewis (1898–1963), conservative Anglican and Oxford don, wrote *Perelandra* (1944), the second novel in a three-part space trilogy. It retells the Garden of Eden story on the planet Perelandra (which Earthlings call Venus), but with a difference. Maledil, as God is called elsewhere in the universe, decides to help evil's intended victims by sending an academic named Ransom to Perelandra. When Ransom arrives there, Lewis gives a brilliant description of an Augustinian Garden of Eden, of a world untouched by sin. Ransom finds that all of his senses have been heightened; he enjoys food in a way he never had before; no animal fears him nor does he fear any animal; death is unknown. When Ransom meets the Green Lady, the Perelandran Eve, he assures her that he comes in peace. Her reply? "What is 'peace'?" (57). Never having known evil, she has no fear of anyone or anything. Peace to her is daily life. Ransom immediately recognizes that not only his senses but also his values need to be reordered.

The serpent in this garden is Weston, a Faustian scientist who has come to extend the blessings of "civilization" to primitive Perelandra but who has also brought a revolver in case the natives fail to see the benefits of doing things his way. As his name suggests, Weston represents all the viciousness and immorality which Lewis deplored in Western society. Taking a colonial attitude, Weston considers the Green Lady, who has no need for clothing, "a naked savage"; like the European imperialists, he has no interest in the rights or thoughts of the indigenous population. Lewis thoroughly demonizes Weston. The Green Lady saw

Weston's space ship fall from the sky, as Satan fell from heaven. He lies as soon as he arrives on Perelandra. Eventually the reader learns that an evil spirit has taken over Weston's body and works through him. Ransom warns the Green Lady about Weston, but he blithely uses lies and half-truths to force Ransom to concede some points. Since no good can come from evil, Ransom cannot respond in kind. He laments to Maledil that the deity has sent him to the contest virtually unarmed.

Lewis shows how insidiously evil works. When the Green Lady tells Weston that she cannot transgress a divine command, Weston replies that she is allowed to think about transgressing it. He also tortures a small frog, leaving it in great pain. When Ransom discovers the wounded frog, he knows that it will never heal but suffer forever. He has no choice but to kill it, thus making himself, the person sent to save Perelandra, the one who brings death to the planet. Eventually Ransom, a Christ-figure, realizes that he must ransom Perelandra from evil and physically battles the demonized Weston. To his surprise, he triumphs. Perelandra is saved, and he, personally redeemed by his triumph over evil, returns to earth to tell his story.

For Lewis, the devil was a real being, but, like the Renaissance scholar he was, he followed Dante in presenting evil as a vicious little beast which had to be fought on a day-to-day basis in numerous little ways. Like Dante, he used a cosmic backdrop for a personal drama, but a drama with cosmic consequences.

Although not sharing Lewis' conservative religious views, the German novelist Thomas Mann (1875–1955) shared his horror of Faustian Western society. He believed that the German people had made a pact with the devil to restore the glories supposedly stolen from them after World War I. For his Faustian figure, he followed a Nietzschean path, choosing the ultimate Overman, the artist. *Doctor Faustus* (1947) traces the career of Adrian Leverkühn, a concert pianist. The novel's narrator is Serenus Zeitbloom, whose last name means "Timebloom," telling the reader that he is a man of his age. Naturally a modern person cannot believe in Satan, and so when Leverkühn has a conversation with the devil, the reader cannot be sure whether or not to take it literally. Mann, like Dostoyevsky, has the demon become real for the central character, but he leaves a way out for the modern skeptic. Leverkühn has contracted syphilis, a disease which eventually destroys him; he collapses at a concert and is taken to an asylum. Does the disease cause him to believe in a devil as his skeptical friends thought? Mann did not expect his readers to believe in a devil, but we see his distress at the modern inclination to explain everything scientifically without looking for any other explanation.

Mann sets his Faustus clearly within German history. The Faust myth first occurs in German literature in the sixteenth century, the century of

Luther, a seminal and disturbing figure for so many German intellectuals. The figure of Faust also recalls Goethe, a giant of German literature. Leverkühn, as an artist, is personally driven and thus represents the Dionysian strain, an echo of Nietzsche's famous theory about the origins of Greek tragedy. The tragic collapse of Leverkühn, destroyed by his own inner demons, represents Germany's destruction through Hitler. Mann makes the connection to German history very clear. Two of the characters are theologians, Kumpf, an arrogant man who actually imitates a legendary act of Luther by throwing a biscuit at a supposed demon, and Schlepfuss ("Dragfoot"), who recalls Medieval portraits of the devil as a lame man, his outside deformity reflecting his inside deformity. Via these two characters, a boor and a demon, Mann suggests that modern liberal Christianity has little to say to modern humanity. In conversation with Leverkühn, the devil actually brags that he understands Christianity better than contemporary theologians. Yet Mann is not completely pessimistic. Leverkühn loves his nephew, and love always points to possible redemption. If an individual can be redeemed, so can a nation.

The American writer Flannery O'Connor (1925–64) also used the Faustian theme. A conservative Roman Catholic, she believed that most modern people deluded themselves with belief in human progress and overlooked the evil that infected their daily lives. She dealt with evil in its endless manifestations in daily life. Her short story "The Lame Shall Enter First" (1962) goes after one of her favorite targets, the secularist do-gooder.

Sheppard is a social worker who has recently lost his wife. He neglects his son Norton and instead devotes himself to Rufus Johnson, an impoverished boy who grew up with his grandfather, a hellfire country preacher. This boy has a clubfoot, recalling Mann's Schlepfuss and the Medieval devil, and the word "rufus" in Latin means "red," another hint of the demonic. Sheppard knows Rufus's problems stem from his background, but O'Connor hints that Rufus's problems have a far simpler explanation: the boy is evil.

Convinced the boy needs full-time attention, Sheppard brings him into his home. The social worker jumps at any sign of interest the boy portrays, but, unknown to Sheppard, Rufus sets out to change his son by telling him about heaven and hell. When Sheppard buys Rufus a telescope, Norton wonders if he can see his mother in heaven. Most parents would recognize a cry for help, but Sheppard is too busy playing God by creating a new human, the reformed Rufus Johnson. But Rufus will have none of it. He scornfully tells Norton, "He [your father] thinks he's Jesus Christ."

Sheppard bets everything on getting Rufus a new shoe so that he could walk more easily and maybe even normally, but Rufus, repudiating redemption, refuses to wear the shoe. When the police charge Rufus with vandalism, Sheppard lies to protect him; the evil is beginning to spread. When the social worker finally realizes that he will not win the boy over, he does not stand up for Rufus when he is again arrested for vandalism. The police car has attracted some attention, and Rufus pays Sheppard back by telling a local reporter that the social worker made "immor'l suggestions" to him. Realizing that his career is finished, Sheppard at last decides to be a good shepherd to his son; as Mann and others had written, love can save even Faustian figures. But O'Connor provides no way out. Caught in some ropes, Norton has hanged himself a few feet from the telescope in an attempt to launch himself into space and be with his mother in heaven.

O'Connor had no illusions about modern readers believing in the devil, but she did want them to believe in evil. Like Dostoyevsky and Mann, she includes enough ambiguity to make the story modern but to still raise questions. Most readers would agree with Sheppard; there is no need to believe in the devil to know why Rufus acts as he does. But O'Connor shrewdly works the reverse of such thinking, showing Rufus immune to all the cures which modern secular society presumes will work. Sheppard is the modern liberal Faustian. He knows what is good for poor people; all they need to do to be happy is listen to him. The boy repeatedly tells him that Satan has him (Rufus) in his power, but Sheppard dismisses this as so much religious superstition which Rufus, like all modern people, must outgrow. O'Connor does not dismiss the harm done by poverty and other social problems, but she sees these as outgrowths of a more fundamental evil.

Other themes besides the Faustian have occupied modern writers. In 1947, the same year Doctor Faustus was published, the Frenchman Albert Camus (1913–60) published *The Plague*. Camus was an atheist, but unlike Nietzsche he did not advocate desertion of society to establish a new human being. Camus' characters get caught up in a plague that infects the city of Oran in Algeria, and they work daily with other citizens to stop its spread and to keep it from destroying the fabric of life in the city.

Camus wrote frequently of the absurdity of life and of the need to combat that absurdity with the affirmation of the human. The plague symbolizes the affliction facing all humans and forces them to confront their mortality. Since the government has to quarantine the city from the outside world, Dr. Rieux, the central character, laments the boredom it imposed upon the city as no new faces appeared on the streets and no new films appeared in the cinemas. There is no escape. The plague has made the citizens of Oran exiles, shunned by the rest of the world: "the feeling of exile—that sensation of the void within which never left us" (60), a good Medieval description of hell.

Traditional sources of hope mean nothing. The priest Paneloux interprets the plague in traditional terms of natural evil; God would not send it for no reason. It warns people to turn away from their sins. Later on Rieux sees a small boy "racked on the tumbled bed, in a grotesque parody of crucifixion" (175). This crucifixion has no redemptive significance; it is just useless suffering which even threatens the faith of Father Paneloux. The state, the traditional secularist French alternative to the power of religion, also offers no help. Civic authorities are slow to react, and Rieux finds himself standing by a statue of the personified *République française* and conscious only of a "bleak indifference" (76). One of the doctor's friends, a civil servant named Grand, has been trying to write a book for years, but he cannot get past the first sentence. This genuinely amusing character underlines a more serious theme, the futility of art in the face of meaningless death. Even the ultimate consolation has no power: "The plague had gradually killed off in all of us the faculty not of love only but even of friendship. Naturally enough, since love asks something of the future, and nothing was left to us but a series of present moments" (150). The plague has become normal life. Pressed to explain how he was standing up to the plague, Rieux tells a friend, "Heroism and sanctity don't really appeal to me, I imagine. What interests me is—being a man" (209). He asserts his humanity against all the absurdity, represented by the plague, which beats him down. Rieux survives the plague, only to learn that his wife, who had been safely away from the city in a sanitarium, has died, and he must face the rebuilding of his life alone.

Camus insisted that people not give in to the threat of extinction but rather assert the dignity of their humanity, in face of a meaningless, absurd existence. Evil was the void, and good was recognizing and facing it squarely.

The empty cosmos of Camus and some other French authors crossed the Atlantic. In 1956 the American poet Archibald MacLeish (1892–1992) wrote a verse drama called *J.B.*, a retelling of the book of Job. It has a complex plot, difficult to retell, and it has an ambiguous ending: the theatergoer cannot be certain whether God exists and makes a difference in J.B.'s life or whether J.B. is merely deceiving himself about God because he needs something to hold on to. MacLeish deals with the effects of evil on people rather than with theories of evil. In the book of Job, Satan destroys Job's children in just seven verses, but the destruction of J.B.'s children reaches through almost two-thirds of the drama. MacLeish shows us what J.B. suffers, but he also forces us to recognize that J.B.'s wife and children are more than just cardboard figures in a theodicy. He gives them names and personalities. J.B.'s wife Sarah has become a major character rather than just the "foolish woman" (Job 2:10) of the biblical book.

J.B. uses the device of a play within a play. Two worn-out thespians play God and Satan and bring the other characters into being. Mr. Zuss (= Zeus), wearing the God-mask, attempts to maintain the biblical view, while Nickles (= Old Nick), wearing the Satan-mask, asks the terrible questions all humans have when facing evil, especially after World War II. When they look for someone to play Job, Mr. Zuss remarks, "Oh, there's always / Someone playing Job." Nickles replies:

> There must be
> Thousands! . . . Millions and millions of mankind
> Burned, crushed, broken, mutilated,
> Slaughtered, and for what? . . . Sleeping the wrong night in the
>   wrong city—
> London, Dresden, Hiroshima (prologue).

Nickles pushes the theme: "I know what Hell is now—to see" (prologue). Hell is facing the world as it is.

Knowing what is to happen, Mr. Zuss and Nickles debate the value of the test. Mr. Zuss: "Would God permit the test unless / He knew the outcome of the testing?" Nickles: "Then why test him if God knows?" (sc. 3). The disasters begin, and MacLeish omits any dignity from the deaths of J.B.'s children. One son, a soldier, dies in an accident after a war is over. A daughter is killed when a wall collapses. The youngest girl is raped and murdered. The two other children die in an automobile accident, and the people who tell Sarah and J.B. are newspaper reporters who plot to get a photograph of the parents' reaction to the news. MacLeish displays all the violence, stupidity, and vulgarity of meaningless deaths.

As the horror sinks in, J.B. falls back on his faith. When Sarah mumbles, "The Lord giveth," J.B. responds piously, "The Lord taketh away." But this piety is more than Sarah can bear: "Takes! / Kills! Kills! Kills!" (sc. 6). God's silence runs through the drama. When J.B. asks God to let him die, Sarah sarcastically observes that God won't even let him do that. When J.B., still clinging to his faith, affirms that "God is just," Sarah hysterically replies:

> God is just!
> If God is just our slaughtered children
> Stank with sin, were rotten with it! . . . They are
> Dead and they were innocent: I will not
> Let you sacrifice their deaths
> To make injustice justice and God good!

The bewildered J.B. clings desperately to his theology: "We have no choice but to be guilty. / God is unthinkable if we are innocent" (sc. 8). Since the reader knows that J.B. and his family are innocent, the implication is that God is unthinkable.

The three Comforters arrive (sc. 9) when Sarah is absent. The biblical three believe that Job must have done something to have suffered so much, and they try to convince him to face the truth of what he has done. The modern three try to get J.B. to face up to his abandonment by God.

> Young men in slaughtered cities
> Offering their silly throats
> Against the tanks in innocence shall perish.
> What's your innocence to theirs?

They do not try to convince J.B. of his guilt; one of them, Eliphaz, even claims that "Guilt is a / Psychophenomenal situation / An illusion, a disease, a sickness." Zophar suggests that J.B. wise up: "Your sin is / Simple. You were born a man!" J.B. holds on: "Yours is the cruelest comfort of them all, / Making the Creator of the Universe / The miscreator of mankind." Zophar: "If it were otherwise we could not bear it / Without the fault, without the Fall, / We're madmen." The modern world cannot explain evil without holding God responsible. Before the play's final scene, Mr. Zuss and Nickles consider what has been said. Confused, Mr. Zuss asks, "Who plays the hero, God or him [J.B.]? / Is God to be forgiven?" Mr. Zuss insists that the final scene, where God restores J.B.'s wife to him and gives him new children, must be played. When he claims that J.B. "gets all he ever had and more / Much more," Nickles snidely replies, "Sure. His wife. His children!" Mr. Zuss defends his view, but MacLeish's stage directions say that he is embarrassed to do so.

In the final scene Sarah returns to J.B. She tells him that, unlike the ironically named Comforters, she was always there for him.

> I loved you.
> I couldn't help you any more.
> You wanted justice and there was none
> Only love.

Invoking the majesty of God and also the traditional philosophical explanations of the deity, J.B. replies, "He does not love. He / Is." "But we do [love]," replies Sarah to this barren creed. Like Camus' characters heroically resisting the absurdity of the humanity-robbing plague with no supernatural or religious consolation, Sarah and J.B. must face a world in which "the candles in the churches are out." J.B. can only conclude, "We'll see where we are. . . . Blow on the coal of the heart and we'll know." Job, the strongest believer in the whole of the Bible, the man who faced unspeakable horrors without losing his faith, has metamorphosed into the modern J.B. who must live in a world without faith and without traditional values. Evil is the false illusion of hope in a just deity; goodness is recognizing who we are and affirming our humanity in the face of an often absurd world. Yet the yearning for faith remains as the characters and author feel the absence of God.

MacLeish had reworked one biblical theme; in his novel *Lord of the Flies* (1954), the British author William Golding (1911–93) reworked another one, setting the Garden of Eden against the backdrop of World War II. Survivors of a plane crash (the plane was shot down), a group of young British boys are marooned on a deserted tropical island just as two other children found themselves in a garden. They go about largely unclothed, they have abundant fruit to eat, and one of them claims to have seen a snake. Their leader, a boy named Ralph, surveys the island and pro-nounces it "all ours" as God had given Adam and Eve dominion over Eden, and, like Satan falling from heaven, a dying pilot parachutes onto the island where his body is mistaken by the boys for a frightful beast.

Eden was a cosmos, and the boys try to establish another one, setting rules for speaking at assembly and assigning tasks to one another. But, even at their young age, they have been corrupted by the values of their elders. Piggy represents rationality and tries to keep the other boys fo-cused on the need to be rescued, but Ralph recognizes the value of ra-tionality too late. Jack, the head of a choir, has fascist tendencies and organizes his singers into killers, first of animals and then of other boys. After one successful hunt, Jack and his group decapitate a pig and put the severed head on a stick, ostensibly to pacify the beast (the dead pilot), but the decaying head, covered with flies, quickly becomes a totem figure, the Lord of the Flies, which is what Beelzebub, one of Satan's biblical names, means. Another boy, Simon, is a mystic who rec-ognizes who the Lord of the Flies really is and has a mystical experience of the evil which is infecting the boys. But in a frenzied dance the oth-ers kill Simon, thinking he, the messenger who warns them about evil, is actually the beast. Simon parallels Christ.

After only a few days, the boys descend into total savagery, killing Piggy soon after they have killed Simon. Jack replaces Ralph as the leader and focuses the boys on hunting and killing rather than on being saved, both physically and morally. He incites them to hunt and kill Ralph. Ralph manages to hide for a while in heavy underbrush, so Jack orders the hunters to set fire to much of the island, hoping to burn him out. The fire will destroy most of the island's food supply, but, driven by the hate and mindlessness of Milton's demons, Jack literally turns the island into a hell in which he will reign. Ralph manages to escape just long enough for all of the boys to be rescued by a crew from a British naval vessel brought to the island by the smoke. A British officer looks at the armed, naked savages, and says to Ralph, "I should have thought that a pack of British boys—you're all British, aren't you?—would have been able to put up a better show." When the boys break down and weep, the embarrassed officer turns around and looks at his battle cruiser as Golding brilliantly aligns the descent of the boys into savagery to the descent of the "civilized" nations of the West into a far wider savagery.

Ralph, the erstwhile leader, thinks he knows what has happened—the loss of innocence. But he is wrong. The boys had no innocence to lose; society had just covered up their intrinsic evil. And, unlike Milton, who ends his Edenic story with the hope of redemption, Golding ends his with the boys boarding a ship with the older savages in hunt of their own prey. Like Frankenstein's creature, the boys never stood a chance; unlike the creature, they will mask their evil desires in the requirements of polite society—they will "put up a better show"—but they are still savages inside. Original sin is not the sin the boys commit but the sin which society committed against them. Like MacLeish, Golding has used a biblical theme to describe a world without God or hope.

In the nineteenth century the emphasis upon human evil was new, a reflection of the declining power of religion and the belief in demonic evil. In the modern era, human evil has practically been the only type of evil present in literature. In the nineteenth century writers focused on an increasingly harsh and empty world in which traditional values were overturned, but the modern era has had a frightening new focus, the incomprehensible genocidal crimes of modern totalitarian states.

Although not a work of fiction, Elie Wiesel's *Night,* first published in French in 1958 and translated and reprinted many times, has been many people's introduction to the horrors of the Nazi Holocaust. Wiesel (1928–) was born in what is now Romania. With his family and the other Jews of his town he was deported to concentration camps, spending time in Auschwitz, Buna, and Buchenwald, until liberated in 1945 by Allied troops. *Night* gives a stark account of his attempt to survive and to help his father survive as well (his father did not make it). He recounts the studied brutality of the Nazi regime and the daily fear of the prisoners that they might be weeded out and gassed if they failed the "selection," when the camp commanders selected those prisoners they thought most fit to work and executed those not deemed fit. The prisoners had no idea when a selection might occur, and they knew every day might be their last.

Wiesel recounts how the Nazis separated families so that people had no idea if their spouses and children were even alive. Guards and commandants believed the prisoners to be subhuman and deserving of nothing except life, and then only if they could work. Every little mistake could be fatal, and the reader is shocked at how a tiny action on the part of a prisoner or a guard could mean the difference between life and death. Courage appeared in seemingly small ways. A young French woman at the Buna camp spoke a few words to him "in almost perfect German," urging him to hold on, "The day will come, but not now." Wiesel was surprised. "She seemed to me to be a Jewess, though here she passed as Aryan" (50–1). She was Jewish and quite literally risked her life because a knowledge of German on the part of a French woman would have raised the suspicions of the guards. Wiesel met her years later in Paris and thanked her for her kind words to him. A few sentences from one stranger to another—so little and yet so much. The book ends in a note of defiance to evil: Wiesel, a theist, survived. He looked in a mirror; "a corpse gazed back" (109). But he survived.

Night is difficult to read and impossible to put down. So is *One Day in the Life of Ivan Denisovich* by the Russian Aleksandr Solzhenitsyn (1918–), first published in Russian in 1962 and, like *Night*, translated and reprinted many times. Solzhenitsyn served as a captain of artillery in what the Russians call the Great Patriotic War, but an indiscreet letter critical of Stalin earned him an eight-year prison sentence in a labor camp, followed by a forced exile. "Rehabilitated" in 1956, he remained on the outs with every regime, publishing his books clandestinely. Even the Nobel Prize for literature in 1970 did not alleviate his situation, and he declined to go to Sweden to receive the award for fear of not being allowed to return to the Soviet Union. He was exiled in 1974 and eventually came to the United States, but returned to Russia in 1994 after the fall of the Soviet regime.

Although based on Solzhenitsyn's experience, *One Day in the Life of Ivan Denisovich* is a work of fiction. The central character is Ivan Denisovich Shukhov, who must grub his way about the camp for his daily existence. Unlike the Jews in *Night,* who could be executed any day, the prisoners in the Soviet camp have been sent to prison for fixed terms, usually not less than ten years, and they expect to be released, if they survive. But survival cannot be taken for granted. The prisoners (all men) work outdoors in freezing weather, have barely enough food, and, for something as minor as an off-hand remark, can be sent to solitary confinement in a freezing cell for ten days or more. A ten-day sentence guarantees the prisoner will get tuberculosis; a longer sentence means death.

What strikes the reader is the oppressive monotony and the reduction of humans to beasts, striving to survive. Prisoners bargain and threaten for cigarette butts. They hide extra bits of food that they manage to steal. One group marches at double time and then begins to run in order to get into formation before another group because the prisoners who get there first will be dismissed first and get out of the cold sooner. The ultimate form of dehumanization is death, robbing us forever of our futures, but the Soviet regime worked to dehumanize its prisoners while keeping them alive for another day's work.

And "day" is the key word. The reader follows Ivan Denisovich on his struggle to get along with the guards and other prisoners, to scratch out whatever meager advantage he can, to hide his extra food, to buy to-bacco on the sly, to keep up his spirits, and simply to keep warm. It is an exhausting struggle, and, Solzhenitsyn reminds us at the end of the book, that this was "Just one of the three thousand six hundred and fifty-three days of his sentence" (159). An epic battle—and for one day.

In recent years, novelists have turned more to evils than to Evil, and especially to demonizing the Other. Toni Morrison dealt with the diffi-culty black people encounter just trying to be themselves in a white so-ciety in *The Bluest Eye* (1970). In *Snow Falling on Cedars* (1994), David Guterson wrote of the World War II American internment of its own citi-zens of Japanese descent. In 1974 James Welch explored the corrosive effects of white society upon Native Americans in *Winter in the Blood,* and in 1993 Larry Watson showed the willingness of white family members to overlook rape and child molestation of Native American girls by a white doctor in *Montana 1948.* Anna Quindlen's *Black and Blue* (1998) is but one of many novels dealing with the insistence of some men to con-tinue demonizing women who must be brutalized to be "kept in line." In *The Poisonwood Bible* (1998), Barbara Kingsolver deals with racism, sex-ism, religious intolerance, and the deadly combination of the three.

Chapter 15

Some Scientific Theories of Evil

> *Natural selection has a malicious sense of humor.*
> —Richard Wright, *The Moral Animal*

Psychological Explanations

Today people often look to scientists to understand the world. A 1998 Arts and Entertainment Network cable-television program on "The Problem of Evil" dealt with evil solely in psychological terms and did not even mention literary or religious approaches to evil. This reflects the growing importance of the social sciences in our understanding of our world and of what it means to be human.

Regardless of what psychologists may personally believe about God or about religion, professionally they do not deal with theodicies, concentrating instead on human motivation. Some psychologists do not feel comfortable with the word "evil," preferring instead "aggression," but many recognize that some phenomena demand the word "evil."

In his 1989 book *The Roots of Evil*, Ervin Staub concentrated on the origins of genocide, the ultimate demonization of the Other and something immensely personal to him. As a six-year-old boy, he was among the thousands of Hungarian Jews saved from the Holocaust by one of the true heroes of the modern era, the Swedish diplomat Raoul Wallenberg. Staub studies not just the Holocaust but also the genocides by the Turks against the Armenians and by the Khmer Rouge against the Cambodians. He finds the origins of genocide not just in group activity but in what he calls "personal goal theory," that is, group evils emerge from individual motives.

Human beings have genetic propensities for both altruism and aggression. Which of these propensities evolves more depends on individual socialization and experience. . . . *Evil* is not a scientific concept with an agreed meaning, but the idea of evil is part of a broadly shared human cultural heritage. The essence of evil is the destruction of human beings (24–5).

Staub accepts as a given that humans have propensities in two directions; the question for him is which direction they will take and why. The book deals with how he believes one propensity comes to dominate. He emphasizes that genocide is not a mass activity but an elaborate plan devised by a few who convince others that their security or way of life is threatened. The bureaucracy is essential because it impersonalizes the process, replacing moral and even immoral actions with the repetitive necessity of keeping the system working. Staub does not expect genocides to cease (he was prescient—both Rwanda and Bosnia occurred after he wrote this book), but he argues for positive socialization and effective parenting as methods of preventing the impersonalization and resentment of others upon which the thugs who plan genocides can rely.

In his *Ordinary People and Extraordinary Evil* (1993), Fred Katz also investigated the Holocaust as well as the massacre of Vietnamese civilians by American troops at My Lai. "I define and use the word *evil* to mean behavior that deliberately deprives innocent people of their humanity, from small scale assaults on a person's dignity to outright murder. This is a *behavioral* definition of evil." Katz acknowledges the value of seeing evil "in religious, moral and philosophical terms," but he considers these in "the realm of the supernatural" and not "in the realm of day-to-day living." What he wants "to accomplish" is to show "that a behavioral view of evil helps us confront it" (5). Katz finds evil arising in the many decisions we make on a day-to-day basis as a consequence of our psychological autonomy, something we do not always realize. "Often we believe we have no autonomy, no freedom to choose, when in fact we have a great deal of autonomy" (43). But too often we follow others who play upon our often legitimate fears, and we do not realize when we slip into evil acts, even horrific ones. In a remarkable statement of secular faith, Katz claims that science "is perhaps our only hope of effectively getting control over evil. It will do so if we allow science to do what it does best—to be dispassionate, creative and committed to truth—in order to address the problem of how evil is actually produced" (133). Science can provide us with the information about evil which we need to make moral decisions.

In 1996 Carl Goldberg published *Speaking with the Devil: Exploring Senseless Acts of Evil*. In spite of using "evil" in the title, he prefers the term "malevolence," which does not carry the religious or super-natural overtones that "evil" does. Goldberg gives a personal definition, "malevolence always involves treating other people without respect or consideration for their humanity," and goes on to a general definition, "malevolence is the *deliberate* infliction of cruel, painful suffering on another living being" (4). Goldberg believes that past explanations of evil, for which he shows considerable respect, had tinges of the de-monic, but today we can understand evil via the behavioral sciences. "Once we understand the paradox—we must be responsible for our-selves, but we are also the responsibility of others—metaphysical mys-teries can be set aside in examining the problem of evil. Rather, it becomes a *practical problem,* whose psychological and social causes can be traced empirically" (26–7). (Philosophers and theologians will feel uncomfortable having their investigations of evil dismissed as "meta-physical mysteries.") Goldberg draws his conclusions from work with patients whom he quotes throughout the book, concentrating on how the individual learns anti-social behavior (for example, outward-directed but defensive contempt, a justification of harmful actions). Evil can only be combated on a social level, and society can only do that by re-turning to person-centered values, hardly a popular view in modern consumerist culture.

In the same year that Goldberg's book appeared, so did *Evil: Inside Human Violence and Cruelty* by Roy Baumeister, who makes it clear that he works only from facts: "In the social sciences, ideas are cheap but facts are precious" (vii). He has "resisted the constant temptation to il-lustrate key points with episodes from . . . fictional entertainments" (viii), an approach which immediately devalues the understanding of evil by Dante or Mary Shelley and which differs from Goldberg's will-ingness to cite Shakespeare and William Golding. Baumeister insists that the scientist must work objectively (386) and must look objectively at both the witness of the victim of an evil and of the perpetrator. For Baumeister, evil arises when individuals break the bonds imposed upon them by society. There are four root causes of evil: the desire for material gain, threatened egotism which forces the individual to defend himself or herself against a perceived threat, idealism which turns those who disagree into the Other and thus makes them targets for violence, and the pursuit of sadistic pleasure. Baumeister takes an often iconoclastic approach, insisting that criminals often have too high a self-esteem rather than too low. Since he insists that he works only from facts, he cannot accept the notion of pure evil, which he calls a myth which shields us from the real causes of evil.

In 1998 C. Fred Alford weighed in with *What Evil Means to Us,* relying heavily upon work with people who committed evil acts and who agreed to be interviewed about their views of evil. Alford declines to define evil but works only from experience.

> Most [of his subjects] approached evil as an experience of dread. From this perspective evil is not a moral or theological problem. It is a problem of life, more practical than theoretical: how to know and live with an uncanny presentiment of disaster which sneaks up on one from time to time (2).

He goes further: "People do not have concepts of evil, or at least that is not on the experiential ground. . . . People live an experience of evil, and it lives in them" (4).

Alford recognizes that people experience evil in many different ways, but he does not find in this grounds for relativism, which he considers, in a telling phrase, "a defense against experience" (9). He discusses the Holocaust, which remains the strongest argument against relativism and against psychological reductionism (the Nazis really weren't bad, they were just misunderstood). By avoiding a single definition of evil, Alford is able to define or characterize it in several ways: as cold, as cheating, as misleadingly attractive but actually boring, as the loss of self, as the loss of boundaries, as the refusal to accept being human, and ultimately as nothing. He quotes one of his subjects: "Self-deception is the root of all evil" (24). Alford himself says that the "problem of evil is at its core a problem of circles and cycles" and that the "first and best thing we can do about evil is to break the cycle" (139). Like Katz and Goldberg, Alford believes that we must study evil people, try to understand why they do what they do, and then treat all people, including evil-doers, humanely.

Two prominent psychologists have taken a very different approach to this problem. In his 1983 book *People of the Lie,* M. Scott Peck takes a frankly religious approach to the question, even to the point of affirming his belief in Satan, although "Satan may be said to be a spirit of mental illness" (207). Yet Peck agrees with many of the views of other psychological students of evil: "The most basic scientific investigator of evil will always be a therapist" (260). Although accepting the existence of God, he does not make belief in a deity essential to wellness. "All adults who are mentally healthy submit themselves one way or another to something higher than themselves, be it God or truth or love or some other ideal" (78). Peck agrees with other psychologists that evil arises from self-deception, the inability to recognize our limits, or the unwillingness to accept those limits. He, too, bases much of his book upon his dealings with his patients, and he considers an example of evil on the large scale, the American massacre of Vietnamese peasants at My Lai in 1968. Yet, almost uniquely, he insists that any psychology of evil "cannot be a purely secular psychology" (45).

As a believing Christian, Peck can accept the insight of the Bible into evil, although most of his biblical examples parallel insights of other psychologists, such as the Genesis emphasis upon evil as self-deception and destructive of humanity. Yet Peck can move outside the Bible and Christian tradition. He does not reject outright the idea that creation should be good as the product of a good deity, but he does ask a fundamental question: "Why is there good in the world? . . . The mystery of goodness is even greater than the mystery of evil" (41).

The last psychologist we will consider is one of the pioneers of the discipline, Carl Jung (1875–1961). Son of a Lutheran pastor and an early disciple of Freud, Jung brought to the question of evil a respect for traditional religious teachings and an insistence on incorporating the latest advances in psychology. He wrote about evil in several of his works, but his views appear most fully in *Answer to Job* (1952).

Jung explained evil in theistic terms: for him God is the coincidence of opposites. Jung often wrote more as a philosopher than a psychologist, but he insisted that he was doing psychology. He believed that the understanding of God as the coincidence of opposites is part of the lived experience of humanity and thus has become part of our "collective unconscious," Jung's famous theory to explain why so many peoples and cultures share the same myths and tales. For Jung, "psychological experience shows that whatever we call 'good' is balanced by an equally substantial 'bad' or 'evil'" (*Answer to Job*, 520). Since there are "psychic truths which can neither be explained nor proved nor contested in any physical way" (522), Jung felt free to look at religious statements rather than just disregard them for lack of empirical verification. All his life he was a student of myth, believing that myth was a valid way although hardly the only way to reach a psychic truth.

In a long analysis of the book of Job, he pointed out that God causes Job's ills and then rebukes Job for his angry response to those ills. This shows both the good and evil side of God, a reflection of the duality in the deity which also appears in his creation of the Tree of the Knowledge of Good and Evil and then his warning to Adam and Eve, two children, not to touch the tree. This duality does not always have a moral context. God creates Adam and then takes Eve from his side, proof that Adam had both male and female qualities, as did God since woman and man are both made in God's image. Jung also asked a damning question for biblical literalists: instead of condemning his son to a painful if redemptive death, why didn't God just forgive Adam and Eve? He didn't forgive them because he wanted to show both sides of his personality; his revelation to humans could not be otherwise.

From the ancient Jewish sages to modern believers, religious people have tried to justify or explain away some of God's apparently negative behavior in the Bible, but Jung accepted it at face value. He did not accept it as historical fact but believed the biblical writers wanted us to see God as genuinely—rather than just apparently—negative. Jung discarded arguments such as the necessity of evil to understand the good but instead insisted that Job "clearly sees that God is at odds with himself" (531). He occasionally made the historical argument that ancient people had less difficulty accepting the coincidence of opposites than moderns, but the heart of the book lies in his understanding of the divine nature: "[God] is everything in its totality; therefore, among other things, he is total justice, and also its total opposite. . . . Job is no more than the outward occasion for an inward process of dialectic in God" (534, 542).

Jung did not consider Satan to be an actual being but understood him as the shadow side of God, a side which the deity does not care to acknowledge and so expels Satan from heaven. But this tack fails; God cannot deny the totality of his own being. "His readiness to deliver Job into Satan's murderous hands proves that he doubts Job precisely because he projects his own tendency to unfaithfulness upon a scapegoat" (555). Jung pointed out that some religious thinkers, like the ancient Gnostics and contemporary Tibetan Buddhists, can accept the duality and can live at peace with a God whom Jews and Christians constantly have to explain.

Jung was a controversial figure in his lifetime and continues to be so after his death. Admired by literary and creative people, he gets a mixed reception from psychologists, psychiatrists, and psychoanalysts, some of whom reject his views completely or deny that they have practical, therapeutic value. Religious scholars, too, are never quite sure what to do with his views, which they initially find appealing when they explain some myth, but which lose their appeal when Jung turns doctrines into symbols. But Jung cannot be ignored, especially on the question of evil.

Although some writers we surveyed have called upon philosophers and creative artists to help understand evil, all insisted ultimately upon psychological definitions or explanations. This reflects the modern approach to evil: an acceptance of evil as a fact of life, a reluctance to try to explain it in metaphysical or theological terms, and a recognition that it is more important for society to deal with evil than to define it. Something else which emerges from this survey is how many modern explanations of evil sound familiar: the lie, the cold, self-deception, inhumanity, nothingness. These explanations appear in much older literature (Dante, Milton, Shelley) and several go back to the book of Genesis. Joseph Campbell (1904–87) in his *The Hero with a Thousand Faces* (1949), studied ancient, primitive, and comparative religions and concluded that people in every era had to deal with the same problems as moderns do, but they could not explain them as modern psychologists do. Lacking explanations, these people still had a sense of the problem which they expressed in their myths. Consider the classic case. To Freud goes the credit for discovering the Oedipus complex, but these lines were written in the fifth century B.C.E. by the Greek tragedian Sophocles in his play *Oedipus Rex* (lines 981–2): "For in dreams many a man has been his mother's mate." Campbell makes his case; we can still learn from the ancients.

Genetic Explanations

Psychological explanations of evil dominated the scientific approach in the twentieth century, but more recently genetics has emerged as a force. The discovery of DNA and the completion of the Genome Project have pushed biochemistry to the front of the sciences in the public mind, and genetics seems to promise solutions to everything, and not just to debilitating diseases or serious cancers like those of the breasts or colon. More and more, genetics moves into realms once occupied by psychology, sociology, and other disciplines which study how people are shaped by their upbringing and environment. Physical problems such as obesity and smoking, long thought to have psychological origins, are now thought to have genetic foundations. Is obesity caused by psychological factors, such as the need for oral satisfaction, or is it caused by a gene? Do people get hooked on nicotine and find themselves unable to quit smoking because they cannot discipline themselves to stop or are they genetically predisposed to nicotine addiction? Maybe Freud's cigar was just a cigar.

Clearly genetics will impact the question of evil. If gene theory can explain so many other human behaviors, why not the ultimate one? This genetic approach has a genuine attraction, partly because, like the theories of Augustine or Leibniz, it offers a completeness and a solidity lacking in so many others theories: evil arises from original sin; evil is built into the cosmos by the deity; evil results from a gene. It also obviates the unease so many people feel about psychological explanations: Can a serial murderer really be explained solely by his or her upbringing or neighborhood? Why don't other people with similar backgrounds commit murder? How much more comprehensible it is to explain such behavior by a gene. But completeness and comprehensibility do not guarantee truth.

The jury is still out, but more and more people today are looking to genetic explanations. Literally decades of research await those trying to explain the interaction of genes on the question of evil. But much evidence is already in, and some writers have ventured ideas about genetics and evil. Actually, the question is not so new. In 1975 Edward O. Wilson published *Sociobiology,* arguing that biological imperatives stood behind many elements in social life; the next year Richard Dawkins published *The Selfish Gene,* which treated, among other things, the genetic role in altruism, but the book was controversial and widely criticized.

Two decades later the world was perhaps more willing to look at the power of genes, and in 1994 appeared Robert Wright's *The Moral Animal.* He got right to the point: genetically the human race wishes to survive and will do what it takes to do that. Many practices we think have a base in moral goodness are really expressions of the genetic will to survive. At the head of the list is altruism, activities in which an individual pays a price (time, money, deferment of satisfaction, even death) for the good of another individual or a group. If parents did not make constant sacrifices, children would not grow up to be productive members of society. Parents believe that they make such sacrifices out of love, but, according to Wright's "evolutionary psychology," parents somehow know that a child who grows up to be a librarian rather than an arsonist will benefit the group, which in turn is beneficial to the parents as individuals. But does any parent actually think like that? "Natural selection tends to work underground, by shaping human feelings, not by making humans conscious of its logic" (173).

Wright offers manifold examples. More than 90 percent of the American prison population is male, and men far more often solve their problems with violence than women do. Psychological factors? Macho behavior expected of men in patriarchies? Maybe, but Wright points out that men's bodies are physically better equipped for fighting than women's are, and that could explain why men resort to physical force more frequently and more quickly than women.

Since genetic transmission relies primarily upon sexual intercourse, Wright has a great interest in sexual behavior, at least of heterosexuals in patriarchies. "Polite" society has generally praised young women who were sexually reserved and frowned upon those who were sexually free, a trait widely associated with women in very low socioeconomic groups. But this behavior has a genetic base. Women whom men find attractive because of their physical appearance, education, cultivation, and social status know that they are desirable and will therefore eventually find a desirable "mate." This, in turn, means that they can be sexually reserved ("coy" is Wright's term) and wait. Women who are less desirable (in men's eyes) do not have that luxury. Since impoverished women rarely meet men with good education, money, and promising careers, genetically they have nothing to gain by being reserved and often engage in sexual behavior the upper socioeconomic classes consider immoral. Male sexual behavior works on the same principles. Male animals want to spread their genes to the largest number of females (a male ape with several females), and thus men have promiscuous urges, tempered by the need to bring up their biological offspring. But this has nothing to do with morality or with any sense of good and evil. "What is in our genes' interest is what seems 'right'—morally right, objectively right, whatever sort of rightness is in order" (325).

Wright even offers a genetic justification for polygamy. Would it not be in the best interest of an impoverished young woman to become the second wife of an educated, wealthy, socially prominent man, and thus get better genes for her prospective children and a husband who will invest time and energy in their upbringing as well as the opportunity to live far more comfortably herself? "In sheerly Darwinian terms, most men are probably better off in a monogamous system and most women worse off" (96). But won't this lead to chaos? No, because in the long run behaviors which benefit others are better for the species. "The new paradigm [evolutionary psychology] will lead the thinking person toward love and away from hate. It helps us judge each feeling on its merits; and on ground of merits, love usually wins" (341).

So how do individuals and society hold people responsible for what they do, especially acts traditionally understood to be evil, such as murder or theft? "'Free will' has been a fairly useful fiction, a rough approximation of utilitarian justice." But if there is no free will, then people are not responsible for horrendous actions? "We must get used to the idea of holding robots responsible for their malfunctions—so long, at least, as this accountability will do some good" (355). At the end of the book, Wright throws a comforting bone to those who worry about what this might do to human relations. "Indeed, if you ponder the ruthlessness of evolutionary logic enough, you may start to find our morality, such as it is, nearly miraculous" (378). Then again, you may not.

Wright believes that if people knew that notions of good and evil derive from genes and environment, they will be more tolerant and forgiving. But critics will worry, first, about any theory that claims to explain everything, and, second, about a theory that diminishes rationality and patronizes the notion of truth. Could not people abandon altruism, claiming indifference to the species? But Wright would insist on an evolutionary psychological reason even for a decision like that.

In 1996 the British biologist Lyall Watson wrote *Dark Nature: A Natural History of Evil*. Watson acknowledges that the question of genetics and evil is still in its infancy but provides a guide to how it might develop.

He quotes the "Victorian scientist and humanist" Thomas Henry Huxley: "Brought before the tribunal of ethics, the cosmos might well stand condemned" (249–50). Nature is amoral. Genes want to survive and to propagate themselves, and they will do whatever it takes to succeed. They follow three basic rules: (1) Be Nasty to Outsiders; (2) Be Nice to Insiders; (3) Cheat Whenever Possible. Watson shows how these rules apply in nature, especially among animals, and then suggests that these traits also apply to human behavior. For example, "Stepchildren are sixty-five times more likely to be murdered than children who still live with both of their natural parents" (120), a ferocious application of rule one.

To establish the parallels, Watson heavily emphasizes male animal behavior, especially the desire to propagate offspring with as many females as possible, a desire often frustrated when a more powerful male establishes a harem and drives away weaker rivals. Occasionally the excluded males will find some weaker females and force themselves upon unwilling and unprotected victims. In his human parallel, a large wallet replaces a large body as a desirable trait, and Watson finds it no surprise that most rapists are men "who have failed to climb the social or economic ladder and have the greatest difficulty in attracting desirable mates in the normal ways." Their victims are "usually poor, helpless, younger women" and rarely "rich, powerful, older women" (178).

> There is a sense in which all behavior is mediated biologically. . . . Our chemical and physical organization . . . determines finally how we respond to any new set of stimuli. We have always been, and probably always will be, at least partly in thrall to our biology. We are only human, which is to say organisms produced by natural selection, anyway (254).

Yet Watson is not a determinist because biology is not the sole factor in human development. "There have been changes in how we use the potential inherent in those brains, changes which depend less on biology than they do on culture" (253). Watson claims that "an informal moral code now exists in which there is an implicit understanding that we ought to be able by now to do better than the genetic minimum. Human nature is no longer inevitable" (270–1). Following Richard Dawkins, Watson uses the term "memes" to describe ideas which survive from generation to generation. "And, like viruses, they are forced to compete with one another in a truly Darwinian fashion, struggling for access to the most successful minds and bodies" (213). The "faith-meme" translates religious ideas and values, such as martyrdom or self-renunciation (celibacy, asceticism), which contradict the immediate demands of genes and prove that culture affects human evolution. Humans, acting in common, established culture as a means for survival, and it has taken on a life of its own, impacting physical evolution and introducing into it a moral element, our ability "to do better" than our genes demand (271).

"Doing better" implies a standard for the good. For Watson, good "can be defined as that which encourages the integrity of the whole" and evil "becomes anything which disturbs or disrupts such complete-ness. Anything unruly or over the top. Anything, in short, that is bad for the ecology" (9). Thus pollution is evil because it disrupts the natural workings of the world. On this standard, senseless violence, from strik-ing someone to genocide, is evil. (He is particularly interested in the 1993 murder of a two-year-old English child, James Bulger, by two ten-year-old boys, whose trial Watson attended.) For reasons yet unknown, humans have been able to evolve past the basic demands of their biol-ogy, for both good and ill. "The choice is ours. It is the capacity to choose that makes us special, giving the ability to select a course for nature, in-stead of just submitting to the course of natural selection" (292).

Maybe. We would like to think that we choose, but could not some radical geneticist claim that Pol Pot did not choose genocide but merely eliminated "weaker" members of Cambodian society who were inca-pable of adjusting to the new environment founded by the Khmer Rouge? Could not this geneticist claim that ethnic cleansing is not a hate-filled choice but just a way of eliminating "inferior" groups the way dominant animal and plant species eliminate rivals? The evidence is still coming in, and we should look at Watson's book as a pioneering effort.

He follows his data thoroughly, even when it leads to a socially un-popular stance. Many ecologists encourage people to return to a more natural way of life, but Watson points out that just hours after birth a baby hyena will literally kill another newborn to guarantee more mater-nal attention and thus food for itself. Nature is indeed red in tooth and claw, and returning to a truly natural way of life involves more than hu-mans often bargain for. Contrary to the views of many educators, social workers, and psychologists, Watson claims that humans never com-pletely escape from those three rules which govern genetic survival and that it is naïve to assume that by changing a person's environment (home, school), that person can change her or his behavior without tak-ing the genetic elements into consideration. Genes do not go away, and he makes the case that evil has a genetic base, although not to the ex-clusion of other factors.

Watson looks like an optimist next to Bryan Appleyard. In *Brave New Worlds: Staying Human in the Genetic Future* (1998), Appleyard explores the vast new power genetics has given to humans, such as designer ba-bies, and the new world view, which he calls genocentrism, which it is imposing upon us.

For Appleyard, geneticists believe that "evolution and the mighty gene give us a scientific basis for the moral and spiritual life of humanity" (92), an abandonment of the old attitude that science as science could not speak about morals. Appleyard takes the big step: if genes determine behavior, can individuals be held responsible for what they do? The law and society say yes, but is that merely because we want to believe that we have individual responsibility? Are we actually just our genes? "[A criminal's] genes made him do it [a crime], but his genes are him." But what about environmental forces, like a crime-infested neighborhood? Those forces are there, but a neighborhood is where our neighbors and their genes live. If our own genes don't drive us to do things, then other people's genes do. "Either way we end up as robots" (96–7).

Appleyard worries that genocentrism will rob us of our humanity, not just causing us to see ourselves as a biochemical collection but robbing us of our will to deal with problems and even forcing us into socially reprehensible actions. If a child is born to a family which has produced generations of criminals, why should society not lock the child up immediately rather than wait for the inevitable criminal to grow up and do something horrible? The child cannot be presumed innocent because eventually she or he must commit some crime; the child's genes guarantee guilt. The child may suffer, but at least the state can prevent one or more other people from suffering. Appleyard insists that such a bleak future is not as impossible as it may sound.

Echoing Watson's views about genes doing whatever it takes to survive, Appleyard claims that genocentrism will destroy psychology as we know it. "We do have a subconscious, but it is not defined by the systems of repressions of which Freud spoke; rather it is simply the realm of naked genetic self-interest which often pursues its goals by deceiving the conscious mind about its true motivations" (115).

Appleyard finds himself puzzled. He accepts the Enlightenment view that science has discredited religion, but he also knows that the genocides of the modern world discredit the Enlightenment view of moral progress via reason. He believes that genocentrism is wrong—"In order to become scientific, we must become inhuman" (166)—but he does not know how to respond to it. He only knows that we must. Otherwise we will turn the defining of human nature over to a small group of specialists who will inform as to what we are, based upon the latest genetic findings. In such a world, how will we even speak of good and evil?

But is this future inevitable? The answer depends partly on future research in genetics and partly upon how many people accept the view of the scientists Appleyard cites and put those views into practice. Many people simply will not do it. They will define life as they have lived it, and they will probably insist that the definition include their own experiences and those shared with others. And even old-fashioned psychology might enter in. Appleyard's scientists share the same set of presuppositions, the most important being that they are objectively analyzing life, yet who is to say that their approach is really objective and not a product of their genes or even of their environment? And are the genes which produced the geneticists any "better" than the genes which produced criminals?

Clearly the relationship between genetics and the understanding of evil has a long way to go, and so likely psychological theories will continue for a while to dominate scientific explanations of evil. Yet, just as clearly, future theories of evil, including psychological ones, must include genetics, and possibly genetics will overtake psychology as the central scientific explanation of evil.

Chapter 16

Modern Religious Approaches to Evil

The most prominent difficulty in Theism is the existence of evil.
—John Henry Newman, *Letter to J. R. Mozley*

Theists have a special interest in the problem of evil because they must reconcile the problem of evil with belief in a good and powerful deity. Since the eighteenth century, another aspect of the problem has become its use by skeptics and atheists to argue that evil calls God's existence into question or actually disproves it. We will examine both aspects of the question.

But first we must note that some theists see no need for theodicy. In 1996 Neale Donald Walsch published *Conversations with God: An Uncommon Dialogue, Book One,* with a New Age approach to evil. "To my surprise, as I scribbled out the last of my bitter, unanswerable thoughts and prepared to toss my pen aside, my hand remained poised over the paper, as if held there by some invisible force. Abruptly, the pen began *moving on its own*" (1, Walsch's emphasis). This arresting beginning introduces "God" to the dialogue. "God" identifies himself as the coincidence of opposites and tells Walsch that the only way to truly know something is to know its opposite. Not only that, "a thing cannot exist without its opposite" (29), so that not only is evil necessary to understand the good, it is necessary for the *existence* of the good. The necessity of evil to know the good obviates any need to reconcile God and evil.

"God" also tells Walsch that "'Rightness' or 'wrongness' is not an intrinsic condition, it is a subjective judgment in a personal value system" (48). "Evil is that which you *call* evil" (61)—in a word, relativism with all its attendant difficulties ["Let's not *call* genocidal murders evil, and then they won't *be* evil"] which do not interest Walsch or "God." Yet, *"if*

213

there were such a thing as sin, this would be it: to allow yourself to become what you are because of the experience of others" (p. 62, Walsch's emphasis). It is scary that this book is a best-seller.

At the other end of the spectrum, Christian fundamentalists also see no need for theodicy. They insist upon a biblical literalist interpretation beyond that of mainline Christians and Jews, and they accept the opening chapters of Genesis as historical accounts. There was a Garden of Eden, and Adam and Eve and the serpent all lived in it. Since the book of Revelation had identified the serpent with the devil, evil came into the world when the serpentine devil tempted humanity's first parents to commit original sin. He has continued his dastardly work ever since, as proved by a fundamentalist classic, Hal Lindsey's *Satan Is Alive and Well on Planet Earth* (1972), which found Satan at work in astrology, rock music, drug use, the media, secularist universities, and mainline Protestantism. No one needs theories to explain evil. It exists because of original sin.

A third "religious" group indifferent to theodicy would be Satanists, who claim to worship the devil. They define good as doing what Satan wants them to do and evil as disobeying him. They have little influence on concepts of evil, but they do serve a purpose, at least in the United States, by providing fodder for television talk shows.

Others

The demonization of Others has infected the West since the ancient world and reached its peak in the last century. Yet if the twentieth century brought the demonization of the Other to an appalling level, it also saw the effective end of justifying such a practice. The Holocaust made it clear beyond doubt what the notion of the Other can lead to, and most Christian denominations have renounced and apologized for anti-Semitism; some others sin by refusing to admit their responsibility. Recognizing the danger of demonizing the Other will soon challenge the United States where the fastest-growing religion is Islam. Since too many Americans unthinkingly link the words "Islamic" and "terrorist," we must avoid another demonization against our own fellow citizens, like the one imposed upon Japanese-Americans during World War II. The modern era has laid the theory of the Other to rest; one hopes the practice will follow.

The Devil and Original Sin

Belief in the devil continues to be strong in Christian circles, including most mainstream ones. Yet, outside fundamentalism, the devil plays no role in modern theodicies. In Christian teaching, the devil is a fallen angel, a created being whom God can control. If the devil exists and promotes evil, the true problem is why does God permit him to. The question of evil still revolves around God, not the devil.

Original sin is meeting the same fate. Biblical scholars point out that original sin was created by Augustine and that it appears in neither the Hebrew Bible nor the New Testament. The ecumenical and scholarly *Anchor Bible Dictionary* (1992) does not even include an entry on original sin, reflecting the consensus of Jewish, Catholic, and mainline Protestant scholars that original sin is not a biblical concept.

Modern theologians interpret original sin as a symbol of the human tendency toward evil, as the rabbis recognized two millennia ago. The Jewish philosopher Martin Buber (1878–1965) maintained the rabbinic tradition. "To the Biblical images of evil corresponds . . . the purpose of man to overcome the chaotic state of his soul. . . . For creation has a goal and the humanly right is service directed in the One direction. . . . [The] commission [of evil] is not doing of the deed but a sliding into it" (*Good and Evil* [1953], 140–2). Most Christian theologians now insist that this tendency toward evil is part of the human fabric and not just a result of upbringing and environment, yet it is not overwhelming and functions in humans alongside the tendency to do good. They also emphasize that original sin symbolizes the divided condition of human nature, living in the world yet separated from full community with the world and its inhabitants by sin. Furthermore, original sin can symbolize human resistance to divine grace and assistance. Most denominations have abandoned predestination in its crudest form. Humans still require the salvation gratuitously offered by God through Christ, but this salvation is available to all, not just a predestined elect.

Consider these passages from theological dictionaries, standard but not innovative works. The mainline Protestant *Westminster Dictionary of Christian Theology* (1983): "At least as an existential fact of the human condition, and *however it may be called,* original sin . . . affirms man's inability to attain his purpose in life without confessing his native inadequacy and seeking his salvation as God's gift through faith" (421, my emphasis). *A Concise Dictionary of Theology* (1991) by Jesuits Gerald O'Collins and Edward Farrugia: "Original sin expresses not only the sinful condition into which all human beings are born, but also the fact that the new life in grace coming through baptism is no 'natural' right but the free gift of God." These works insist upon a fidelity to biblical teaching without passing that teaching through an Augustinian filter.

Feminist Views of Evil

Because of the strictures of a patriarchal society, few women contributed to Western notions of evil before the twentieth century. Today women contribute in two ways, by following the mainstream path and writing theodicies (as we shall see later in this chapter), or by contending that the mainstream path is a male path, indifferent to women's concerns, ignorant of women's understanding evil, and even inimical to women. We will consider two significant works from the latter group.

In 1973 Mary Daly published *Beyond God the Father: Toward a Philosophy of Women's Liberation*. Daly concentrates on the influence of organized religion upon women, claiming that Western religions have imposed patriarchy on society and in so doing have made women symbols of evil. "The image of the person in authority . . . has corresponded to the eternal masculine stereotype," thus forcing women to give up their wholeness to correspond to a destructive ideal (15). "If God is male, then the male is God" (19). Women should not cooperate with sexism by trying to update or reform religious teaching but rather must break free from it.

She insists that what religions call "God's plan" is a mask for men's plan, that talk about a happy afterlife deters women from doing anything about their subordinate status in this life, and that the image of God the judge "confirms the rightness of the rules and roles of the reigning system" (19). Religious institutions and most social ones exist to protect and prolong patriarchy, and their values, including their explanations of evil, are neither fair nor objective. Some forces which social institutions have identified as evil, such as war, are indeed so, and the institutions are capable of reform, but, as they exist today, these institutions promote the evil of patriarchy and women should be wary before accepting what the institutions define as evil.

Daly focuses on the Genesis creation myth. She complains that people no longer take it seriously today, which blinds them from seeing its historical and continuing impact on the West. It "takes on cosmic proportions since the male's viewpoint is metamorphosed into God's viewpoint. . . . As long as the myth of feminine evil is allowed to dominate human consciousness and social arrangements, it provides the setting for women's victimization" (48). This myth has had such deep influence that "repudiating the myth of feminine evil will require a corporate redemptive action by women" (55). Christian tradition created the myth of the fallen woman and then established as her opposite a woman who was both virgin and mother, but this "impossible ideal has a punitive function since, of course, no woman can really live up to it" (62). Women can only define good and evil when they have liberated themselves from patriarchal oppression, at which point men will also be liberated from the false values patriarchy has imposed upon them. Only in a yet-to-be-realized post-patriarchal world can all humans work a true and just understanding of good and evil.

In *Women and Evil* (1989), Nel Noddings challenges the general philosophical approach to evil which stressed theory over experience or which fitted experience into theory. When the classic explanations of evil came into being, "human" experience was men's experience, but evil must also be seen "through the eyes of people who bear and raise children, try to maintain a comfortable and stable home, feed and nurture the hungry and developing" (19). She cites the excesses of past thinkers on evil. "Scholars have concentrated on the terror induced by disobeying a father, god, or authority and thereby incurring its wrath. They have paid relatively little attention to the desire for goodness that is aroused by loving relations with the mother" (9). Male theodicies insist that innocent suffering must be accepted as a mysterious element in an otherwise benign divine plan, and this justifies suffering. No one wishes to suffer or to see others suffer, but, if it is part of a divine plan, then we will just have to tolerate it. But, Noddings asks, why should we ever justify or even tolerate suffering? And why should the believer have to justify God? Who wants a deity whose conduct has to be explained away?

Theodicy reflects another male value. It promotes the control of others. "Since God presents the world to us in an impenetrable mystery, there is precedent for mystification, and the dependent and powerless must learn to trust authority" (20). The authority to be trusted is, of course, male.

In this society, women find themselves relegated to the home, yet Noddings finds some goodness in this. Caring for children is a positive contribution to society, far more positive than finding ways to intimidate weaker nations or to make money. She wants women to have the option of pursuing any career, but she will not write off as irrelevant the personal experiences of billions of women throughout history. She recognizes that the traditional definition of the "good woman" fits the male definition of a good woman, but to dismiss all the elements of this definition, such as caregiving, is a terrible mistake.

> This is a trap that feminists as well as other social meliorists are
> likely to fall into. We are simply not going to make the world better
> by making it possible for women to live like traditional men—that
> is, to escape the vocation of caregiving—for then *no one* will live
> with the assurance of compassion and the security of devoted love
> (177, Noddings' emphasis).

Noddings defines evil in several ways. She designates three categories of evil: pain, separation, and helplessness. She also redefines traditional categories of evil: natural evil consists not of the earthquakes and floods of classical theodicy but rather of the daily evils of illness and death. She defines moral evil in a traditional way, the willful infliction of pain, but, in place of metaphysical evil, she speaks of cultural evils, that is, evils endemic to society, such as poverty, war, and sexism. She knows most classical theories of evil, and she finds them wanting in people's experiences.

Yet Noddings is always careful not to reject out of hand all values traditionally understood as masculine, nor does she assume that women's values will necessarily solve society's ills. She calls for a serious reassessment of values in terms of their presuppositions (theory) and effects (experience). She follows her own advice and takes a good look at the effects of traditional notions on men. "Men too have suffered psychological abuse from societies that have created uniform expectations for them, and this fact is often overlooked" (225). Noddings proves a traditional feminist claim—women's liberation is men's liberation.

Writers such as Daly and Noddings make it clear that any modern theory of evil must take into account the views of that half of the human race that has historically been so systematically excluded.

Evil and the Question of God's Existence

Modern theologians and philosophers have continued the long tradition of trying to reconcile God and evil or to prove that evil and God cannot coexist and, since evil obviously exists, God cannot. These attempts fall into several categories, and we will look at some of the most prominent ones.

The Logical Problem of Evil

David Hume framed the problem. If God is good, he does not wish evil to exist. If he is omnipotent, he has the power to eliminate evil. But evil exists, implying that God does not exist. In 1955 J. L. Mackie (1917–81) wrote a seminal article, "Evil and Omnipotence," in which he argued that evil and such a deity are logically inconsistent. If humans *often* choose the good, why could they not *always* do so? Mackie contended that a truly omnipotent deity could create intellectual creatures who would always *freely* choose the good, that is, they would always do the good but would not be moral automatons. To say that God could not create such beings is to say that God is not truly omnipotent. Such a view is inconsistent with the traditional understanding of God. Since God did not create such beings, Mackie contended that theists would have to abandon either God's goodness or his omnipotence, that is, to abandon the accepted notion of God, or they would have to conclude, as he did, that God logically cannot exist.

The traditional response to this has been the Free Will Defense, that God must create rational creatures with free will, even if they would use that will to choose evil. The leading modern exponent of this approach is Alvin Plantinga (1932–), who insists that it is logically possible for God and evil to coexist. (Since Mackie contended that it is not logically possible for God and evil to coexist, Plantinga does not have to prove that they do but only that it is logically possible that they do.) In *God, Freedom, and Evil* (1977), he makes extensive use of Anglo-American logic. His arguments cannot be recounted fully, but basically he argues that God loves his creations, and he wants them always to choose the good, although they must make that choice freely. But, Plantinga points out, if God created creatures in such a way that they *always* chose the good freely, he thus caused or determined what they would do, and any kind of determinism destroys human freedom. God must create beings capable of moral evil as well as moral good; otherwise, they are not completely free. Therefore God must allow evil to occur.

The logical problem of evil does not command the attention it used to, but the questions it raises are still pertinent.

The Evidential Problem of Evil

While the logical problem of evil debates whether the coexistence of God and evil is illogical or inconsistent, the evidential problem questions how reasonable or indeed plausible that coexistence is. Augustine, Luther, and Milton argued that God can bring good out of evil, Leibniz and Pope argued that "partial evil" succumbs to the "universal good." They take the same basic approach—even evil acts have meaning in a world guided by divine providence. But scholars like Edward Madden and Peter Hare (see bibliography) consider this approach specious.

Most people can accept the coexistence of God and evil if the evil is something like a stolen wallet—the loss is real but we have learned to be more careful in future, thus preventing an even worse loss. But the Holocaust? the Gulag? the Killing Fields? What kind of divine plan requires the violent extermination of tens of millions of people? Theists answer that they do not know, but they are sure God has a plan, yet any sensitive and sensible person has to ask what kind of God would have a plan like that. And what good is the divine plan if it causes such sufferings among God's creatures who can see the horrors and yet never perceive the goodness emerging from them? To be sure, some goods came from them, such as the awareness of the true evil of demonizing the Other and the determination to combat it. But can any good arising from such suffering justify its extent? In his *Faith of a Heretic* (1961), Walter Kaufmann asserted, "The theism preached from thousands of pulpits and credited by millions of believers is disproved by Auschwitz and a billion lesser evils" (139).

Theists cannot claim to explain much less justify such horrors, but the approach they use against the logical problem of evil is applicable here. When God gave his creatures free will and thus the opportunity to do evil, he did not put a limit on the evil they would freely do. Yet even theists would concede that the genocides of the modern era make this a difficult doctrine, and they share with Job the agony of God's apparent absence. (As we shall see further on, there are *theological* responses to this question that have meaning for believers but would not answer atheist critics.)

The Problem of Gratuitous Evil

The problem of gratuitous evil is a subset of the evidential problem in that it does not use evil to disprove God's existence but rather raises serious questions about the plausibility of theism. Gratuitous suffering differs significantly from innocent suffering. In theodicy innocent suffering means that the person who suffers an evil did nothing to deserve it, but that God will somehow bring some good out of the event. Gratuitous suffering means that the person who suffers an evil did nothing to deserve it but no good came from the evil event. Theists cannot accept gratuitous suffering because they accept the existence of a beneficent being whose motives they cannot fully understand. Thus any evil event, no matter how horrendous, can be part of a divine plan. But to critics, this seems like an eternal excuse that can be universally applied to any event to justify or at least mitigate its severity.

In *Philosophy of Religion: An Introduction* (1993), William Rowe offers the example of a fawn which had been badly burned in a forest fire and which lingers for several days in terrible agony before dying (80–1). On the surface, no good seems to have come from the fawn's suffering. The theist could argue that God brought out of that suffering a good of which we are unaware, but Rowe effectively asks how often that argument can be used. "But even if we should think it is reasonable to believe that [the] fawn's suffering leads to a greater good unobtainable without that suffering, we must then ask whether *all* the instances of profound, seemingly pointless human and animal suffering lead to greater goods" (81). Literally billions of evil acts occur without apparent good arising from them, and theists must somehow justify every last one of them. Rowe concludes that although one cannot prove that any particular act of suffering was gratuitous, it is reasonable to believe that such acts occur. And if any suffering is purely gratuitous, then the theist must acknowledge that God permits it, thus altering the traditional view of a deity who can bring meaning out of suffering, or the theist must even concede that God does not exist.

The argument for gratuitous evil presents the most formidable modern challenge to God's existence. Although not insuperable, it does manifest the tenuousness of theistic explanations of evil that ultimately rest on the incomprehensibility of God.

Modern Theodicies

Process Theodicy

Some theistic thinkers offer an important approach which obviates the problem of how to explain the coexistence of evil and a good, omnipotent deity. The Anglo-American philosopher Alfred North Whitehead (1861–1947) founded process theology, which claims that God is not immutable but instead is growing as we are, and, furthermore, that he is not omnipotent, a key element in Hume's and most atheist criticism of theistic approaches to evil.

For generations Western theists had accepted the Greek notion that God could not change because he was perfect and thus the only way he could change was to become imperfect. This is logical but not biblical. In the Bible, God changes his mind (he regrets he created the human race and so sends the Flood) and becomes emotionally involved with his creation. To many theists, this represents a primitive anthropomorphism, which intellectuals should discard. But process theists take the biblical texts more seriously, not in a fundamentalist way, but by accepting that God can be affected by what humans do. The unchanging deity of tradition was, in a sense, not alive, because to be alive is to grow and change. God grows with the human race and with the expanding cosmos.

Biblical tradition identifies God as a loving parent. People feel anguish when someone they love hurts them, and so, too, does God, the process theologians say. When humans do evil, they turn their backs on the deity. The traditional deity could inflict apocalyptic disasters upon humans, but a loving God rejects force and tries to win humans over with love and persuasion. Furthermore, when someone we love suffers, we suffer with her or him. The traditional God of Western philosophy and theology could not suffer; his omnipotence and perfection put him beyond that. But, say the process thinkers, he must suffer if he loves us. Whitehead defined the process deity as "the fellow-sufferer who understands" (*Process and Reality,* 532).

Process thinkers such as Charles Hartshorne and David Griffin challenge the traditional notion of divine omnipotence. If God were omnipotent, then he would have all the power and no other being would have any, and any interaction between a being with all power and a being with no power would be meaningless. Furthermore, if we have no power at all, then we could not really be free because God could dismiss our freedom whenever he chose. For the process thinkers, we must have an inherent freedom and the power to resist God, who must respect us and try to win us over to the good. One consequence of this is that the traditional problem of evil does not apply to the process deity because the problem assumes an omnipotent God. Since God is not omnipotent, there are events that he cannot prevent, including gratuitous evils. Process thinkers accept the free will defense for evil, but not as Plantinga understands it. A noncoercive deity cannot create us so that we will always do the good; he must give the ability to choose and then try to win us over so that we freely do the good. Every evil act is a tragedy, but we can learn from tragedies. God helps us to understand the harm of evil and shares the pain that evil causes for us and others. Most process theologians reject the notion of personal immortality (although humans survive objectively as elements in the divine eternal reality), and so there can be no postmortem reward or punishments. Humans must actualize their potentialities here and now, and God will aid them to do so. Failure to self-actualize is evil.

Any theory this broad naturally has critics, who form a wide band, from theologians who object that process theology inconsistently abolishes an all-powerful God but keeps a morally perfect one, to atheists who consider this view of the deity to be illogical and apologetic. Many traditional theists question whether process theology can stand in the biblical tradition with a rejection of omnipotence and a personal afterlife. The debate will go on, but the process thinkers have established an innovative theodicy which goes beyond traditional categories.

Irenaean Theodicy

John Hick's *Evil and the God of Love* (rev. ed. 1978) has dominated much thinking about theodicy, especially in the English-speaking world. Hick (1922–) argued that humans are not the finished moral products of Augustine's Eden but rather are always in the making, an idea he got from the Early Christian writer Irenaeus of Lyons (d. ca. 202). Hick claims that the traditional notion of the fall distorts our view of our nature, but the term has been around for so long that it cannot be dropped. He reinterprets it as the yawning gap between what kind of persons we actually are and what God hopes we will be. For Hick, humans come to moral maturity through experience, an experience guided but not determined by God, a process Hick calls "soul-making." Soul-making occurs in a social environment; other moral agents interact with the individual and even the physical environment plays a role. God presents the individual with moral choices and tries to win the person over to the good.

Hick concedes a remarkable point to atheist critics who use evil to argue for God's nonexistence. He says that God could have created a world in which humans could freely have always chosen the good, thus rejecting a central pillar of the Free Will Defense. God did not do so because an environment of challenge enables humans to become morally mature, whereas if we always chose the good, we would be morally weak, never having known what it was like to make a real moral decision.

Furthermore, our decisions would be of less value to God because they were not the products of mature people but of moral children.

Plausible as this sounds in Hick's context, it does raise the question of the amount of suffering in the world. Hick admits that God could obviate suffering, so he must concede that God allows it. What can one think of a deity who could have stopped but allowed the genocides of the modern world? Hick replies that the suffering is relative to an ideal which humans establish, and so God really cannot eliminate suffering from the world. A believer might pray for a loved one who was critically injured in an accident; if that person survived the accident, the believer might pray for her or his survival from cancer; if the loved one survived that, what next? At some point people die, and we cannot reasonably expect God to spare us and those we love from all suffering on earth.

Because of human evil and natural disasters, the deity often seems distant to the individual, but, for Hick, this is not all bad. If we knew God to be present, we would not require faith. This "epistemic distance" requires the individual to nurture faith and trust in God. Here Hick answers Job—the absence of God necessitates faith on our part. Some individuals prosper in this demanding environment and move to moral maturity; in other words, soul-making succeeds for them. Clearly it does not for others, yet God does not abandon them. Hick believes in universal salvation, so if God cannot attract individuals in this life, then the process will continue in a postmortem existence until God has won all intelligent creatures to the good. This is not a variation on purgatory. Hick argues not for a postmortem restitution for earthly sins but for a continuing process that was uncompleted in earthly life. Not surprisingly, this contention has brought significant criticism upon Hick. More traditional thinkers insist that the Bible says that we can do enough in this life to be saved or that God can save us by reckoning us righteous. Other critics insist that Hick has devalued the moral efforts of humans by stretching these efforts into a hypothetical or at least unprovable future and that his transference of the solution to the problem of evil into a postmortem world weakens any imperative to solve problems now. Furthermore, if we can profit from adversity, does this not imply the Leibnizian best of all possible worlds and make God responsible for every evil since we can presumably profit from them?

Hick insists that evils are real evils that we should work to eliminate, but he insists that we must encounter them for spiritual growth. He cannot prove the deity will work with people in a postmortem existence, but he sees this a logical possibility, especially since God will not desert his creatures, now or in the future. There is no way Hick and his critics can meet on the question of a postmortem continuation of the soul-making process, a point central to Hick's theory, which falls apart without it.

Hick's theory is just that, a theory which demands acceptance or rejection; most people doing theodicy have chosen the latter but have had to sharpen their own arguments in response to him.

The original Irenaean theodicy focused on recapitulation, that in Christ God brings to fruition the past and future and that at the end of time and in Christ he restores the human race to the glory it had before Adam's sin. Pierre Teilhard de Chardin (1871–1955), a French Jesuit and anthropologist, revived that approach. Classic Darwinism says that life evolves according to natural selection toward no goal and without the guidance of an intelligent being. Teilhard believed that under divine guidance the cosmos was actually progressing toward a goal, the Omega point, which he identified as Christ. (Omega is the last letter of the Greek alphabet, and the book of Revelation identifies Christ as "the Alpha and the Omega, the beginning and the end" [21:6].) Teilhard expressed his views in many of his writings but most especially in *The Phenomenon of Man* (1955).

Teilhard believed that God's creation went through a series of creations, from cosmogenesis to geogenesis on to biogenesis, followed by hominization as creatures in the divine image began to inhabit the earth and next by noogenesis as the power of thought transformed humanity.

> Noogenesis produces reflective persons which converge upon the Omega point and will do so much more after the final threshold of the biological collective is crossed. So, in a sense, Omega is the culmination of the series. Yet Omega . . . is outside space and time, and so is transcendent to all series. This transcendence is the final property of Omega (Edward Dodson, *The Phenomenon of Man Revisited*, 200).

All of evolution points toward the transcendent Omega-Christ and is moving toward it. Evil can be understood as part of a world of becoming rather than of being, and evil cannot stop the world's progress toward the Omega point. When creation is joined to God, evil will disappear. Teilhard took evil very seriously, and in an appendix to *Phenomenon* he discussed several types of evil, including disorder, decomposition, anxiety, and even growth, but not moral evil.

Teilhard provided not so much a theodicy as a vision, but one that situated evil in a developing cosmos and one created by a scientist with a first-hand knowledge of evolution that was so often lacking in his many critics.

"Are You Glad That You Exist?"

William Hasker ("On Regretting the Evils of This World," 1981) based his approach to evil upon the question, "Are you glad that you exist?"

Like most modern theodicies, this uses Anglo-American logical terms and should be read in its entirety. I will summarize the argument.

Are you glad that you exist? Not, are you happy with your life as it is; not, do you wish to change your life; just the basics—are you glad that you are in existence? Among the world's billions, presumably there are some who are not, but to quote Alexander Pope, "Hope springs eternal in the human breast." We can all hope for something better and most of us are glad that we exist.

We are in existence because of our parents, which in turn means we owe our existence to the forces that brought our parents together. This realization introduces us to a much larger picture. We are all aware of the interconnectedness of events in history. We are all in existence because of a multitude of factors, and many of those factors were evil. The Irish people in the nineteenth century had to endure oppression, poverty, and starvation, factors which drove millions of them to emigrate to the United States. If they had not emigrated, my wife and I would never have existed because our parents would not have existed. Had we not existed, our children would never have existed. I and people I love dearly are in existence because of the suffering of the Irish people.

This question need not be set on so large a scale. Consider a man who deeply loves his wife and children. This is possible only because his first wife died in an automobile accident a few months after their wedding. This tragedy cost a young woman decades of life and left a young husband desolated. Yet had the accident not occurred, he never would have met his current wife and their children would never have existed.

Thus the dilemma: Since we or persons we love could not exist unless some horrible event had happened and since we are glad that we or they exist, are we therefore glad that the event happened? The answer would be no in the sense that we would not be "glad"; we would certainly wish that this good had a different origin. But since this good depends at least partially on an evil event, is it really possible for us to wish our own and our loved ones' nonexistence? This ingenious argument appeals to theists who are constantly defending the possibility of God's existence in the face of seemingly gratuitous evil. If we can recognize that good things arose from some genuinely evil event, then the event is not totally without meaning.

But does the existence of an evil event that resulted in a good require a theistic explanation? Ultimately not. Atheists or skeptical theists might ask, could not the constellation of events, negative and positive, which brought us and our loved ones into existence, simply have happened, much the way evolution proceeds without a guiding intelligence? The answer, of course, is yes; we and our loved ones benefited from the accidents of history. Yet this argument can have a theistic application. Gratuitous evil represents the strongest use of evil against the existence of God, but this argument can reconcile God with evil by showing that he can bring good out of evil and that no event need be gratuitously evil. This argument provides a logical and an intriguing method of reconciling God and the existence of evil.

Traditional Theodicy, Updated

The Western religious tradition of theodicy has its modern supporters. The German Jesuit theologian Karl Rahner (1904–84) linked traditional Augustinian and Thomistic teaching with modern philosophical insights, but he remained first and foremost a theologian.

Many modern theistic writers, such as Plantinga, have tried to reconcile the existence of God and of evil by means of the Free Will Defense, but Rahner would have none of it.

> According to Christian understanding, . . . the freedom of men and angels is a created freedom, sustained in its existence and nature always and everywhere by God's supreme providence, in its power and action, in its capacity and concrete decision. . . . Our free decision as such is nevertheless in every respect and in its whole reality dependent upon God ("Why Does God Allow Us to Suffer?" *Theological Investigations* 19, 201–2).

He considered and rejected a variety of explanations for innocent human suffering, such as evil as a product of freedom or as a way to produce morally mature creatures who struggle against it. He concluded that suffering is incomprehensible, but

> this mystery of God's incomprehensibility, however, is not merely the mystery of a being to be understood as static, but is also the mystery of God's freedom, of his underivable disposition, which has not to be justified before any other authority. . . . Suffering, then, is the form . . . in which the incomprehensibility of God himself appears (206).

Believers can only approach God in love, a love "dispossessing man until he is absorbed selflessly into the mystery of God" (205). Rahner did not hide evil behind God's incomprehensibility but rather argued that God in his essential being is beyond our comprehension, and evil manifests this reality.

He brought another element to the discussion:

> The mystery of God's incomprehensibility, however, is not merely the mystery of a being to be understood as static, but is also the mystery of God's freedom, of his underivable disposition, which has not to be justified before any other authority. . . . If [his freedom] wills the

suffering of the creature [it] is incomprehensible, since it could achieve without suffering the sacred aims of the freedom that wills suffering (206).

Human acceptance of this is more than just a way to explain the coexistence of God and evil; it is how we approach God in his totality. "In our present concrete state, the acceptance of suffering without an answer other than the incomprehensibility of God and his freedom is the concrete form in which we accept God himself and allow him to be God" (207). Incomprehensibility is part of God's being, not a deficiency.

Many contemporary theistic thinkers still work in the eighteenth-century mode, trying to avoid reliance upon faith while answering criticisms of secular thinkers. Rahner spoke openly as a theologian, although he also spoke to and learned from other traditions. For him God's incomprehensibility is an essential element of his relation with humans; furthermore, even in heaven when believers encounter God directly, he will still be incomprehensible although at that stage believers will be able to accept that. (Although Rahner did not cite him, Martin Buber shared his views. "Good conceived thus cannot be located within any system of ethical co-ordination, for all those we know came into being on its account and existed or exist by virtue of it" [*Good and Evil,* 142]. Human freedom functions within the context of the divine.)

Rahner offered a sophisticated Roman Catholic updating of traditional theodicy, and the Canadian author John Stackhouse updates traditional Protestant teaching.

In his *Can God Be Trusted? Faith and the Challenge of Evil* (1998) Stackhouse presents the challenges that evil presents to the Christian, next reviews the response to evil in other religions, considers the theistic responses (Plantinga, Hasker), and finally concludes, as did Rahner, that evil can only be approached by faith—which includes a belief in Satan and a rather historical understanding of the Gospel narratives.

Disappointed that Christian scholars usually leave Jesus out of their attempts to answer the problem of evil, Stackhouse turns to the Bible and points out that it contains no comprehensive theodicy (92). Instead the Bible deals more with how to respond to the challenge of evil than to explain it. Not that Stackhouse ignores the problem. "God must provide us with grounds to *trust* in spite of evil, and in spite of our lack of a complete understanding of it" (99). God does this in the person of Jesus: "We can respond properly to evil in our lives *because we know that God is all-good and all-powerful because we know Jesus*" (104, Stackhouse's emphasis). He relates the problem of evil to the doctrine of the Trinity. God knows what it is to suffer because, "If the doctrine of the Trinity is stoutly affirmed, however, then it is God who hangs on the cross" (118). In the person of Christ God intimately experienced the physical and emotional suffering of humans. Stackhouse insists that the real problem for Christians is not evil but sin, and he recommends ways to overcome, especially becoming part of a worshiping community—"ask [its members] to introduce you to Jesus" (171).

Although a professor himself, he concludes that the academic response to evil must always fall short. He insists that faith is not an abandonment of knowledge but rather increases our knowledge, allowing us to know truths unreachable by reason alone. In more than just a pastoral sense, faith is the only true theistic response to evil, and faith includes more than just assent to dogmatic propositions—it includes love, trust, and sometimes suffering, all under the guidance of divine providence.

The last author we will discuss is also a theologian, but Marilyn McCord Adams is an American woman in holy orders, whose book indicates how future discussions may develop and whose person suggests who will be increasingly shaping those discussions.

Adams works within the Christian tradition, although she uses much of *Horrendous Evils and the Goodness of God* (1999) to debate the merits of various philosophical theodicies, all of which she finds wanting. She concentrates on horrendous evils, which she defines as "evils the participation in which (that is, the doing or suffering of which) constitutes prima facie reason to doubt whether the participant's life could (given their inclusion in it) be a great good to him/her on the whole" (26). She goes on: "I find this criterion for horrendous evils to be objective, but relative to individuals. . . . I define the category of horrendous evils as I do because I wish to focus on precisely those evils, Divine permission of which clearly calls into question Divine goodness towards the individuals who participate in them" (27). She insists that God has to defeat evil but not in the sense of abolishing it or somehow making it just, but rather by having the experience "relevantly integrated" into a person's "relation to a great enough good" (29). Only God can provide such a good to persons, and, "at a minimum, God's goodness to human individuals would require that God guarantee each a life that was a great good to him/her on the whole by balancing serious evils" (31). She works out these themes in the rest of the book.

As a theologian Adams uses the resources of Christian faith, and she recognizes that God's goodness may not be apparent but also that God can make our lives worthwhile after death. She shows other traditional themes. On the question of the extent of suffering, she insists that God would never permit more suffering than he could defeat (54), and she agrees with Rahner that God is not "a cause among others, alongside all others," but rather, "divine causal power operates on a different level, to empower finite causes by virtue of being the power through which they exist" (65). Like Job, she acknowledges an unbridgeable gap between the divine and the human from the human point of view (191), but God can bridge the gap.

But Adams fears the traditional imagery of divine power overcoming evil. Instead she points to the model of Christ, who gained power through suffering, who changed the world by giving up his life, not by forcing others to give up theirs. She believes that a divine being became human in Jesus and, like Stackhouse, she claims that "it is God's becoming a human being, experiencing the human condition from the inside, from the viewpoint of a finite consciousness, that integrates the experience [of evil] into an incommensurately valuable relationship" (168). To those who would claim that her view of divine activity compromises human freedom, she uses an untraditional image for theological writing, invoking "the mother-infant analogy to make room for particular Divine providence without the phenomenon of created voluntary action" (104).

Adams acknowledges and discusses the familiar philosophical arguments, but she concludes that they can no longer advance the question. She uses familiar biblical and theological arguments, but she concludes that she must go beyond them. In a very modern stance, she insists on who she is, a theologian, and will let her philosophical critics reject that if they wish. She also incorporates pastoral themes into her argument. Like Nel Noddings, she does not care for a God whose actions have to be explained. Rather, she insists on a deity who cares for humans, and who cares for them as individuals. In a remarkable statement she asserts: "I assume that for an individual's life to be a great good to him/her on the whole, it is not enough for good to balance off or defeat evil objectively speaking. The individual must him/herself also recognize and appropriate at least some of those positive meanings" (82). Modern theodicies and traditional faith explanations for evil fall short if they prove that God has objectively overcome evil but individuals continue to suffer.

Epilogue

The truth is out there.
—Fox Mulder

The attempt to understand evil has a long history in the West, from Job through Augustine, the scholastics, the Reformers, the Humanists, the *philosophes,* the Romantics, the social scientists, and now the geneticists. All of these people "solved" the problem of evil, but contemporary and later thinkers disagreed with them. The search for the answer goes on.

Like most historians, I do not feel comfortable writing about the future, but some trends suggest the direction in which theories of evil will go. Many traditional ideas will persist, such as belief in the devil and also in hell (Jeffrey Walls, *Hell: The Logic of Damnation* [1992]; Jonathan Kvanig, *The Problem of Hell* [1993]). Relativism is here to stay but in a modified form; few will say the Holocaust was not truly evil and that it depends on how you look at it. Demonizing the Other will also persist but with no intellectual credibility. Women will have much more to say about evil. Some will understand evil from women's perspectives, while others will defend traditional approaches but insist that they take a more pastoral and personalist approach by emphasizing the redemptive aspects of suffering and of integrating it into one's whole life. More and more a concern for the human impact of evil will emerge. Lisa Barnes and Michelle Shattuck raise the humane question of *God and the Victim: Theological Reflections on Evil, Victimization, Justice, and Forgiveness* (2000).

Marginalized groups will speak forcefully on the matter of evil. An example of this is liberation theology, a movement by Latin American Christian thinkers who contend that any Church ethic or polity must speak to the evil of economic and social deprivation in Latin America; otherwise any discussion will be irrelevant. This demand for immediacy runs counter to the traditional European and Anglo-American approach of discussing such matters on a theoretical level, not to the exclusion of practical application but without specific concern for it. The liberation theologians insist that Latin America's poor are poor now, and it is an evil to debate philosophies and theodicies and expect the poor to wait for North American and European thinkers to decide what to do.

Western views of evil will also be influenced by the views of other cultures and religions. In the Cleveland area, what had been a traditional, Roman Catholic, working-class suburb now boasts a Buddhist temple that attracts many people who are not Buddhists. While many non-Buddhist visitors may stay within their own traditions, they will still pick up elements of Buddhist teaching, one example of what will become a larger trend. For example, Buddhism focuses on liberating people from ignorance, not from sin. To know one's self is to know others and to transcend the barriers between humans, barriers the biblical religions believe are erected by sin. The coincidence of opposites has always played a marginal role in the West, but it plays a great role in Asian explanations of evil. It will likely play a greater role in the West.

The fastest growing religion in the United States is Islam. Muslim theology of evil involves a belief in Satan and in the *jinn* or evil spirits. As Islamic influence spreads in the United States, and as Jews, Christians, and Muslims interact, all may have to rethink notions of evil. (As for how this might happen, I learned about Islamic theories of evil from a Muslim graduate student pursuing a degree in religious studies at my Jesuit university.)

Many groups will rethink evil. In "The Usefulness of Sin" (*World: The Journal of the Unitarian Universalist Association*, winter 1999), Philip Simmons urged UU readers to rethink evil, claiming that accepting the existence of sins allows people to acknowledge their interdependence with other people and with all existence. Simultaneously, the winter 1999 issue of *Parabola*, journal of the Society for the Study of Myth and Tradition, focused on evil, with articles ranging from Medieval demonology through Jungian concepts to Asian experience and finishing with modern film—myth and tradition encounter high tech in the search to explain evil.

For theists, theodicy will continue to offer explanations for evil and to attract atheist critics of these explanations. But they will have to reevaluate their approaches in light of such developments as feminism and scientific insights. Psychology will continue to contribute to our understanding of how and sometimes why people are evil, but genetics seems poised to take a larger share of the scientific explanations of evil. Yet genetics will raise many other questions about good and evil, such as whether there will be a place in genetically-engineered societies for the less than genetically perfect (Hans Reinders, *The Future of the Disabled in Society* [2000]).

At some point, theories of evil will encounter the final frontier. The University of California at Berkeley has a chair for the Search for Extraterrestrial Intelligence, funded by two members of the group SETI (Search for Extra Terrestrial Intelligence). Skeptics abound—*Rare Earth* (2000) by Donald Brownlee and Peter Ward claims intelligent extraterrestrial life may be very unlikely—but the attempt to find intelligent life outside our solar system has clearly moved past science fiction and is now being taken seriously by scientists who believe that in the billions of galaxies in the universe there must be some form of intelligent life. When we do make contact, what will we find? Are there totally good or totally evil beings anywhere in the universe? Will the extraterrestrials be like us, a mix of both? In *The War of the Worlds* (1898), H. G. Wells portrayed hostile, merciless aliens intent on conquering the earth, while in *Perelandra* (1944) C. S. Lewis pictured a perfectly good world threatened by humans. Popular television series, like the undying Star Trek and its progeny, have shown good, evil, and mixed beings like ourselves. Will the aliens need redemption? Will they need to redeem us? And when we do encounter intelligent extraterrestrial life, what will that do to our understanding of evil on earth or at least among our species?

The truth is out there, but future generations will have to find it.

A Personal Reflection

After reading this book, the reader is entitled to know the author's personal view of evil. My view is really quite simple. I am a theist, a Christian, a Roman Catholic, and thus must reconcile my belief in God with the existence of evil. In a word, I cannot. In spite of years of teaching and thinking about this topic and of learning from these many authors and from my students, I still cannot reconcile the existence of a good God with the existence of evil. Therefore, my personal view is that of the anonymous Jewish author who wrote the Book of Job. Like him, I cannot fathom why God does what he does, and thus I will never understand why this God permits evil. The author of Job had to accept his ignorance and trust in his God. So do I.

Select Bibliography

Ancient World

General

Bernstein, Alan. *The Formation of Hell: Death and Retribution in the Ancient and Early Christian Worlds.* Ithaca, N.Y.: Cornell University Press, 1993.

Ferguson, Everett. *Demonology of the Early Christian World.* New York: E. Mellen Press, 1984.

Forsyth, Neil. *The Old Enemy: Satan and the Combat Myth.* Princeton, N.J.: Princeton University Press, 1987.

Russell, Jeffrey Burton. *The Devil: Perceptions of Evil from Antiquity to Primitive Christianity.* Ithaca, N.Y.: Cornell University Press, 1977.

————. *Satan: The Early Christian Tradition.* Ithaca, N.Y.: Cornell University Press, 1981.

Particular Topics

Altaner, Berthold. *Patrology.* Trans. Hilda C. Graef. New York: Herder and Herder, 1960.

Chadwick, Owen, ed. Monastic texts in *Western Asceticism.* Philadelphia: Westminster Press, 1958.

Fitzgerald, Allan, ed. *Augustine Through the Ages: An Encyclopedia.* Grand Rapids, Mich.: Eerdmans, 1999. (A guide to Augustine's thought offering extensive bibliographies.)

Floyd, W.E.G. *Clement of Alexandria's Treatment of the Problem of Evil.* London: Oxford University Press, 1971.

Malchow, Bruce. *Social Justice in the Hebrew Bible.* Collegeville: The Liturgical Press, 1996.

Pritchard, James B., ed. *The Ancient Near East: Supplementary Texts and Pictures Relating to the Old Testament.* Princeton, N.J.: Princeton University Press, 1969.

Sparks, H.F.D., ed. *The Apocryphal Old Testament.* Oxford: Clarendon Press, 1984.

Wise, Michael, Martin Abegg Jr., and Edward Cook, eds. *The Dead Sea Scrolls: A New Translation.* San Francisco: HarperSanFrancisco, 1996.

The Middle Ages

General

Russell, Jeffrey Burton. *Lucifer: The Devil in the Middle Ages.* Ithaca, N.Y.: Cornell University Press, 1984.

Particular Topics

Aquinas, Thomas. *Basic Writings of Saint Thomas Aquinas.* 2 vols. Ed. Anton Pegis. New York: Random House, 1945.

Boethius. *Consolation of Philosophy.* Trans. V. E. Watts. Baltimore: Penguin Books, 1969.

Dante. *The Inferno.* Trans. Mark Musa. New York: Penguin Books, 1984.

Gregg, Joan. *Devils, Women, and Jews: Reflections on the Other in Medieval Sermon Stories.* Albany: State University of New York Press, 1997.

Kennedy, Charles, ed. *Early English Christian Poetry.* London: Hollins & Carter, 1952.

Lambert, Malcolm. *Medieval Heresy: Popular Movements from the Gregorian Reform to the Reformation.* 2d ed. Oxford: Blackwell, 1992.

Russell, James. *The Germanization of Early Medieval Christianity: A Sociohistorical Approach to Religious Transformation.* New York: Oxford University Press, 1994.

Reformation to the Nineteenth Century

General

Russell, Jeffrey Burton. *Mephistopheles: The Devil in the Modern World.* Ithaca, N.Y.: Cornell University Press, 1986.

Particular Topics

Appleman, Philip, ed. *Darwin.* New York: Norton, 1979.

Barbour, Ian. *Religion in an Age of Science.* San Francisco: Harper & Row, 1991.

Blake, William. *The Marriage of Heaven and Hell.* New York: Oxford University Press, 1975.

Brooke, John H. *Science and Religion: Some Historical Perspectives.* New York: Cambridge University Press, 1991.

Browne, E. Martin, ed. *Religious Drama 2: Mystery and Morality Plays.* New York: Meridian Books, 1958.

Byron, George Gordon Noel. "Cain." *The Complete Poetical Works of Lord Byron.* Ed. Jerome J. McGann, 232–95. Vol. 6. Oxford: Clarendon Press, 1991.

Coleridge, Samuel Taylor. *The Rime of the Ancient Mariner.* New York: Dover Publications, 1992.

Denis Diderot's The Encyclopedia. Trans. Stephen Gendzier. New York: Harper & Row, 1967.

Dostoyevsky, Fyodor. *The Brothers Karamazov.* Trans. Constance Garnett. New York: Modern Library, 1950.

Erasmus, Desiderius. *Ten Colloquies.* Trans. Craig Thompson. New York: Liberal Arts Press, 1957.

Freud, Sigmund. *The Basic Writings of Sigmund Freud.* Trans. and ed. A. A. Brill. New York: The Modern Library, 1938.

Gay, Peter. *Deism: An Anthology.* Princeton, N.J.: Van Nostrand, 1968.

———. *The Enlightenment: An Interpretation.* 2 vols. New York: Knopf, 1966–69.

Goethe, Johann Wolfgang von. *Faust, Part One* [German-English]. New York: Bantam Books, 1985.

———. *Faust, Part Two.* New York: Penguin Books, 1959.

Hawthorne, Nathaniel. *Young Goodman Brown, and Other Short Stories.* New York: Dover Publications, 1992.

Hume, David. *Dialogues Concerning Natural Religion.* Ed. by Henry D. Aiken. New York: Hafner Pub. Co., 1948.

Jefferson, Thomas. *Notes on the State of Virginia.* New York: Harper & Row, 1964.

Klaits, Joseph. *Servants of Satan: The Age of the Witch Hunts.* Bloomington: Indiana University Press, 1985.

Kramnick, Isaac, ed. *The Portable Enlightenment Reader.* New York: Penguin Books, 1995.

Leibniz, Gottfried Wilhelm von. *Theodicy: Essays on the Goodness of God, the Freedom of Man, and the Origin of Evil.* Ed. Austin Farrer. Trans. E. M. Huggard. La Salle, Ill.: Open Court, 1993.

Malthus, Thomas. *An Essay on Population.* London: Dent, 1958.

Marlowe, Christopher. *The Tragical History of Doctor Faustus.* New York: Appleton-Century-Crofts, 1950.

Milton, John. *Paradise Lost.* Ed. Roy Flannagan. New York: Maxwell Macmillan International, 1981.

Moore, James. *The Post-Darwinian Controversies: A Study of the Protestant Struggle to Come to Terms with Darwin in Great Britain and America, 1870–1900.* New York: Cambridge University Press, 1979.

Newton, Isaac. *Newton's Philosophy of Nature: Selections from His Writings.* Ed. H. L. Thayer. New York: Hafner Pub. Co., 1965.

Nietzsche, Friedrich. *Twilight of the Idols; and The Antichrist.* Trans. R. J. Hollingdale. Harmondsworth: Penguin, 1990.

Oberman, Heiko A. *Luther: Man between God and the Devil.* Trans. Eileen Walliser-Schwarzbart. New Haven, Conn.: Yale University Press, 1989.

Pope, Alexander. *An Essay on Man and Other Poems.* New York: Dover Publications, 1993.

Sade, Marquis de. *Justine, Philosophy in the Bedroom, and Other Writings.* Trans. by Richard Seaver and Austryn Wainhouse. New York: Grove Weidenfeld, 1990.

Scarre, Geoffrey. *Witchcraft and Magic in Sixteenth- and Seventeenth-Century Europe.* Atlantic Highlands, N.J.: Humanities Press International, 1990.

Shelley, Mary. *Frankenstein.* New York: Dover Publications, 1994.

Shelley, Percy Bysshe. "On the Devil and Devils." *The Complete Works of Percy Bysshe Shelley.* Ed. Roger Ingpen and Walter Peck, 87–104. New York: Gordian Press, 1965.

Stevenson, Robert Louis. *The Strange Case of Dr. Jeckyll and Mr. Hyde.* Lincoln: University of Nebraska Press, 1990.

Trachtenberg, Joshua. *The Devil and the Jews.* Philadelphia: Jewish Publication Society of America, 1943.

Twain, Mark. *The Mysterious Stranger and Other Stories.* New York: Dover Publications, 1992.

Voltaire, Francois. *The Portable Voltaire.* Ed. Ben Redman. New York: Viking Press, 1949.

Winstone, H.V.F. *Uncovering the Ancient World.* London: Constable, 1985.

Wollstonecraft, Mary. *A Vindication of the Rights of Women.* Buffalo, N.Y.: Prometheus Books, 1989.

Contemporary Era

General

Delbanco, Andrew. *The Death of Satan: How Americans Have Lost the Sense of Evil.* New York: Farrar, Straus, and Giroux, 1995.

Peterson, Michael. *God and Evil: An Introduction to the Issues.* Boulder, Colo.: Westview Press, 1998.

Peterson, Michael, ed. *The Problem of Evil: Selected Readings.* Notre Dame, Ind.: University of Notre Dame Press, 1992.

Particular Topics (Literature)

Camus, Albert. *The Plague.* Trans. Stuart Gilbert. New York: A. A. Knopf, 1948.

Golding, William. *The Lord of the Flies.* New York: Paragon Books, 1954.

Lewis, C. S. *Perelandra: A Novel.* New York: Macmillan, 1944.

MacLeish, Archibald. *J.B.: A Play in Verse.* Boston: Houghton Mifflin, 1958.

Mann, Thomas. *Doctor Faustus: The Life of the German Composer, Adrian Leverkuhn, as Told by a Friend.* Trans. H. T. Lowe-Porter. New York: Knopf, 1948.

O'Connor, Flannery. "The Lame Shall Enter First." *The Complete Stories.* New York: Farrar, Straus, Giroux, 1971.

Solzhenitsyn, Aleksandr. *One Day in the Life of Ivan Denisovich.* Trans. Max Hayward and Leopold Labedz. New York: Praeger, 1963.

Wiesel, Elie. *Night.* Trans. Stella Rodway. New York: Hill and Wang, 1961.

Particular Topics (Science)

Alford, C. Fred. *What Evil Means to Us.* Ithaca, N.Y.: Cornell University Press, 1997.

Appleyard, Bryan. *Brave New Worlds: Staying Human in the Genetic Future.* New York: Viking, 1998.

Baumeister, Roy. *Evil: Inside Human Violence and Cruelty.* New York: W. H. Freeman, 1997.

Campbell, Joseph. *The Hero with a Thousand Faces.* Princeton, N.J.: Princeton University Press, 1973.

Dawkins, Richard. *The Selfish Gene.* 2d ed. New York: Oxford University Press, 1989.

Goldberg, Carl. *Speaking with the Devil: A Dialogue with Evil.* New York: Viking, 1996.

Jung, Carl. "Answer to Job." In *The Portable Jung.* Ed. Joseph Campbell. New York: Viking, 1971.

Katz, Fred. *Ordinary People and Extraordinary Evil: A Report on the Beguilings of Evil.* Albany: State University of New York Press, 1993.

Peck, M. Scott. *People of the Lie.* New York: Simon and Schuster, 1983.

240   *The Problem of Evil in the Western Tradition*

Shakur, Sanyika. *Monster: The Autobiography of an L. A. Gang Member*. New York: Penguin Books, 1993.

Staub, Ervin. *The Roots of Evil: The Origins of Genocide and Other Group Violence*. New York: Cambridge University Press, 1989.

Watson, Lyall. *Dark Nature: A Natural History of Evil*. New York: HarperCollins-Publishers, 1995.

Wright, Robert. *The Moral Animal: Evolutionary Psychology and Everyday Life*. New York: Pantheon Books, 1994.

Particular Topics (Religion and Philosophy)

Adams, Marilyn McCord. *Horrendous Evils and the Goodness of God*. Ithaca, N.Y.: Cornell University Press, 1999.

Buber, Martin. *Good and Evil: Two Interpretations*. New York: Scribner, 1953.

Daly, Mary. *Beyond God the Father: Toward a Philosophy of Women's Liberation*. Boston: Beacon Press, 1973.

Dodson, Edward. *The Phenomenon of Man Revisited: A Biological Viewpoint on Teilhard de Chardin*. New York: Columbia University Press, 1984.

Freedman, David Noel, et al., eds. *The Anchor Bible Dictionary.* New York: Doubleday, 1992.

Griffin, David. *God, Power, and Evil: A Process Theodicy.* Philadelphia: Westminster Press, 1976.

Hartshorne, Charles. *Omnipotence and Other Theological Mistakes*. Albany: State University of New York Press, 1984.

Hasker, William. "On Regretting the Evils of This World." In *The Problem of Evil*, ed. Peterson, 153–67.

Hick, John. *Evil and the God of Love*. Rev. ed. New York: Harper & Row, 1977.

Howard-Snyder, Daniel, ed. *The Evidential Argument from Evil*. Bloomington: Indiana University Press, 1996.

Kaufman, Gordon. *God the Problem*. Cambridge, Mass.: Harvard University Press, 1972.

Kaufmann, Walter. *Faith of a Heretic*. Garden City, N.Y.: Doubleday, 1961.

Lindsey, Hal. *Satan Is Alive and Well on Planet Earth*. New York: Bantam, 1973.

Mackie, J. L. "Evil and Omnipotence." In *The Problem of Evil*, ed. Peterson, 89–101.

Madden, Edward, and Peter Hare. *Evil and the Concept of God*. Springfield, Ill.: Thomas, 1968.

Noddings, Nel. *Women and Evil*. Berkeley: University of California Press, 1989.

O'Collins, Gerald, and Edward Farrugia. *A Concise Dictionary of Theology.* New York: Paulist Press, 1991.

Petrik, James. *Evil beyond Belief.* Armonk, N.Y.: M. E. Sharpe, 2000.

Plantinga, Alvin. *God, Freedom, and Evil.* Grand Rapids, Mich.: Eerdmans, 1977.

Rahner, Karl. "Why Does God Allow Us to Suffer?" In *Theological Investigations* 19. Baltimore: Helicon Press, 1983. 194–208.

Rowe, William. *Philosophy of Religion: An Introduction.* Belmont, Calif.: Wadsworth Pub. Co., 1993.

Sartre, John Paul. "The Humanism of Existentialism." *Philosophy: A Literary and Conceptual Approach.* Ed. Burton Porter. New York: Harcourt Brace Jovanovich, 1974.

Stackhouse, John. *Can God Be Trusted? Faith and the Challenge of Evil.* New York: Oxford University Press, 1998.

Teilhard de Chardin, Pierre. *The Phenomenon of Man.* Trans. Bernard Wall. New York: Harper & Row, 1965.

Walsch, Neale Donald. *Conversations with God: An Uncommon Dialogue.* Vol. 1. New York: G. P. Putnam's Sons, 1995.

Whitney, Barry. *Theodicy: An Annotated Bibliography on the Problem of Evil, 1960–1990.* New York: Garland, 1993.

———. *What Are They Saying About God and Evil?* New York: Paulist Press, 1989.

Index

Abraham 172, 179
Adam 18–19, 23–4, 30, 34, 39–41, 44, 46, 53–7, 59–61, 64–6, 75, 82, 84, 88, 90, 97, 100, 102–10, 124, 139, 150, 156, 159–60, 172, 174, 176, 181, 196, 204, 214
Adams, Marilyn McCord 228–9
Albigensian Crusade 73
Alford, C. Fred 202–3
Amos 14
angels 15–16, 53
Anselm of Canterbury 75–6
Antony 47–9, 65
apocalypticism 21–5, 33–5
Appleyard, Brian 210–2
Aristotle 59, 74–8, 80, 82, 91, 111, 117, 120
Athanasius 48–9
Athena 104
Augustine 51–61, 63, 66, 70, 74–7, 79, 82, 90–1, 93–6, 100, 104–6, 109, 111, 122–3, 125, 135–6, 138–9, 155, 176, 181, 184–5, 206, 215, 219, 230

Baal 9–10
Balaam 16
Babylonian Theodicy 9
Bacon, Francis 4
Barnes, Lisa 230
Baumeister, Roy 202

Baur, Friedrich 178
Bede 67
Beelzebub 104
Benedict 67
Beowulf 64–6
Black Death 87
Blake, William 155–6, 158
Boas, Franz 182
Boethius 62–3
Bonaparte, Napoleon 179
Bosch, Hieronymus 97
Brownlee, Donald 232
Buber, Martin 215, 227
Byron, George Gordon, Lord 156–7

Calvin, John 95–6, 109, 138
Campbell, Joseph 205–6
Camus, Albert 192–3, 195
Cathars 5, 72–3
Champollion, Jean-François 179
Charlemagne 68–9
Christ and Satan 64–5
Chronicler 17
Clement VI 88
Clement of Alexandria 41–4
Clement of Rome 38
coincidence of opposites 6, 204–5
Coleridge, Samuel Taylor 154–5
Comte, Auguste 183
Copernicus, Nicholas 113, 117, 119
Cuthbert 67

Daly, Mary 216, 218
Daniel 22, 25, 34
Dante 48, 79–86, 102–4, 109, 145,
    151, 158, 161–2, 190, 202, 205
Darwin, Charles 153, 174–6
Darwin, Erasmus 174
David 11, 13, 16, 88
Dawkins, Richard 207, 209
Dead Sea Scrolls 25–6
demon 22–7, 31, 43
Descartes, René 125, 141
devil *see Satan*
DeWitte, W.M.L. 178
D'Holbach, Paul-Henri 133–4
Diderot, Denis 126, 134, 136–7, 182
Dominic de Guzman 68
Dominicans 72–4
Dorner, Isaak 181
Dostoevsky, Fyodor 164–7, 169–71,
    190, 192
Dryden, John 136
Dualism 5, 52, 60, 72–3
Durkheim, Émile 183

Enoch 23
Enuma Elish 8
Erasmus 93–6, 112
Eve 9, 18–19, 23–4, 30, 34, 39–41, 44,
    46, 53–7, 59–61, 64–6, 71, 75, 82,
    84, 88, 90, 97, 100, 102–10, 124,
    150, 156, 159, 161, 172, 174, 176,
    181, 189, 196, 204, 214

Farrugia, Edward 215
Faust 98–101, 109
Fitzgerald, F. Scott 188
Flagellants 88
Francis of Assisi 72
Freud, Sigmund 184–6, 206, 211

Galileo 113, 117, 119
Genesis A 65
Genesis B 65
Gibbon, Edward 134–5, 177–8
Gilgamesh 9, 179
Gnosticism 37, 39, 42, 52, 72, 205

Goethe, Johann Wolfgang von
    149–52, 191
Goldberg, Carl 201–3
Golding, William 196–7, 202
Gospels 29–33
Gottschalk 63–4
Gregory Nazianzen 59
Gregory the Great 67
Griffin, David 221
Gunkel, Hermann 178

Hare, Peter 219
Harrowing of Hell 88
Hartshoren, Charles 221
Hasker, William 224–6
Hawthorne, Nathaniel 162, 164
Hemningway, Ernest 188–9
Herder, J. G. 178
Hick, John 39, 222–4
Hitler, Adolf 1, 191
Homer 82, 102, 177
Hume, David 129–34, 137, 140–3,
    146, 148, 156, 164, 176, 218, 221
Huxley, T. H. 208

Incubus 25
Innocent III 73
Inquisition 73–4, 87
Irenaeus of Lyons 38–9, 57, 222
Isaiah 10–11, 14–15, 49, 67, 88, 156
Israel 8–11

Jacob of Voragine 67–8
Jefferson, Thomas 126, 137, 142
Jesus 29, 31, 46, 49, 88, 181
Jews 69–70, 87–8, 97
Job 10, 17–21, 49, 54, 66, 78, 122,
    125, 135, 149, 179, 193–5, 204–5,
    220, 223, 228, 230
Jubilees, Book of 23–4, 34
Jung, Carl 204–5
Jungmann, Bernard 181
Justin Martyr 38–9

Kant, Immanuel 131, 148
Katz, Fred 201, 203

Kaufman, Gordon 189
Kaufmann, Walter 219
Kepler, Johann 113, 117, 159
King, William 125
Kvanig, Jonathan 230

Lactantius 45–6
Lamarck, J. B. 174
Leibniz, Gottfried Wilhelm von
    121–3, 125, 128–9, 164, 206, 219
Lewis, C. S. 189–90, 232
Lindsey, Hal 214
Linnaeus, Carl 174
Louis XIV 115
Loyola, Ignatius 117
Lucifer 44
Luther, Martin 94–6, 100, 109, 113,
    170, 185, 191, 219
Lyell, Charles 173–4

Mackie, J. L. 218–9
MacLeish, Archibald 193–7
Madden, Edward 219
Malleus Maleficarum 112
Malthus, Thomas 152–3, 175
Manichaeism 52, 60, 72
Mann, Thomas 190–2
Map, Walter 111
Marcion 37, 39
Marduk 8, 179
Marlowe, Christopher 98–101, 103,
    105, 109, 156, 159, 168
Mastema 23–5, 34
Mead, Margaret 182
Melville, Herman 167–8
Mephistopheles 98–100, 149–52
Micah 14–15
Michelangelo 91
Milton, John 18, 102–10, 154–6, 158,
    160–1, 168, 205, 219
Mohammed 69
monks 46–50
Moses 120, 126
Moses Maimonides 76
Muslims 68–9
mystics 89

Newton, Isaac 117, 119–22, 124–5,
    145
Nicholas of Cusa 91–2
Nietzsche, Friedrich 169–71, 191–2
Noah 172
Noddings, Nel 217–8, 229
nominalism 89–91

Ockham, William 90–1
O'Collins, Gerald 215
O'Connor, Flannery 191–2
Origen 42–5, 49, 53
Orphism 35–6

Paley, William 176
Pambo 46
Pan 49
Pascal, Blaise 140
Paul the apostle 29, 91
Paulus, H. E. 178
Peck, M. Scott 203–4
Pelagia 68
Pelagius 52–4, 56, 58, 139
Phelps, William 115
Philo 26–7, 43–4
Plantinga, Alvin 219, 222, 226
Plato 36, 141, 146
Pol Pot 210
Pope, Alexander 120, 123–5, 127–8,
    137, 219, 225
prophets 13–15

rabbi(s) 27–8
Rahner, Karl 226–7
Raphael (angel) 106
Rawlinson, Henry 179
Reinders, Hans 231
Revelation, book of 33–5, 49
Rousseau, Jean-Jacques 119, 137–9,
    143, 146–8, 175
Rowe, William 220

Sade, Marquis de 145–8, 158, 185
Sartre, Jean-Paul 148
Satan 15–19, 21–7, 30–4, 38–50, 53,
    57, 64, 69–71, 75–81, 84–5, 88–90,

93–4, 102–18, 125, 135, 140–1, 150, 152–3, 156–61, 166, 168, 176, 181, 185–7, 190–4, 196, 203, 205, 214–5, 231
Schleiermacher, Friedrich 141–2, 178, 181
Semyaza 23, 25
Shakespeare, William 97–8, 114, 202
Shakur, Sanyika 183
Shattuck, Michelle 230
Shelley, Mary 158–61, 164, 202, 205
Shelley, Percy 154, 157–8, 186
Sheol 22
Simmons, Philip 231
Sirach 24
Smith, George 179
Solzhenitsyn, Alexander 198–9
Song of Roland 68–9
Sophocles 206
Spencer, Herbert 175
Spinoza, Benedict de 141, 177
Stalin, Joseph 1, 198
Staub, Erwin 200–1
Stevenson, Robert Louis 162–4
Stockhausen, John 227–8
Stoicism 36
Strauss, David 178

Teilhard de Chardin, Pierre 224
Teresa of Avila 117, 185–6

Tertullian 40, 70
Thomas Aquinas 76–79, 82, 181
Tiamat 8–9, 11, 179
Tindal, Matthew 126
Toland, John 126
Tolstoy, Leo 167
Twain, Mark 168

Ussher, James 172

Vergil 81, 102
Voltaire 119, 121, 126–9, 132, 134–5, 137–9, 142, 146
Voyage of Saint Brendan 67

Wallenberg, Raoul 200
Walls, Jeffrey 230
Walsch, Neale 213–4
Ward, Peter 232
Watcher Angels 23, 25, 40, 44
Watson, Lyle 208–10
Wellhausen, Julius 178
Wells, H. G. 232
Whitehead, Alfred North 221
Wiesel, Elie 197–8
Wilson, Edward 207
witches 110–8
Wollstonbecraft, Mary 143–4
Wright, Robert 207–8

Zechariah 16